Globe-Trotting Abe the Newsboy, carrying his clippings and
autographed photos in his world-trotting bag.

THE LIFE STORY OF

Abe THE Newsboy

HERO OF A THOUSAND FIGHTS

By

ABE HOLLANDERSKY

Published by ABE THE NEWSBOY

LOS ANGELES, CALIF.

*Dedicated to my
Dearest Friends*

THE PRESIDENTS

and

OFFICERS AND MEN
of the
U. S. NAVY

This educational book, my life's work, contains 538
pages and is fully illustrated with photos of our old
and new Navy.

First Edition 1930

Second Edition 1936

Third Edition 1937

Four Edition 1939

Fifth Edition 1940

Sixth Edition 1942

Seventh Edition 1943

Eighth Edition 1943

Ninth Edition 1944

Tenth Edition 1945-46

Eleventh Edition 1947

Twelfth Edition 1949

Thirteenth Edition 1949

Fourteenth Edition 1951

NOTE

The editor is grateful to his many friends for information furnished in compiling this book. Due to the many promotions and changes in Navy personnel, mistakes are bound to appear. The editor begs your indulgence.

PREFACE

The United States Navy was the making of Abe, the Newsboy. And Abe fully appreciates this. To the officers and men in the Navy, past and present, whose sympathetic kindness enabled young Abraham Hollandersky to have a career worth writing about, he dedicates this book.

From Roosevelt's time down to the present, Abe, in his capacity as newsboy on the battleships, and favorite boxer of the Navy, has met all the Presidents in their capacity as Commander-in-Chief of the Navy, and received their autographed photographs as their contribution toward illustrating this book. From the time he received friendly recognition from Admiral "Fighting Bob" Evans and President Theodore Roosevelt, he had the intention of writing this autobiography. Everybody in the Navy has encouraged him in the long struggle and presented him with autographed photographs, from the Admirals down to the enlisted men, and hundreds of these photographs, Abe has reproduced in this book.

As an example of what the Navy can do for the enlisted men, Abe often proudly refers to his friend, Captain Fried, now world-famous for rescues at sea, where twice, with the vessel under his command, he was able to rescue the passengers of liners that were sinking. Abe first knew Fried when he was chief quartermaster on the U. S. S. Hartford, stationed at New London, Conn. Now he is a great Captain and a world-famous hero. The Newsboy says:

"My advice to the poor or rich boy who wants to rise in the world, is to join the Navy, where he will learn a trade, see the world, gain a wide education, and have an

I

opportunity for a career that will gain him glory in time of peace as well as in war.

"My career with the Navy gained me my greatest glory in time of peace, like the great feats of Captain Fried. I am glad I was enabled to spend a life-time with the Navy and do a lot of fighting in time of peace. My eyesight was defective and I could not qualify as an enlisted man, but the Navy found use for my talents, and let me serve as a newsboy, a boxer and a boxing instructor.

"The Navy is a pleasant home, where men are well fed, well cared for and given plenty of amusement aboard and ashore. Every ship has a good library. Their Christmas celebrations are home-like, and every ship has its illuminated Christmas tree. At the mess table, any day in the year—morning, noon, and night—the boys will always crowd over and make room for a hungry visitor. Many a time I have had my first full meal for a week when a ship came in to the Naval base at New London and I went aboard with a bundle of newspapers.

"Now it is the greatest pride of my life to have my own autobiography among the books that are read on shipboard in our Navy."

Abe wishes to extend his thanks for hospitable treatment by the Panamanians, among others, Dr. J. J. Vallarino, Senor Dave Cordosa, Senor Raul Espinosa, Senors F. Arias, Pancho Arias, Luis F. Clement, Ricardo J. Alfaro, Maduro Brothers, Juan de la Guardia and Mr. Gus Eisman, Congressman Alvarado and the Duane family (whose father originated the Pam Lottery), Mr. McIllvaine, and a host more whose names he does not know.

"Now," says Abe, "there are a great many citizens who do not know what the Navy does. The Navy boys spend thirty to forty thousand dollars or more on Christmas. They buy presents of clothing and other gifts for the orphan children, wherever they are anchored at the Christmas season, and they give the children a good dinner also. This entertainment is given the children on board the ships, and the children are then safely conducted back to their homes. God bless the Navy for all the good things they do for everybody and what they have done for me.

"I want to pay tribute to the memory of our dear friend, Mayor B. F. Mahan, of New London, who was responsible for the Million Dollar State Pier, and I'm also thankful to our Mayor Waldo E. Clarke, who is taking care of the Pier now, for the kind-hearted favors he has done for me, when I operated the canteen on the Pier."

And he also wants to thank all his dear friends in his home town of New London, which he calls the greatest little town in the world. New London produced the late James O'Neil, the great actor, also the late Richard Mansfield, the great actor, and James Hammond, who still lives there, and that great sports lover, my good friend the late Harry Bond. We also had the largest drawbridge in the world, in that beautiful bathing beach, and the largest American submarine base.

It is the scene of the annual Yale-Harvard boat races. And don't forget that the German submarine, the Deutchsland, landed there before we entered the European war. Abe calls himself the World's Greatest Newsboy for living in such a great little town and selling newspapers to great people all over the world. That's what makes him the World's Greatest Newsboy.

I want to say a word of thanks to some friends from Los Angeles, San Diego, and Long Beach, Calif., who have been very kind and encouraging. Mr. E. G. Peck is the man who prints my great book. He is not only a great printer, but a great fellow. I am grateful to my friends at the Fountain Pen Shop in the Grosse Bldg. in Los Angeles. These boys always see to it that my pen is in

III

good working order, to autograph my books. I also wish to thank Mr. Lester D. Lawson, who is well liked throughout the Navy for his good-fellowship; Nat Baranov and I. Glaser and family, San Diego, Calif.

His brother, Sol, is given full credit for faithfully encouraging Abe until the work was done. "As two brothers, we are living up to the full meaning of brotherhood, as taught to us by our parents, and we hope to remain true to these ideals until the end," says Abe.

"Good advice how to keep physically fit: Go to bed early, arise early, keep the body clean, do plenty of walking, so you will always feel good, and never neglect your meals. Now, to the whole world, remember that everything physical or material wears out in time, but honesty never wears out. And it always pays in the end. And, above all, fellows, remember your dear old mother and father." This is the parting advice of

ABE HOLLANDERSKY, *The World's Greatest Newsboy.*

CHAPTER ONE

WHEN I was talking to President Roosevelt on the yacht Mayflower, in 1906, something happened that had never happened before in history. A cross-eyed stranger, who had forced his way into the presence of the Commander-in-Chief, made a dive at the President and hit him with his fist.

Secret service men jumped and grabbed the fellow who had taken a wallop at the President. That fellow was me. A tough kid.

I had come aboard the Mayflower telling the guards I was Abe, the Newsboy, and I said I wanted to sell the President a paper.

When I came up on the quarter deck where Roosevelt was standing on the starboard side, he looked at me very solemnly and dignified, as if he was greeting an admiral. But he couldn't get my goat. So I sold him a paper.

Then Roosevelt laughed and started kidding. He pulled my ear with his right hand and said:

"Where did you get that cauliflower?"

"I got it this way," I said, and I squared off and ducked under his guard and gave him a little poke in the ribs. It was a pretty good sock at that. It made him grunt and cover up. And that's when the secret service men rushed me.

1

"The kid's all right," the President said, and waved the guards back. Then we talked together for quite a while. And he was my friend ever after.

This had happened while the President was reviewing the Fleet under Fighting Bob Evans at Oyster Bay. When Roosevelt got back to the White House, he permitted the Admiral to create the post of Newsboy of the Navy for me, which is the same as creating an honorary cabinet position. The President could do this without the aid of Congress because the position carried no salary. It gave me the right and privilege to go anywhere in the world on U. S. Naval vessels and sell papers.

This Newsboy pass was sent to me through my friends at the Navy Yard, and when the officers explained to me what it was, they were so solemn and blew their noses so often that I looked at them sharply to see if they were trying to kid me.

They told me that when I had laid a violent hand on the person of the President of the United States—that's what they called the little sock in the ribs I had handed to the Great Teddy—I had done something which in any other country on earth would have got me shot at sunrise or sent to Siberia for life.

Now listen. Get this. I had committed one of the greatest crimes in the world, and I didn't know it. I always say: If you die the day you're born you will die a fool, and if you live a hundred years you will die a fool. And there are lots of things we don't know in this life, so what t'hell's the difference?

When the sailors found out what the President had done for me they gave Abe a big hand, and I'm not lying. But those naval officers were almost crying because a poor little cross-eyed Jew boy had been given the biggest boost by the Commander-in-Chief. Everybody liked Roosevelt and everybody liked me.

The month of January in 1912 was a very cold and dreary month. I had given a pint of blood to help a poor newsboy who was in the hospital. The doctors had asked for somebody to donate blood. So they tested my blood and found it was all right, and took a pint of it. But the poor kid died anyhow.

But I couldn't hardly keep warm that January, although I had swell clothes and an overcoat. I had been boxing around the New York clubs and getting ten or fifteen dollars for a fight. I met a Naval friend on Fourteenth Street, and he said:

"Why don't you go down to the Tropics and let the sun warm your hide, Abe, while you build up your blood?"

"Who do you think I am—J. Pierpont Vanderfeller?"

"You've got a Naval pass. Go down to the Canal Zone. There are forty thousand men down there building the Canal and they crave entertainment. If you get a bout there, you will be in the big money."

I didn't know what the Canal Zone was; but I would go against anything. I wrestled a bear once for five dollars a minute.

Whatever my Naval friends tell me to do, I know is right. So I asked him if any Naval vessel was sailing for Panama. But there wasn't any at that time.

So I bought passage on a Royal Mail Steam Packet Liner to Cuba. The fare was nearly forty dollars, the most money I had ever spent at one time in my life. And it took all I had. But I was game.

I found that everybody on board had heard of Abe, the Famous Newsboy, and those that hadn't heard about me, I told them. They soon had me relating my adventures all over the world. And believe me, I found that every man on board from the richest passenger in the first cabin, down to the greasy-handed workers in the engine room, was my friend.

Of course they all wanted to see Abe in action.

I said, "All right, I would box any man on board, passenger or crew." They canvassed the boat for the best man. Gus Schwartz, the ship's butcher, was a strong fellow with ring experience, and he weighed about two hundred pounds. He was chosen to be my opponent.

The bout took place on the third day out, and it was scheduled to go six rounds. There was no betting on the result, because everybody agreed on what the result would be. Nobody could expect me to knock out a 200-pound man, when I weighed only 145, and had gone outside my class merely to furnish some sport for the passengers because they were friends of mine.

Mr. Butch rushed me for two rounds, and he was a tough customer, believe me. He was the charging slugging type, like Sailor Tom Sharkey and later Wild Bull Firpo; and for two rounds Abe had a hard time holding his own. But I soon found out that the Rushing Butcher didn't know much about the finer points of scientific boxing. In the third round we got a chance to do some in-fighting. And that's where I punished the butcher's liver, kidney and short ribs, like a hungry mut in a basket of sausages.

The big fellow got seasick and asked permission to quit. I was generous. We shook hands, and I got a great ovation.

Everybody said that I must have the best steaks the butcher cut from then on. And sure enough, they served me prime beef steaks such as I had never tasted before—I had seen them in the restaurant windows where the swells eat. I had never thought that Abe, the Newsboy, would eat meat like that. I mention these things because I want this book to be a lesson to the boys of America. Always fight square, keep your shoes shined, have a clean collar, and always take care of your mother, and you're going to have good luck. I believe that, and no lying. In Ripley's "Believe It Or Not," you read where he said: "Abe, The Newsboy, fought a thousand fights." And Ripley is a man that proves what he says.

Arrived at Guantanamo, Cuba, on January 21. The weather was wonderful, so warm and different from the cold New York climate. After a fond farewell to my fellow passengers, I at once got busy getting my baggage to the railroad station. For I was going to Santiago and visit

San Juan Hill, where Theodore Roosevelt, my great friend, had fought an uphill battle. The people on the boat had told me about it, and as they had given me a purse of five dollars for my bout, I had the means of visiting that historic spot. I got to Santiago and found several friends from New York.

We went out to the battlefield in a mule-driven bus. There was a bronze tablet inscribed with the names of many Spanish American war heroes. There was a monument to Theodore Roosevelt put up in 1923. I put a wreath on that monument, and one of my friends, with a camera, took a picture of me doing it. I have that picture yet. It is one of the most historic pictures in the world, because it shows Abe, The Newsboy, paying tribute to his Greatest Friend, on the spot where he won his first fight.

After this ceremony I returned to the hotel and met with good luck. Father Reney of the U.S.S. Utah was there, and he gave me the low-down on the situation. He told me the U. S. Battle Fleet was holding Winter manoeuvers off the port of Caimenero, Cuba, and if I could get there I would find a host of my friends. I counted up my money, and the priest lent me a dollar and a half. So I bought a ticket and went back to the Winter base of the fleet with the Catholic chaplain.

"I have known you, Abe, for twenty years," he told me. "And I know you are absolutely reliable. Now, if you think you can rely on me, I will undertake to get you started in the big

This great flag is designed out of sailors, in the Great Lakes Training Station.

Abe says: "We have a number one Leader, our President, a number one Navy, and number one men in the Navy.

GOD BLESS AMERICA!

Our beloved President, Theodore Roosevelt, who gave me my start with the Navy, and was always glad to see me at the White House.

Award OF Merit

with best wishes and Congratulations to Abe —
C.W. Nimitz
"Fleet Admiral"

with regards to Abe the Newsboy
James Forrestal
Secretary of the Navy

Congratulations and best wishes. William D. Leahy

OF THE UNITED STATES NAVY RECRUITING SERVICE

Abe Hollandersky

This is to certify that _____"Abe the Newsboy"_____

of ____Long Beach, California____ is awarded

this certificate in acknowledgment of his patriotic

contribution to the war effort in obtaining the enlistment

of _OVER 1700_ recruits for service in the United States Navy

OFFICER-IN-CHARGE

Issued   UNITED STATES NAVY RECRUITING STATION
7 Dec. 1943 Los Angeles, California
DATE

I am proud of this award of merit given to me by the Navy Department for recruiting over 1,700 men and helping to sell millions of dollars worth of bonds.

From recruit to chief warrant and from ensign to captain, 2-star, 3-star, 4-star, and 5-star admiral and the Commander-in-Chief from Theodore Roosevelt to Harry S. Truman are all my friends.

I have served the Navy fifty years as a newsboy and as a bumboat man and boxed and have always been ready to assist in the morale of the Navy. . . . With so many good friends in the Navy I hope to continue for fifty more years. God bless the Navy.

THE WHITE HOUSE
WASHINGTON

December 20, 1935

My dear Abe:

I take pleasure in enclosing herewith
a photograph of the President which he has been
glad to autograph for you.

Sincerely yours,

M. H. McINTYRE
Assistant Secretary
to the President

Our Fighting late President. He was loved by the Navy, and that goes
for me, too.

Our President, Harry S. Truman, who is trying his best to keep peace all over the world.

Josephus Daniels

Franklin D Roosevelt

This photo was presented to me by my two friends, Josephus Daniels, Secretary of the
Navy in 1917, with Franklin D. Roosevelt, Assistant Secretary of the Navy.

Our Late President Taft, Late Supreme Court Justice O. W. Holmes,
and George Brandeis.

13

Our beloved President Wilson, to whom I have sold newspapers while on the President's yacht, "Mayflower," in New London, Connecticut.

14

To "abe"

Herbert Hoover

President Herbert Hoover, whom I met in the White House, where
he presented me with his autographed picture.

With good wishes to "Abe, the Newsboy."

Warren Harding

Our beloved President Harding, a great admirer of Abe the Newsboy,
who was always glad to see me at the White House.

Our beloved President Calvin Coolidge, whom I met in the White House during his administration—and he sure was a good President!

17

My good friend, the late Secretary of Defense, James Forrestal.

Fleet Admiral and Fleet Newsboy. Photo taken at Hotel Huntington, Pasadena, on New Yar's Day. Adm. W. F. Halsey, one of our great heroes, who helped make a happy victory. I sold papers to him and Dad Captain Halsey over 40 years. A good guy and a good fellow.

To my old friend and the newsboys
William D. Leahy —

My good friend, the retired Fleet Admiral William D. Leahy, Chief of Staff to the President of the United States, formerly Chief of Naval Operations, Governor of Porto Rico, Ambassador to France.

20

My good friend, Fleet Admiral Chester W. Nimitz and Fleet Newsboy.

My good friend, Five-Star Admiral Ernest J. King, who helped us to win the war as Chief of Naval Operations.

money."

"If you have found out I am reliable and like me for it," I replied, "then that shows you're reliable, and that's the kind of man for me to tie to."

So every morning I brought a paper to Father Reney on the Utah and we had breakfast together, while he scanned the sporting pages to find a bout for me.

"You are in the land of bull fights now," he said. "Few of these Spanish countries have boxing."

"I'll fight a bull," I said, "if they'll cut his horns off. I once licked a bear that was muzzled."

Finally he found news of boxing in the British West Indies; the welterweight champion was a Jamaica colored boy named "Young Jack Johnson." Father Reney told me to go to Kingston, Jamaica, when I felt that my blood was restored to its usual vigor.

"With all the good steaks they fed me on that British boat," I said, "I feel strong enough now to lick the British Empire. And all these big-time breakfasts you have been giving me makes me want to be a credit to you."

"You have to eat in order to fight, my boy." And he patted me on the shoulder.

"I have always had to fight in order to eat," I replied.

I had always been a pork-and-beaner. That's what they call a preliminary fighter, who is glad to get a couple of dollars for a six-round fight. He has to live on fifteen-cent meals until he can get in another bout. I didn't eat pork and beans, but I used to order a cheese sandwich and a cup of coffee when I really could have eaten a ten-pound turkey at one sitting. Fellows, if you think I'm lying about the ten-pound turkey, just keep reading till we come to it.

I arrived at Kingston, Jamaica, and stopped at the Marine Garden Hotel, as Father Reney had advised. I went to the office of the Jamaica Gleaner, and told the sporting editor:

"I am Abe, the Newsboy, welterweight champion of Connecticut, known as the Connecticut Tiger. I live in New London, Conn." And I showed him my clippings.

He was glad to meet me. He said a fight could surely be arranged for me. He called in the leading promoter, and I was matched to meet the champion. The winner was to get 35 percent of the gate. I asked what the prices were, and they told me one and six, top.

Two dollars had been the top at the New York clubs where I had appeared as a pork-and-beaner. One time they promised me three dollars for a six-round prelim, and I was so eager to get my money and go out and eat, that I knocked my man out in the first round. And they only paid me a dollar and a half, because they had to put on two more pork-and-beaners to fill the gap in the program.

Now I was to fight in the British Indies for six dollars ringside, and the lowest admission a dollar. And it wasn't any prelim for two or three dollars, either. I was to fight the champion in the principal go, and if I licked him, oh, boy! I was to get thirty-five percent of all that gate.

I was in the big money at last.

And those generous steaks they had given me on the British boat, for licking their bloody butcher, were now growling inside of me for a chance to lick their bloomin' champion himself.

Let's go.

CHAPTER TWO

 WENT back to the hotel and got a friend to write a letter to Father Reney, telling him about my good luck. He had refereed many of my bouts on the U. S. battleships, and he believed I was a coming champion. He had told me:

"You can't make any money out of these sailor bouts on ship-board. But if you can get bouts with the champions of other countries, the whole Navy will back you to a man. That means gate receipts. And you need the money."

He knew I had supported my mother and my blind father as best I could since I was six years old. That's why I had never before made connections with the big beefsteaks.

So I wrote the good priest how happy I was. I was going to knock the Jamaica champion for a row of beefsteaks that would reach from here to Panama.

The British promoter was a good guy. He got out some swell posters with my picture and everything. Under Young Jack Johnson's picture was a British flag and the statement that he was the champion of the West Indies. Under my picture was an American flag.

Say, when I saw the old Star Spangled Banner depending on me to uphold her glory, I was the

proudest Jew boy in the world. Now I saw why
Roosevelt had made me Newsboy of the Navy.
My cauliflower ear was good news to him.

He told me at that time that lots of people
believe that "a Jew won't fight." But my cauliflower ears showed I could take it, and my jab to
his ribs showed I was boring in for more. Roosevelt was a great man, take it from me.

The night of the fight came and I was in good
condition. The amphitheatre was packed full of
people, most of them black. When I entered the
ring and looked at that sea of faces, it looked like
the sea on a dark night — just a white surf in
front of you, and back of that you couldn't see
much, but you knew it was there.

But those white folks in the six-dollar seats
were enough to make my fortune without counting those tropical, sunburned Britishers back
there in the dollar seats. But Lincoln said, don't
fail to count the common man, because God made
so many of them. So I made a quick guess as to
how much money that colored multitude would
bring me, as I advanced to the middle of the ring
to shake hands with my colored opponent.

He said:

"Boy, whah you get dat eye?"

I didn't answer him because I thought he was
kidding like Roosevelt when he asked me where I
got that ear. I was wondering where those colored fans all got that dollar to go to a fight.

The gong rang. We squared off and we went
to it. He was a tough order, that fellow Johnson.
But I believed I could lick him. I had to. I represented the American flag, and wouldn't quit:

he'd have to kill me. Besides, there was all that money in the house, and my Naval friends had sent me to the Tropics to get in the big money.

I went boring into Young Jack Johnson with all the confidence in the world. I never dreamed of the disaster that was to overtake me.

The smell of his body was good to me as we milled and mixed it. The sound of his clicking teeth when I chugged his ribs was sweet music to my ears. His big eyes and those white ivories were good to look at, for he was a well-built man, about one-fourth English and three-fourths colored bear-cat.

But I found out he was afraid that I was trying to hoodoo him.

He kept talking all the time we were fighting. He was worrying because I was cross-eyed. When I found out what was worrying him, I told him:

"I have worried all my life because I am cross-eyed. But don't let that worry you. It's me that's cross-eyed, not you."

It was a whirlwind fight. There wasn't much chance for talk. Bim, bim. Biff, biff. The black boy was scared, and when they're scared they fight like wildcats. But they don't use their head. I was using my head to keep him from getting to my chin. I was ducking and glancing his blows off my skull. He believed in magic and voodoo and all that jungle stuff. He was afraid I had the Evil Eye.

It was the fifth round of a scheduled ten-round battle, and I got wise to myself. In the next clinch, I said to him:

"If you don't like my cross-eye, knock it straight. If I didn't like your straight eyes, I'd knock you cross-eyed."

He was no good after that. He was a tar baby in my hands. I felt safe then in stalling along, for it was to be only a ten-round go, and all his friends had come there and paid the big money. They were entitled to a full program.

Right there is where I made my mistake, see?

I remembered when they cut my three-dollar guarantee to a dollar and a half payment because I knocked out my man in the first round. I didn't want them to cut this three-thousand-dollar house in two because I licked my man in the middle of the fight. So I decided not to floor him till the tenth round. I needed the money.

And do you know what happened?

When the promoter and the box office man began counting out my share as the winner— which was 35 percent—I found out that the prices were not one to six dollars. The top price, ring-side, was one and six, that is, one shilling and six pence—about thirty cents.

Can you beat it?

Those dingies out there in the bleachers had got in for a dime. I had put on this great show of the white man whipping the negro—regular Uncle Tom's Cabin stuff—at the regular old Tom show prices of ten, twenty and thirty. The joke was on me.

I went back to the hotel and paid my bill, which took more than half of what I had got for the championship battle. I had been eating all I wanted instead of sticking to sandwiches and

coffee. It was a lesson to me. I had thought I
was a great man and was entitled to eat beef
steaks. When I told the promoter I understood
that the prices were six dollars ringside, he said:

"But that's your fault, me lad; the prices were
printed on the posters. Can't you read?"

"No, I can't read," I told him. He thought I
was lying.

But, anyhow, I won the fight. What t' hell's
the difference? After I saw the American Flag
printed under my picture I didn't look for anything else. I'll bet that colored Britisher couldn't
read, either. But I spoke a universal language.
A wallop on the jaw that makes you know nothing is understood by men of every country and
every race.

So I checked out of my hotel owing nothing,
and went to the dock and bought intermediate
passage to Colon, Panama. Panama was where
Father Reney told me to go, and if I hadn't forgot myself and ate all I wanted in the Jamaica
Hotel, I would have been going there with money
in my pocket.

A great crowd was down to the dock to see
me off. Newspaper men, city officials, and business men with sporting blood surrounded Abe,
the Newsboy, and made him promise that he
would return to Jamaica as soon as he filled his
engagements in Panama.

I didn't have any engagements in Panama. I
was going to find some. But I didn't tell these
Britishers that the American champion would
land in Colon broke and would have to go to
selling papers.

But I promised on my word of honor I would come back to Jamaica and meet the next good man they could find for me. The reason they were so eager to entertain Abe, the Newsboy, in their hospitable island again was because Abe was carrying away their championship underneath the red-white-and-blue sash at his belt, and they were anxious to get it back, under the British flag, again.

And the reason I intended to come back as I promised, was to let them try and get it.

So I boarded the steamer Prince Joachim and sailed for Panama with thirty-eight cents in my pocket. And a million dollars worth of pride.

I got off at Cristobol, a port adjoining Colon, in the Canal Zone. I was carrying a fine traveling bag, which was a gift from the boxing fans of Kingston. Those Britishers are pretty smart fellows. They gave me that swell luggage so that wherever I travelled I would always be reminded of my promise to come back to Jamaica. They didn't give me a medal; they didn't give me a belt. They gave me that traveling bag to indicate that their welterweight championship was merely traveling.

The British were the greatest world travelers in those days. But the Americans are now.

I was walking up Front Street in the city of Colon, wondering how I could get started again. I had been off the boat five or six hours and was hungry enough to eat the brass buckles off that leather bag.

I was still hoarding that thirty-eight cents in

capital. A newsboy never eats his capital, no
matter how hungry he gets. Else he couldn't
buy any more papers to sell, and he would be
out of business.

"Hello, Abe. What are you doing here?" said
a Naval Officer.

I was known by everybody in the Navy because of my hundreds of bouts. Sometimes they
used to introduce me as "the homeliest man in
the world." I took it good naturedly because
they were all my friends.

"I just got in from Jamaica," I replied.
"What ship are you on, Sir?"

"The U.S.S. Severin. We have about four
hundred men with us, Abe."

"How about letting me do a little bumboating
on your ship?"

"Sure thing, Abe. Anything I can do for you,
I'm glad to. Are you short?"

"I've got thirty-eight cents. Could you lend
me ten or fifteen dollars to stock up with supplies?"

"Here, take this fifty, Abe. There is lots of
American activity here, and you'll need a big
stock."

Did I thank him? Oh, boy! Then he asked
me why I bought such swell baggage when I
didn't have anything to carry in it. Just kidding,
of course, to find out about that English bag.

"That leather is made out of the hide of a
sun-burned Jamaica ginger baby," I said, and
told him how I had won the Island championship and had come off with a great big leather

bag full of glory and no money.

He was gladder than ever that he had staked me, and I started on my way to find a supply depot where I could get the papers and magazines to sell on the ship. As I was passing the Lobby Cafe, two gentlemen that had the unmistakable air of the sportsman, took notice of me. One said:

"Look at that little pug. He must be a new fighter on the Isthmus; I've never seen him before. Have you?"

"No. But he must be a tough baby."

So I stopped and told them who I was. They told me their names; one of them was Mr. James Daly. Mr. Daly asked me:

"How much money have you got?"

"Thirty-eight cents," I told him, for that was all I had of my own money.

Mr. Daly put his hand in his pocket and pulled out some coins. He picked out one of them and handed it to me. It was a twenty-dollar gold piece.

"Go and get a place to eat and sleep. And come back and see me tomorrow at eleven o'clock.

CHAPTER THREE

 WENT to the Washington Hotel and got a good comfortable room. The words of Father Reney came back to me: Abe, you will make plenty of money in Panama.

I had found an Irish sportsman to back me in the ring game and a Navy man to back me in the newspaper business. Abe, the Newsboy, was meeting good luck at last.

I decided to take the good priest's advice again about eating: If a man is to fight at his best, he must have enough to eat. I went into the dining room and ordered a steak for four. I was the four.

But that's what the Irishman had given me that twenty-dollar gold piece for. The Irish are a smart race.

I bought my news stand supplies and had them transported to the Severin, and I did a rushing business. The boys had found out that I had taken the measure of the best man the British had in the Tropics, and everybody, from the Captain down to the mascot, wanted to be able to say that they had bought a paper from Abe, the Newsboy.

That night, when I retired to my luxurious bed in the Washington Hotel, I could not sleep.

I was too excited and happy. I have slept sound-
ly in doorways, without an overcoat, in cold
weather, on an empty stomach. And here I was
in a fine bed, down in sunny Panama where it is
Summer time all of the year, and I wasn't sleeping. I was sure losing money on that investment.

But, on the other hand, that bed wasn't paid
for out of my money. The Irish sportsman had
staked me to that bed so that my head would
be clear on the following day when he wanted
me to talk to him about my chances of conquer-
ing Panama. He had read my clippings, and he
must have thought I had a chance, or he would
not have staked his money on the little Jew boy.

He had told me that Panama was full of
boxers. And he said it was the custom of the
Americans employed on the Canal to back their
favorite boxer strong, and give him a share of
their winnings.

Sweet Papa! Here I was right in the midst
of it. Why, one time in New York, when I had
fought a prelim for the promise of five dollars,
they handed me an envelope and it had only one
dollar in it. I went out and tried to find the
promoter and he was gone. And when I got
back to my dressing room, someone had stolen
my clothes. I had my overcoat with me, wearing it for a bath robe, so they didn't get that.
So I had to go out into the cold, cold world
wearing an overcoat and with nothing under it
but ring tights and a dollar in my hand for licking a big palooka that weighed almost as much
as the butcher boy on the boat. Of course, a Jew

always says he loses money on the goods, but
I'm asking you: how did I make any money
on that fight? And now I was in Panama where
they throw money at you if you win. Try to
picture me, boys.

Would I win?

Sure. But what would I get for my first
fight? Would it amount to a thousand dollars?
Who would be my first opponent? How long
would it take me to get a crack at the champion?
They told me that a tough Spanish-Indian, named
Jack Ortega, who had mopped up everything in
California, was now heavyweight champion of
Panama.

That won't do. Panama is under the American flag. Nobody with a Spanish flag on his
belt can be the champion boxer of the American
Canal Zone. I had a lot of things to think of
that night before I went to sleep.

But soon I was in Dreamland. And what I
mean, boys, is that I did have a dream that night.
Some dream! It might have been caused by
that big steak, four meals in one, that I put
away in a hurry when I struck the good luck.

Shall I tell you about that big dream? Sure,
you must hear it.

I dreamed I was matched to fight this big
Greaser, the champion of the Isthmus. It was
to be a twenty-five round go and the purse was
to be ten thousand dollars. And winner take all.

The arena was packed to the doors, as I came
down the aisle to crawl through the ropes. I
asked the referee, "Is this American dollars or

British pence?" And it was American mazuma. The dollar seats were American dollars, and they were filled with Spanish Indians only.

I said "Hurrah for America."

The front seats were full of Naval men and Canal builders and Panamanians. And they were betting their money like throwing confetti at Coney Island.

The bell rang. I walked out and met the big Spanish guy.; I could not see him very plainly, so I can't describe what he looked like to me, but it seemed all right at the time.

The champion led with a right, but I side-stepped it and planted a lulu over his heart. We clinched and were doing lots of damage in short order, while the crowd arose and yelled in Spanish and American: "Kill him, kill him!" The champion had an awful wallop if he could connect.

Then he landed, full force, behind and under my ear.

Down I went to the canvas. I could hear the referee counting, One, two, three . . . while the whole Navy was yelling "Get up, Abe, get up!" I tried to get up, and just then I heard the bell ring, the end of the round.

Well, reader, that was the first round of this fight in my dreams. The battle went on, round after round. I didn't have sense enough to wake up and save myself all this needless punishment.

In the fifteenth round I began to get him groggy, but I couldn't put him away. But I had ten rounds yet. He lasted four more rounds and then he was so punch drunk that I could hardly see him; he was like wavering smoke. I was very hazy myself, but I knew he must drop in a second. Then I began to wake up . . . I tried to stay asleep long enough to get him . . . but I was half awake and he had faded out so I couldn't quite see him . . . As I strained my sleepy eye to spot him for one final bingo, I found myself looking into the eyes of an Army Officer.

I was awake and looking at a portrait on the wall. It was a picture of Colonel Goethals, the man who was building the Panama Canal. A ray of Tropic sunshine was glancing off the glazed picture and hitting me in the face.

He seemed to say to me: "Get up, Abe, get up." And I jumped up and went about the business of the day.

There was something in the air to whisper of good luck. The chimes of the Colon Cathedral were sending forth their sweet notes. Cabs drawn by miniature ponies were traveling two abreast, and the streets were full of people of all nationalities and all colors, busy, hustling and happy. This lovely Tropical city was under the sanitary regulation of the U. S. Navy, so the people were happy because they were healthy.

Abe got in a good half-day's work selling papers before the hour of his conference with Mr. James Daly.

As I was crossing the Plaza, on my way to the Lobby Cafe, a little old wrinkled woman in a green and red dress, bright as a parrot, approached and wanted to sell me some little papers

U.S.S. Connecticut and our late Admiral Fighting Bob Evans. On this ship the late
President, "Teddy" Roosevelt, received a twenty-one gun salute. At
the time, I was getting aboard from the port gangway with my
newspapers. It was my good fortune, as a civilian, to be
present at this presidential salute.

To Abe Hollandersky
with best wishes
Forrest Sherman
Admiral, U.S. Navy

My good Naval friend, Chief of Naval Operations Admiral Forrest Sherman.

40

To Abe Hollandusky
with best wishes
L. D. McCormick
Vice-Admiral, U.S.N.

One of my good Naval friends, Vice-Admiral L. D. McCormick.

To:- Abe the Newsboy,
With warm personal
regards.
Louis Denfield
Comdr. in Chief, Pacific.

My good friend, Admiral Louis E. Denfield, Former Chief of Naval Operations.

To "Abe" with warm good
wishes and deep appreciation
of your friendship
Dr E. Ramsey
Admiral, USN

Admiral DeWitt C. Ramsey, Retired, one of my great admiring friends.

To
Abe Hollandersky
with best
wishes.
Thomas C. Kinkaid
Admiral, U.S.N.

Admiral Thomas C. Kinkaid, one of my great hero friends.

File No OOR-3002

Admiral R. A. Spruance, one of my friends, who helped achieve victory.

To Abe the Newsboy
With best wishes
V. H. P. Blandy

Admiral Wm. H. P. Blandy, one of my many Navy friends.

46

I have many pleasant memories of Admiral Dewey, many of my papers were sold on his flagship.

47

My very esteemed friend, Arthur Brisbane, who is one of the greatest writers.
He is loved by everyone. I am proud to have his autographed picture.

Abe, the newsboy of New London, Conn.
best wishes. Geo W Goethals

The late Colonel Goethals, one of the most brilliant men in America, who
engineered the construction of the Panama Canal. Loved by all
the Canal diggers; a great friend—always ready to do
something for Abe the Newsboy.

To Abe the Newsboy
with best wishes
yours faithfully
Thomas Lipton

The late Thomas Lipton, one of the gamest sportsmen—he never quit.

Two of the greatest fighting Presidents we have ever had, says Abe.
Franklin and Teddy.

(Top): Rear Admiral L. E. Gregory and Rear Admiral T. T. Craven. (Center): Watching a ball game. (Left to right): Late Rear Admiral Ridley McLean, Admiral J. M. Reeves, Captain H. M. Jensen, and Captain L. M. Stevens. (Bottom): The three generations of Sterling's Navy family—(left to right). Retired Admiral Yates Sterling (son), the late Admiral Sterling (father), and Lt. Paul R. Sterling (grandson).

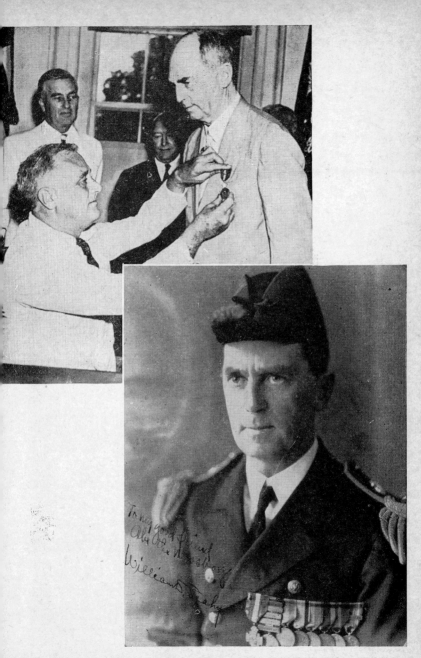

Top: Admiral William D. Leahy receiving another medal from the President of the
United States. Admiral Leahy was Chief of Naval Operations, Governor of
Porto Rico, and was Ambassador to France and Naval advisor to the
President. I hope my friend has retired with a bucket full of medals.

(Top): Admiral William H. Standley with Abe on the U.S.S. Chicago. (Bottom): Admiral Joseph M. Reeves and Brig. General Douglas C. McDougal inspecting the Marine Base in San Diego, California.

she carried in her hand. I can't read, but I was going to buy one anyhow. It was the first time I had been taken for a gentleman that buys papers instead of selling them.

I saw a lot of numbers on the bundle of papers she held out, and then I realized they must be lottery tickets. The one I took was number 5813, and the day was the thirteenth of February. It cost fifty cents.

I took it off her hands because I knew that nobody else would buy it; gamblers are very superstitious. So I was doing a good turn by taking that hoodoo number out of her hands. And I believe that if you do some poor fellow a good turn it will bring you good luck.

If I won the grand prize it would be fifteen hundred dollars. I could always read numbers and count; a newsboy has to know that trick. Young Griffo was one of the world's greatest fighters, but he couldn't count. Often, after he had won a fight for a thousand dollars, the promoter would come to him and say: "Here's your thousand dollars; count it yourself if you don't trust me." And they would fill his hat and his pockets and his shoes with quarters, half dollars and dollar bills. And Griffo would think he must have fully a thousands dollars; but it didn't amount to two hundred dollars.

Mr. Daly was waiting for me, and he had several of the leading fight fans to meet me. He said he had talked over the phone with the leading promoter, who lived in Panama City, and the promoter was coming over on the noon train to meet me.

That's getting fast action, isn't it? Panama City is on the Pacific Ocean, and Colon is on the Atlantic. A business man was coming across a continent to meet Abe, the Newsboy.

The sports at the Lobby Cafe opened wine for me, but I didn't drink any. A boy who has never been able to buy all the coffee and sandwiches he wanted certainly never had a chance to learn to like champagne. So I stuck to coffee.

But, fellows, I want to tell you no wine that was ever crushed from the grape could have made Abe feel any happier than he did at the dinner given him by those good sports. I began to believe I was a great man.

But we had a disappointment. The promoter didn't show up when the train came in. He sent word that unexpected business kept him in Panama City. But he asked us to come over to that city next day and see him.

My chance to break a record by having a promoter cross the continent to see me had flopped on me. That was hard luck.

I want to tell you now how my number thirteen ticket, bought on what I thought would be my lucky day, also turned out. The drawing took place after I had gone to Panama City. It was held in front of the lottery office, where a large crowd had collected. A huge hollow ball was opened, and inside of it were placed small balls numbered from 0 to 9. These were spun around inside the big ball. Then a girl was selected from the crowd and blindfolded.

The little girl began taking out the balls. The first was 4, the second 8, and then 1 and 3. This constituted the winning number, 4813. My ticket was 5813.

"I'm out of luck," I said, and threw my ticket away.

One of my new friends that I had met at Mr. Daly's place picked up the ticket and said:

"You're crazy, Abe. This wins fifty dollars."

"Why?"

"The last three numbers are correct and it wins the second prize. Take it in the office and cash it."

I took it in, and sure enough, they handed me fifty dollars in gold. Lady Luck was with me in Panama. Some people believe that a Jew is lucky, but if every Jew was lucky, there wouldn't be any poverty among the Jews, and no Russian pogroms. Lots of people believe a goat is lucky. Every ship in the Navy has a goat for a mascot. One time I put fifty dollars worth of papers and magazines aboard a ship when the fleet was sailing from New London, and when I went to get them, the goat had chewed them all up. Now, the Jew boy and the goat couldn't both have been lucky on that job. Abe may have been good luck for that hungry goat, but the goat mascot wasn't good luck to Abe, the Newsboy.

But the fifty dollars I had won in the Panama lottery evened me up with the Navy goat. I paid back the fifty dollars which the Naval Officer so kindly lent me, and still had about seventy dollars in money and stock supplies. I was on my feet already and doing a big business. It seemed that everybody liked me, and I was the happiest man in Panama. Until suddenly something happened that took all the joy out of life for me. An attack on Abe, the Newsboy, appeared in the Panama Journal, and it was the most terrific blow that ever hit me.

CHAPTER FOUR

THE thing that gave me such an awful pain in the neck was to find myself selling a newspaper to the gobs of the Navy with a big article in it saying that Abe, the Newsboy, was a hunk of cheese.

I had gone aboard the U.S.S. Severin with a hundred copies of the Panama Journal and had sold about a dozen papers when my friends showed me a big article on the sport page with these headlines:

CHAMPION ON THE WAR PATH: ORTEGA
SAYS HE WILL STOP ABE, THE NEWSBOY,
IN ONE PUNCH: SUGGESTS NEW ARRIVAL
PUT UP THOUSAND DOLLAR SIDE BET.

Those were only the headlines, stretching clear across the page. The article went on to say that Champion Jack Ortega had just learned that Abe, the Newsboy, had invaded the American Canal Zone pretending to be a fighter. "Abe is a cheese champion," said Ortega. "The Newsboy pretends to have whipped Young Jack Johnson, champion of the British West Indies, but he is trying to kid the sports in order to advertise his business which is that of a peddler. If he ever gets in the same ring with me," said the champion, "I will kill him with one blow of my fist. And I could kill six more peddlers like him at the same time so as to make seven at a blow. I am itching to get at this big hunk of cheese and eat him. They say that he is cross-eyed, but that won't injure my appetite. I will gouge out his eyes and eat them for grapes."

When my friends read me that much of the article I felt sick. Oy yoi! What a headache! Here I had invested my money in these papers and now I would have to throw them overboard. Or else peddle these papers to get my money back. Insult, would I have to carry this greaser's insult with my own legs at my own expense among my friends while it cost him nothing but the wind of his lungs?

After I had sold all the papers, I ran as fast as I could for the Plaza to catch the afternoon train for Panama City. I had forty-four dollars in my wallet, and I decided to go and look this bear cat over on his own grounds.

I missed the train by half an hour. Then I tried to call Mr. Daly on the phone and couldn't get him. I tried to locate my Naval Friend next, and couldn't get him by phone either.

I decided to go down to the Canal and find some of the friends that had been introduced to me at the Lobby Cafe. One was named Jim something— all I remember is his first name. They also called him "Snappy," because he used to tell the workmen under him to "Make it snappy," and thus he first introduced the word into the Army and Navy. He had told me that he would give a thousand dollars to see Jack Ortega given "the hell of a good beating that is coming to him."

Now I wanted to look on "Jim's" face again, because it looked sweet to Abie.

When I left the station plaza to go toward the Canal Zone, I was followed by about fifty kids of all the different colors of the rainbow. They were every kind of mixture of Spanish, Indian, Chinese, White and Negro. I have seen a crowd of American newsies trail Jim Jeffries like that when he was champion. Us kids all admired Big Jim.

But the bunch of kids trailing Abe, the Newsboy were sore on me.

They were cursing me in pidgin English and Spanish, calling me a big bladder full of sewerage. Nobody can curse as dirty as a Spanish kid, it's a gift with them. And when I tell you how big a hit it made with me, you can figure it out yourself.

They would yell "Gringo Champion," then squeeze their noses and give me razzberries. "He come to fight Senior Ortega:" the way they said it you would have thought I had hurt that big stiff's feelings some way. The big man-eating Mexican gorilla had told the world he was going to eat me. Maybe he had a sweet tooth and these kids realized if he ever went to chewing my ears he would get a toothache.

You know, the newsboys can make you or break you. Imagine how I wanted to get rid of that bunch.

The mob kept increasing and had grown to a hundred by the time I got in sight of the Canal Zone. I have told you that Cristobol and Colon are not American territory, but are under U. S.

Naval sanitary administration. That is, the Navy keeps them clean so no plague can start there and endanger health conditions in the Canal Zone.

But this crowd of jeering kids was a plague, believe me, and the Navy couldn't do anything to stop it. The tough bunch followed right at my heels until I crossed the railroad tracks which are the dividing line between their country and the Zone.

A big American cop loomed in sight. The kids turned and ran a Marathon back to their native city.

"Hello, Abe. What are you doing down in this God-forsaken country?"

The policeman was smiling as I approached him. I asked him how he knew me.

"I did a hitch in the Navy and met you at New London ten years ago."

He had been working for the Canal Commission as a cop for several years and was homesick for the States. I told him how my Navy friends in New York had advised me to come down and give the homesick Canal workers a chance to see some boxing like I showed to the men in the Navy.

He cheered up right away. And when I told him I had glommed the championship of the British Indies on my way, he wanted to do whatever he could for me.

"Buddy," I told him, "you have already done for me more than anybody in the Navy could do. You chased that bunch of kids."

The cop and I walked on down to the new pier that the Panama Railroad and American

Line was building. The Panama Railroad par-
allels the Canal. Hundreds of Jamaica negroes
were carrying bags of cement on their shoulders
and pouring them into the forms at the end of
the pier. The straw bosses directing the negro
laborers were white boys from the states. They
set a fast pace which kept the colored brothers
on the jump.

I heard one big Jamaica tar baby singing:

> *"God ain't good to black man,*
> *God ain't good to black man.*
> *Let he get thirteen cents the hour,*
> *American man get seventy."*

Most of them were singing some Spanish and
English song and it sounded good enough. I
heard one American darky shoving a wheelbarrow of lumber singing:

> *"Las' old dollar done gone,*
> *Las' old dollar done gone . . ."*

He kept singing that over and over, "Last old
dollar done gone."

"What's it all about?" I asked friend ex-gob,
the policeman.

He told me that the American negroes on
the job kidded the Jamaica smokes. The Jamaica
darkies had been under the British Flag all their
lives and were not as wise as the coons who
grew up in Dixie Land under the Flag That
Makes You Free.

"All the American laborers get seventy cents
an hour, white or black," said the Canal Cop.
"If they ain't worth seventy cents, they send
them back to the U. S. A. to be educated. We

can get plenty of jungle darkies from the British Indies at thirteen cents an hour. If that Jamaica dingie would quit moanin' low about an American nigger being worth seventy cents an hour to his thirteen cents an hour, and begin to thank God that the Americans had come—and were giving him thirteen cents an hour in American money, he would be on the right road to salvation. For he couldn't make thirteen cents a day, in our money, in Jamaica."

"Kid," I said. "Now you're talking."

And I told him how I shed about a pint of blood whipping the champion of Jamaica and received so little pay that I might better have given the blood to some poor guy in the hospital where they ask for free blood donations.

I was eager to get to Panama City and look at this Senior Ortega who was going to eat my eyes for grapes. The Americans put me aboard a work train that was going back to Panama City. So I was all set.

All along the way we passed deep cuts through the mountains or giant locks on the flats as big as skyscrapers. Swarms of men were working on the locks "like spiders aloft," as my mother used to tell me about the carpenters on Solomon's Temple. And in the cuts I heard explosions that shook the earth under the railroad. But they rambled right along.

The Americans were building the Canal, and they were making it snappy.

Gee, ain't it great to be an American. Abie decided that Senior Ortega could kill him but he couldn't lick him. He might try to eat my eyes for grapes, but like the fox in the fable he might find out they were sour grapes.

I never tried to put out an opponent's eyes. Lots of crooked boxers will put alum and ammonia on their shoulders and rub it into an opponent's eyes, and blinding him by this trick, knock him cold. The only strange experience I ever had with an opponent's eyes was one time when I had been in a wrestling match. I failed to throw my man and didn't get a cent. I had no place to sleep that night and was looking for a hall way to flop in when I ran onto my late opponent and he told me I could sleep with him.

We hit the hay together, but I noticed he did not close both his eyes. He kept one eye partly open. I thought he was afraid I would steal his money, and it hurt my feelings. Finally I went to sleep. When I woke up early the next morning, he was still asleep with one eye open watching his money.

When he woke up I told him he didn't need to fear I would rob him. Then I found out he had a glass eye. He wore it while he slept with me but he didn't wear it while he wrestled with me. He kept that eye shut. But wasn't he a good guy to share his bed with me after such a bitter struggle on the mat to win those few dollars?

And I was sure glad to find out he wasn't watching his money.

So the train rolled into Panama City. A beautiful old Spanish town looking out onto the blue Pacific. I started across the Plaza, when a tall, well-built gentleman came up to me and said:

"Aren't you Abe, the Newsboy?"

I replied that I was. He shook hands and said:

"I am Albert Gutberlet, proprietor of the Normandie Hotel. It is the leading hostelry and all the Americans stop there.'"

"But Mr. Gutberlet," I replied. "You understand that 'Abe the Newsboy' is not the ring name of some traveling duke. I sell papers for a living and don't make enough money in a week to stay at your hotel one day."

"And you understand, Abe, I am inviting you as my guest. It will cost you nothing as long as you stay. It will be my pleasure."

Gee.

We got into a swell coach and rode to the Normandie. Mr. Gutberlet told a clerk to notify the newspapers that I had arrived, then he ordered a lunch served for two. We had barely sat down to eat, when a visitor came.

It was Mr. Charles Jones, sporting editor of the Panama Journal. Abe is sure getting up in the world. After the introduction, the first thing Mr. Jones asked was:

"What are you going to do about Ortega's challenge?"

"The only reply I can honestly make is that I will fight him any time for any number of rounds he will name. I came in today on a work train, after inspecting the Canal, to look him over. But I have no money. I cannot meet his terms for a thousand dollars side bet."

Mr. Jones replied:

"Why, boy, you've got plenty of money behind you. Mr. Daly phoned from Colon that he was depositing a thousand dollars with me. And Jim —— (he mentioned the Canal digger whose name I have lost, but whom I will call Jim Snappy) has notified me he would do the same. And just before I left the office a dispatch came from the Naval Reservation at Cristobol saying the sailor boys had got together the one thousand dollars which the champion demanded as a side bet."

I was knocked for a loop.

It was a good thing I had peddled those papers. The challenge of the Champion had made the boys as mad as it did me. And wasn't it great to breeze into the capital city of the Republic of Panama with a backing like that.

And that is what had got me this glorious reception. All the Panamanians were glad handing me, although I had never showed my stuff yet in Panama. But that thousand dollars from the U. S. gobs is what told the story. That was showing the stuff.

Telegrams had been flying back and forth while I was bumming across the Isthmus. They had razzed me out of the city of Colon and three hours later I came into Panama City and they met me with a band. It's hot stuff, ain't it?

CHAPTER FIVE

EVERYBODY I met in that Spanish-American city treated me royally. That is, with one exception. You can guess who that was. My first introduction to the Champion will never be set down as a pink tea affair.

I was seated in the Cafe that evening surrounded by a big bunch of Americans who were employed in hoisting a few cold beers and giving Abe the once over. In the patio behind us a band was playing. Evening in the Tropics is the best part of the day, and there was laughter and lightheartedness all around me, and that sweet music droning in my cauliflower ears.

In through the front door strolled a big husky fellow, a checkered cap pulled down over a brown scar-pitted brow, and a big cigar sticking out of his mouth at a saucy angle. Six or seven tough-looking sporty pals were with him.

The boys around the tables made way for him as he signified his intention of going to the bar.

I will never forget the look of hate on that big boy's face.

The bartender asked:

"Well, Jack, what are you going to have?"

"Give the gang a drink."

They ordered various drinks of the strong stuff. The Champion never looked at me, but I wasn't dumb enough to think he didn't know I was there. One glance at me tells you I am a pug, and a tough one, too. I had already fought more than seven hundred fights in the last eleven years, and still had another fight or two in me.

The Americans steered him over to where I was and introduced him, saying:

"This is Senior Ortega, heavyweight champion of Central America and South America."

I didn't feel scared. I simply said:

"I am glad to meet you."

"You will be sorry you ever met me when I get you in the ring, Jew. Say your prayers, for it will be the last of you. Get me?"

I just sat there and grinned. I wouldn't talk to him. I wasn't going to get into a fight until I was matched. The matchmaker of the National Sporting Club was there, and he set a date for eleven o'clock next morning, at which time articles would be ready for signing.

I bid the boys good night and retired to my room. It was fine enough for an Admiral. I got into a big bed with smooth white linen that crackled like silk under me. I said to myself: "Now, Abe, don't be a fool again and dream you're fighting this big Ortega all night and wake up so tired you can't get out of bed to sign articles with him."

I slept dreamless. I was getting used to good beds. They say that Daniel Boone, the great Indian fighter, slept on the ground for so many years that he never could get used to sleeping in beds. Abe was going him one better, for Abe had learned how to sleep in beds.

I got up late, and after a big breakfast, I journeyed down to the National Sporting Club. A great crowd had collected, and I realized for the first time that this was an important match

The Champion was there, smoking another big cigar. He shook hands with me this time, as everybody did, and we sat down to a table on which lay a set of articles all ready to be filled out and signed.

"How much do you weigh, Abe?"

"One hundred and fifty pounds," I replied, "but I will make one hundred and forty-two the day of the fight."

"Why the Champion weighs one hundred and eighty," said the matchmaker.

He hesitated to make the match. I realized that I might get killed if the Champion was as vicious as claimed to be. As I look back on it now I wonder how I had the nerve to take him on.

"You will be giving away about thirty-five pounds," the matchmaker warned me.

"I gave away about fifty pounds to the big butcher on a British boat, and got back a hundred pounds of his best beef steaks," I replied.

"You realize Ortega is a tough Champion. He has put away some mighty good boys in his class."

"He is only human, ain't he?"

"All right, Abe," the matchmaker replied. "I will do the best thing I possibly can do for you.

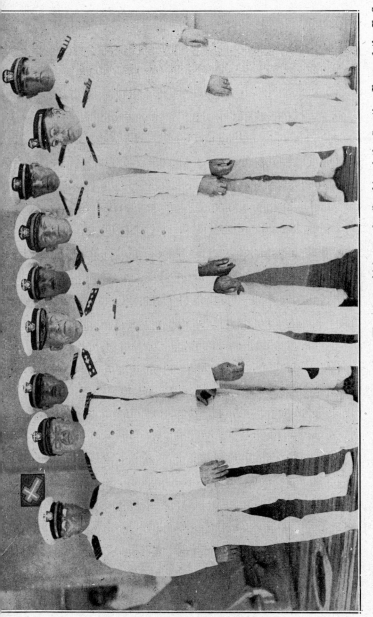

This picture was taken on the quarter-deck of the U.S.S. Wyoming, which was the flagship of the Scouting Force of the U. S. Fleet, 1929-1930, in Guantanamo Bay, Cuba. Vice Admiral W. C. Cole, USN, was Commander Scouting Force, and Chaplain E. A. Duff was the Force Captain. Names of above officers (left to right): H. E. Rountree, Chaplain, USN; E. A. Duff, Chaplain; H. R. Trump, Chaplain; Vice Admiral W. C. Cole, ComScoFor; E. W. Davis, Chaplain; R. D. Workman, Chaplain; S. W. Salisbury, Chaplain; W. L. Steiner, Chaplain; J. T. Casey, Chaplain.

(Left to right): Rear Admiral Walter N. Vernou, Rear Admiral Clark H. Woodward, Rear Admiral Alfred W. Johnson, Vice Admiral Henry V. Butler, Admiral Joseph M. Reeves, Rear Admiral Adolphus Andrews, Vice Admiral William T. Tarrant, Rear Admiral C. W. Cole, Rear Admiral Charles Courtney, Rear Admiral Sinclair Gannon. I have known — also sold papers to these Admirals for over thirty-five years since they wore Ensigns

For: Abe the Newsboy
With best wishes
D.B. Beary. Rear Adm. U. S. Navy

Vice Admiral Donald B. Beary, U. S. Navy
Who I have sold many newspapers to and known since his midshipman days.

Admiral Richard E. Byrd, on arrival in New York City, on his first
trip from Little America. One Admiral who cannot quit.

74

(Top): My friend, Admiral A. J. Hepburn, and I shaking hands on the U.S.S. Texas. (Bottom): An autographed picture of my friend, Admiral A. J. Hepburn, sent to me from Turkey for my great book.

(Top): Admiral William H. Standley, Chief of Naval Operations. (Bottom).
Admiral J. M. Reeves, formerly C. and C. of the U. S. Navy.
Two of my dear friends.

Rear Adm. W. L. Friedell, whom I have known since a Midshipman, and sold him papers on many ships. Always glad to see me.

Rear Admiral F. A. Daubin, whom I have also known since Midshipman days. A very good friend of mine.

(Top left): "On the Sidewalks of New York"—Ex-Governor Al. Smith. (Top right): Theodore Roosevelt, Jr., Governor General of Porto Rico and Philippine Islands. He is a very dear friend of Abe, the Newsboy. My friend, Bernarr MacFadden, Publisher and Sportsman.

To Abe the Newsboy
with sincere regards
U.S.S. Augusta
Shanghai China
Dec. 19, 1938
H. E. Yarnell

My great friend, Admiral H. E. Yarnell, who has done great work for Uncle Sam
in China, and who was good and kind to refugees of all nations.

Read Rig for Church by Captain William A. Maguire, Fleet Chaplain, Pacifc Fleet.

(Top): On the White House steps, before entering to pay my respects to the President. (Left to right): Captain Clarence L. Dairymple, Abe, and Larry M. Seaman. (Bottom): Abe on the White House steps with his treasure of autographed pictures.

Placing a wrearth on the monument of my beloved friend, the late
Theodore Roosevelt, in Santiago de Cuba.

Vice Adm. J. B. Oldendorf, one of my hero friends. Did a splendid job in the last war and took a chance and made good. A good guy and a great sport.

To my good friend and real Navy man Abe the Newsboy
W. S. DeLaney
Vice Admiral U.S. Navy

Vice-Adm. of the Navy W. S. DeLaney—another of my treasured friends and a good fellow. (Bottom). Adm. John H. Towers—once Cmdr. in Chief of the Pacific Fleet, who did a great job in the Navy and is well liked.

Two of my Navy friends, Vice Admiral Frederick Sherman of the U.S.S. Lexington, looking at all my autographed pictures. (Bottom): Vice Admiral Montgomery looking at my award of Merit which I received for recruiting over over seventeen hundred men into the Navy for the war.

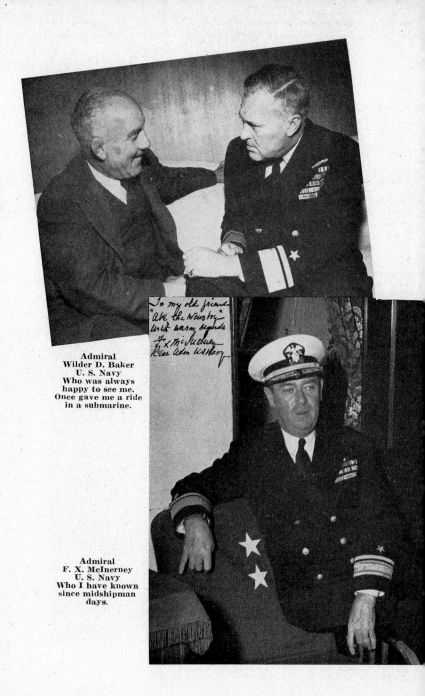

To my old friend
"Abe the Newsboy"
With warm regards
F. X. McInerney
Rear Adm. U.S. Navy

**Admiral
Wilder D. Baker
U. S. Navy**
Who was always
happy to see me.
Once gave me a ride
in a submarine.

**Admiral
F. X. McInerney
U. S. Navy**
Who I have known
since midshipman
days.

I'll book you and give you fifty percent of the gross gate, win or lose."

The Champion's manager objected to that.

"Where does our cut of the gate come in? The Club will probably take the other fifty percent of the gate."

"You've got your side bet of one thousand dollars. It has been increased to three thousand dollars. How much do you want for whipping this newsboy?"

After some arguing I agreed that we would split the fighters' share of the gate any way they wanted it.

The Champion chewed his cigar viciously and said:

"We'll split the way you want it."

"Sixty and forty will satisfy me, or seventy-five and twenty-five."

"All right, seventy-five and twenty-five."

He thought he had bluffed me into these terms by his sneering attitude. But I came right back at him and said:

"I would like it better if winner take all. For after this bout I will be Champion, and when I dictate lousy terms, the people will say I'm a smart man like Jack Ortega."

Yes, boys, we hauled off and signed articles that day for a twenty-five round go to be held before the select sporting fraternity in the aristocratic old City of Panama on May 30. That would be Decoration Day in the United States.

Gee, wasn't this a great day for decoration. Just look what I had done. Abe, the Newsboy, who sold papers on the United States battleships, weight 150 pounds, was signed to fight Jack Ortega, Champion of Panama and Central and South America, weight 180 pounds.

I had been on the Isthmus three days and either stood to be killed, or become the heavy-weight boxing champion of more countries than I had ever heard of.

The very next day a dreadful thing happened, the like of it never happened before nor afterward in my ring career. A big Spanish American worked his way into my affections, his name was Antonio, a handsome big two hundred pound man, a perfect athlete. He came up to me at Pedro Miguel, one of the giant locks of the Canal.

Antonio introduced himself to me as the heavy-weight wrestling champion of the Isthmus. He was working as a skilled mechanic on the locks, and when the noon hour came, I took him to lunch. He and I became friends at once, and I had no premonition of the trick that Fate was going to play on me through my sudden friendship with this Spanish stranger.

During the meal he suggested that he would be willing to take charge of my training camp. I am an old veteran wrestler myself, as I have hinted when I told you that I once wrestled a bear for big money. So I was glad to secure this able fellow as the head trainer for my bout with Ortega.

After lunch he went back to his job as riveter working high up on the steel work of the towering lock, but we had arranged that he was to join me at the Hotel Normandie that night and spend all his time with me until the fight. I never thought there could be any treachery, and was congratulating myself on finding such an able and likeable trainer.

His parting words, as he went back on the Canal job were:

"Well, Abe, I know we are going to have a lot of fun working out together."

Less than an hour later, from where I was standing at one side of the giant gate, I saw an excited crowd collecting about a hundred yards down the north side of the lock. Curious to find out what it was all about, I hastily joined the crowd, and worming my way into the center, I saw something that horrified me.

I have seen some gristly things in my time, but this unmanned me.

The scaffold on which Antonio and his two colored helpers were working had shifted; one end tipping down so the men slid off and fell two hundred feet to the bottom of the Canal. They landed on piles of concrete and scrap iron.

There lay my friend and his two colored boys, mangled, the life crushed out of them in an instant. The tears gushed from me. I had not cried in so many years that I had forgotten that I could cry.

But the Canal employees were crying, too.

"He was the purest and kindest boy that ever lived," they said.

There at my feet lay this splendid athlete who had been my living friend an hour ago. The Grim

Reaper had wrestled him to his last fall. How uncertain this life really is. What can you do? I have seen friends die before, but never did such deaths affect me as this one did. The nobility of nature in that Spanish-American workman had made him beloved by everybody.

Returning to Panama City I had to go about the business of trying to pick my own trainers. Mr. Gutberlet of the Normandie was as helpful as he could be. He suggested that I pitch my training camp at Bella Vista beach, on the outskirts of the Capital, where I would be away from the noise and crowds of the city. There was a dairy near Bella Vista where I could get plenty of fresh milk.

Now to get trainers. I circulated around the popular cafes where the men with cauliflower ears could be got in touch with. I selected three big husky colored lads. I am accustomed to doing everything for myself. A newsboy has to have self reliance, and Abe had been at it so long that he had become a regular one-man organization. Most fighters have a manager and a press agent and a whole staff, but if I live a hundred years I will probably never learn to depend on anybody but myself.

These negro pugilists that I selected turned out to be good men, as I expected they would. One of them turned out to be so good that I could see championship caliber in him. His name was Fitz.

Every morning I used to go three rounds with him, and they were so fast that I did not want to go four rounds. The other two men I would box with until I tired them out, but Fitz was so clever and strong that it would have been foolhardy to try to put him out in a mere training exercise.

I wondered why a man with such brilliant ability would be content to labor as a trainer for the Gringo at two dollars a day. Panama City was the hottest sporting center I ever saw, and thousands of dollars were wagered every Sunday on cock fights, dog fights, bull fights and horse races. Why didn't Fitz get a match with some near champion and make some real money?

I was to find the answer to this riddle a few evenings later.

When Saturday came, my negro trainers had to go to town to have their fun. All the Canal workers got their pay every Saturday, so naturally it was a glorious night in that wonderful Tropic Town. So I let my willing trainers off and they beat it for the white lights.

As soon as they were gone, I slipped into one of those pony-drawn cabs and rolled into the Panama tenderloin incognito. You know the Oriental Moguls always make it the practice to put on citizens' clothes and mingle along Broadway in their home town, like the Cailif of Bagdad in the story. Because you can't trust nobody if you can't trust yourself; so why not get the low down yourself and believe it or not?

I oozed into several cafes and saw what the betting odds were. Offers to bet were chalked up on the mirrors. "Five hundred, even money is offered on Ortega." Every time a bet was coppered, the bartender piled the gold coins up on the shelf under the mirror, back of the bar. Betting was very active and I was pleased to find that the Panamanians wouldn't bet more than even money on their big man-killer. But maybe they were outsmarting the patriotic sailor boys and the Canal builders, who were betting like a "drunken sailor."

Leave it to Abe to find out.

About nine-thirty I was spying around the National Sporting Club. I lamped the Champion, and saw him glide into the darkness of an alley way. And do you know who was at his heels?

My wonderful trainer, Fitz, had got in touch with the guy who was going to eat my eyes for grapes. So that's the lay, is it? Both of them were so eager to get together that they went to talking and I laid down in the shadows and they didn't see me.

Fitz began telling him all about my points, and in the darkness I could see him jumping around and showing my style to his boss. The upshot of Fitz's information was that in a feint with the left, Jack could draw a lead which he could dodge right or left, but either way the counter with the right could take me.

"He's wide open for your right, Mr. Jack," Darky Fitz said gleefully.

CHAPTER SIX

NOW I knew what I was up against. This man Ortega had a staff; he was using every means to get the advantage of me before the bell rang. Not satisfied with his superiority of thirty-five pounds which made him a heavyweight champ, while I was only a welterweight champion, he had got into my camp to learn my style of fighting. Abe was fighting a lone fight with all the wisdom of the sporting Spaniards, all the tricks and intrigues of a thousand years against him. While my backers, the Yankee boys of the Navy and of the Canal, knew nothing of any kind of fighting except square fighting.

And they were betting even money on me. What a shame. These good fellows didn't know what they were up against. The odds ought to have been three to one that this heavyweight with his tricky staff would get me.

But it was too late to notify my backers.

Anyhow I made up my mind I would have revenge on that senegambian wise guy . . . and this resolve later on had its effect when I met Kid Norfolk, one of the greatest and squarest colored fighters known to fame.

I went over to the Normandie and entered the Cafe. I was at once surrounded by Americans and they made it known by their loud shouts that their champion was in the crowd. Pretty soon this smart tar baby, Fitz, edged into the crowd grinning like a hero and said to me:

"Mistah Abe. I wants to play de lottery and I would appreciate you pay me fi' dollars."

I replied:

I owe you for four days training at two dollars a day. Is that right?

That's right."

"When you joined my camp you said you had no decent clothes, so I bought you a jersey and a pair of white duck pants and running shoes. You can have them as a gift. Here is eight dollars, full pay to date, and you are discharged. If I ever see you around my camp again I'll kill you. Is that satisfactory?"

"Dat's satisfactory," he said and took the money. He went out cake walking and clowning. And if the boys had known what was up, they would have lynched him. I didn't tell anything. The whole thing now depended on Abe alone. But Abe wasn't born yesterday. When the Spaniards threw the Moors out of Spain they didn't throw Abe out of Panama. Not yet, but soon.

I replaced this spy with another colored boxer in my camp and he turned out to be a good one. He was not nearly as clever as Fitz, but he was brave and loyal. He was called Lobo, and I want to tell you about a break of luck that this big black boy got.

We were all running along the road one evening after the Tropical sun had hidden his dangerous face behind the sheltering shadow of Ancon Hill. You have to train in the morning and evening in Panama; if you got out at midday it would kill you in an hour. We were in our running tights, treading it off at a good pace, me and the three chocolate colored athletes, when we passed a party of young ladies on horseback with their riding master.

They were strung out along the bridle path and we caught up with one of them and passed her. The horse took fright and jumped side ways. The girl fell off and her long riding skirt caught on the saddle or in the stirrup. The horse ran, dragging the girl.

At every jump her head hit the roadway.

The runaway horse was going to drag her to death. I tried to run to her rescue, but couldn't catch up. Lobo raced like a greyhound and dived in a flying tackle and grabbed the girl in his arms.

Her skirt tore loose, and the horse ran on without her.

The girl was semi-conscious, but we revived her. The riding master and the others came back and found she was not badly hurt. They asked what the darky's name was and he told them. They asked his address, and he said at my camp. This brave colored man had no name but Lobo and no home except where he slept from day to day. Abe, the Newsboy could sympathize with him. I was afraid they would accuse him of laying hands on a white girl, and I was determined to tell the world the circumstances and get justice for this black boy.

But he got better justice than I thought. The next day a Spanish-American gentleman came to my camp and inquiring for Lobo, found that boxer and presented him with a hundred dollars in gold. He then said to me:

"Senor from the bottom of my heart I thank you. I know I can never repay you. How can I show my gratitude?"

These Spanish-Americans are not bad sports after all; I felt it was our fault that the girl's horse got scared. But all this gentleman saw was that we were able to rescue her after the accident happened. He was right, at that.

"Ask the young lady to pray every night that I win my fight," I answered. "They say that the prayers of a virgin are always answered."

He assured me that the prayers would be said gladly.

This happened three days before the fight. Callers began arriving in increasing numbers at the camp to wish me luck and tell me how much they were betting on me. Jimmy Snappy came and told me he had bet seven hundred more in addition to the first thousand he had put up. "Beat him to the punch every time, Kid," he said. "And out game him. So mean a guy as Ortega must have a yellow streak in him if you ever dig down to it."

Word came from Colon that another ship had come in and that the sailor lads on it had raised a pool of a thousand to bet at even money. On the morning of the fight more than a hundred backers called on me. The Canal Commission ran special trains, although it was a holiday, so everybody could get to the celebration of Decoration Day. Three rich Chinamen came from Guatemala as the guests of a Panama Chinaman who ran a string of chop suey restaurants in the American Zone. A Turk who ran a fruit store near the National Sporting Club had bet three hundred dollars on me. The mobs came from Los Casadas, Gorgona, Empire, Corozal and surrounding towns. Every creed, color and nationality was represented. Mr. Charles Cantor, who ran the American Hotel, a rival of the hotel where I was a free guest, raised a big pool and bet it on me.

The Isthmus had gone crazy.

But that was just the lay-out that the Spanish gamblers were playing for. You can't blame me, boys, because I never told them I could lick this heavyweight. I had intended to fight several bouts with men in my division and give the fans a chance to size me up.

But I was rushed into this fight by insult. And that's the way the men who backed me were rushed into betting foolishly. It takes a lot of taunting to make a Jew lose his head. But why these old Turks and Chinamen and Naval officers and canal builders should have gone goofy is not to be blamed on me. It must have been the tropical heat.

The Ancon Hospital sent word they would give me free treatment, and two of the internes came and examined me before the fight. The only offer lacking was an undertaker to give me free burial. The docs pronounced me in perfect condition.

I ate a lunch of a roast chicken, six boiled eggs, buttered toast and a quart of milk. A big feed for a little fellow. Then I slept till two p. m. The fight was billed for three.

I arose and put on my fighting togs and donned a bath robe. I sat on the hotel veranda and chatted with friends till two-thirty. An automobile, donated by Smallwood Brothers, was ready for me. I arose and was ready to face the man killer.

The least I could do was die fighting. The greatest chance of my life awaited me. I had never learned to read and write, nor had any of the advantages that come to most American boys, because I arrived from Russia at six and had to start out at once to support my father who had worked himself blind to get mother and me to this land of opportunity.

My friends and I piled into the automobile and we were off for the battle ground. Along the way hundreds of colored folks who didn't have the price of admission had turned out to wave us good luck.

We swung into Central Avenue and approached the stadium, the very first words I heard as we slowed up in crossing the railroad tracks was the challenging cry:

"One thousand dollars to eight hundred on Abe, the Newsboy."

For the love of Mike, I was going into the ring

a favorite over the heavyweight boxing champion of Panama. Something was wrong with their heads but evidently nothing was wrong with their hearts. If heart could win, I would win. Fellows, I felt eager for action. Abe, the Newsboy was ready.

We were halted at the door, me and my training squad. What do you know about that? They told us we couldn't go any farther until a dozen Panama policemen could assemble and escort us to our dressing room. Those Spanish-American cops regarded it as an honor, and the Spanish police are as keen for honor as all policemen are. Well, fellows, we took our place between the double line of cops, and all of us strutted to the dressing room like a French king going to the guillotine.

A dozen Congressmen, direct from Washington, D. C., with their wives, came in and occupied boxes in the grand stand draped with the American Flag. It was a committee inspecting the Canal and they had come down in the Mayflower, the Naval yacht on which I had got my start in boxing line by sparring with President Roosevelt.

It was a good luck omen, anyhow. Decoration Day, and somebody is going to get decorated soon. I sat down in my dressing room and Lobo massaged my calves just to be doing something in that nervous moment. Reader, did you ever wonder what a fighter thinks as he waits for the opening gong. Plenty of noise and excitement came to our ears from the arena. Suddenly it increased to a terrific steady roar and I knew some fighter was down and being counted out. Then I heard the announcer in a clarion voice yell above the noise:

"Soldier Cumberly wins by a knock-out in the fifth round." Well, the Army had come through all right on our national memorial day. Lobo began fanning me with a towel and rolled his eyes and seemed to be saying prayers and incantations. I remembered the Jamaica laborer who sang: "God not good to black man," and thought of Lobo and the hundred dollars that brave fellow had picked up by good luck.

The cheering had died down. Then it suddenly broke out with an awful noise. One of my boys said:

"Ortega has just entered the ring."

Can you imagine how words like that thrill a fighter? I will admit that I was excited, my heart beat very fast and I quivered like a banjo string.

Joe Engelberg, the announcer, put his head inside the door and I jumped. He asked:

"All ready, Abe?"

I replied I was all set, and so our procession started for the ring. On our way it seemed that fifty hands were extended to me, and I heard a hundred say:

"Good luck, Abe!"

I crawled between the ropes and received a grand ovation.

The Champion sat in his corner with a sneer on his face; and fanning him at a mile a minute clip was my former trainer, Fitz. Remember, this was in the Tropics at the last of May, so you can guess why they fanned a fighter before he even started.

We were first called to the center of the ring to have our pictures taken, after which we returned to our corners to tape and bandage our hands. I could see that Ortega was a little bit plump. He was nearer 190 than 180 pounds. He was depending on this extra poundage to bear me down in the clinches.

I was trained down to a feather edge.

Ortega now jumped from his stool and with a big green bouquet in his taped hand, strode over to me like a great sport. He waved this wad of greenbacks in my face and hissed in my ear:

"Five hundred dollars I knock your head off inside of fifteen rounds."

"People make mistakes. That's why pencils have rubbers on 'em," I replied, encouraged by his grand stand play.

The referee gave us instructions, and we were ready for the gong . . . Bell . . .

He came bounding at me like a tiger, and missed his left thrust at my head. We clinched and he put all his weight on top of me. It was like carrying a 200-pound bag of cement. As the referee broke us, I shot a right uppercut to his jaw, and the crowd went wild. Rushing me into a corner he landed a good left to the stomach and a right to the head. I started a fast one toward his chin and missed, and he ran into a clinch. Again he tried to bear me down with his weight, but I pecked away at his ribs and he lightened up.

As the referee broke us he landed a mean left

jab to my face and yelled:

"Fight! You're yellow."

He thought I was a cover-up defensive boxer who had nothing, and merely wanted to stay the limit. His contempt was real this time.

I feinted him into his own corner and missed a left to the stomach but connected on a terrific right uppercut to his jaw. A surprised look came over his face. It shook him up, boys. He had called me a peddler, and now he knew what kind of goods I peddled.

The bell rang.

During the minute of rest the betting ran riot. "Hundred on Ortega." "Fifty on Abe." "Five hundred even money the fight don't go ten rounds."

The second round continued the fast pace. In a clinch he punished me badly by pounding on my kidneys with both fists. I was no match for him in bombardment at close quarters. Again we boxed to the center of the ring, and encouraged by the crowd, I rushed him. He whirled in a pivot and his right took me behind the ear. For the first time in my ring career I was out. As I stood there stunned and helpless he failed to recognize it. Instead of finishing me he clinched. My head cleared and we fought like wildcats. At the end of the round he was breathing hard and I was easy.

The third round was as fast as before. Both of us gave and took some bad ones. I got in a perfect right hook to the center of the stomach. Before I could follow up he clinched himself out

For "Ike"
with best regards
and wishes
F. S. Low
Com dr Pac.
Nov. 1946.

Two of my great Navy friends, whom I have known since midshipman days.
(Top): Rear Adm. F. S. Low and (Bottom) my other good friend,
Vice Adm. J. W. Roper—both great and good men.

Having a cup of coffee with my old friend, Rear Adm. Oscar C. Badger, talking over the olden days. Have known the Admiral since 1912. Met him on the old U.S.S. Kansas on which his great father was an Admiral, who I served papers, and also was a good friend of mine.

To Abe the newsboy from his old friend Oscar C Badger, Rear Admiral USN.

To my old friend "Abe the Newsboy" Oscar C Badger Rear Admiral USN.

My hero friend, Rear Adm. Oscar C. Badger, who did a good job to help win the war. (Bottom): Official Navy photo U.S.S. Iowa

THE WORLD

Rear Admiral Lawrence F. Reifsnider who I boxed with in Midshipman days.
He is a good boxer and a good fellow.

★ ★ ★ ★

My old friend, Captain James E. Maher, whom
I have known since Midshipman days. He has two
fine sons, who I hope will follow in his footsteps
—and become heroes in the Navy.

With best wishes to my friend of old Abe, The Newsboy whom I first knew when I made the 1905 Midshipman Cruise on the U.S.S. Chesapeake a square rigged Sailing Ship—

Harry A. Badt
Commodore U.S.N.
August 5, 1954

Commodore Harry A. Badt, retired, who I have known since 1905, and never failed to bring him a newspaper.

To my old friend
"Abe the newsboy"
whom I first knew
in 1912 when I was
an Ensign. A lot
of water has
passed under the
dams but Abe
remains
unchanged.
M. S. Tisdale
Rear Adml
U. S. Navy

My old Navy friend, Rear Adm. M. S. Tisdale

Rear Admiral J. L. Holloway, Jr., one of my Navy friends.

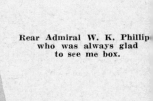

Rear Admiral W. K. Phillip who was always glad to see me box.

With best wishes to my old friend of long standing "Abe the Newsboy"
James Fife
Rear Admiral U.S.N.

My good friend, Rear Adm. James Fife. Known since Midshipman days.

To My long time friend "Abe the News Boy"
O.N.Read

Rear Admiral O. N. Read, whom I have known since Midshipman days.

Three of my great Navy friends (top, left to right): Admiral C. C. Bloch and Vice-Admiral E. C. Kalbfus: bottom): Rear Admiral R. S. Holmes.

Four of my dear Admiral friends who are retired now. (Top left): Hugh Rodman;
(Top right): W. S. Crosley. (bottom left); J. V. Chase; bottom right):
R. H. Leigh.

Captain
Ray E. Arison
My good friend who
I have known for
many years.

Best Regards to
Abe [signature]

For Abe who
the news boy who
sold many papers
to the Sharps
LD Sharp Jr

Captain
Louis D. Sharp, Jr.
One of my good
friends of the Sharp
family, some of
whom have made
Admiral.

114

Above—Captain H. G. Bruton. Three of my Navy friends.
Below—Captain J. T. Acuff, USN, Captain R. A. Dierdorff, USN.

Always a pleasure to meet up with Rear Admiral John P. Wamble.

My good friend Rear Admiral Bernard H. Bieri.

My old friend, Captain J. A. Connoly, who is doing a wonderful job at the Naval Training Center, San Diego.

of danger. We broke and he hit me fully six inches below the belt. I winced in pain and the referee cautioned him against fouling.

In the fourth round he stunned me again just as the bell rang. In the fifth we were still going at that mad pace, and the Tropical sun had cleared the awnings and was shining on our tortured bodies. What a terrible contest. He rushed so madly we both fell to the canvas, me on top. We got up and stood slugging toe to toe, madder than hornets. Bang, I popped his nose for the claret. I believed he was growing weak. I landed another to his stomach as the bell rang, and he went wobbly to his corner.

The crowd had nearly worn themselves out betting and yelling. Five such rounds of fighting had never been seen in Latin-America. Men were too excited to talk. I saw men here and there buy a bottle of beer from the vendors, take one swallow and throw the bottle away because they were too excited to drink it.

The sixth round was slower. Three times he set himself and delivered his knock-out wallop, but there was nobody at the door to sign for it and take it. He had started his big artillery too late.

In the seventh round he was about all in. I punished him all over the ring. A hard wallop to the heart, and his eyes went glassy!

Grapes, boy, grapes.

I set myself for the put-over. But he lifted his leg and put his knee in my groin like a battering ram. As the kick bore me back dizzy with pain, the referee grabbed me in his arms, and lifted up my right hand, signalizing to the crowd that Abe, the Newsboy was now heavyweight champion of Panama and Central and South America.

Decoration day was drawing to its close, and the Navy boys that backed me had cleaned up. And a Soldier boy had won the preliminary.

"Three cheers for the Red, White and Blue."

CHAPTER SEVEN

YOU can't realize what it is like to become a champion. I couldn't realize it. I had been plugging, plugging, plugging all my life. Just like a thousand other boys. Just like a million. The best I had ever hoped for was to get an even break some day, so there would be a chicken in the pot.

And now I was being carried on the shoulders of men mad with joy. Those men were well to do and could eat prime steak whenever they wanted to. Why were they so glad that Abe had won? It must have been partly because they liked me.

They carried me to a big car which the Panamanians had hastily prepared for me. It was draped with American flags and had a big banner on each side which said: THE NEW CHAMPION. The mayor's son, Dave Cordosa, put me and my training staff in this automobile and drove through all the main streets of the capital city and then took me to the City Hall and presented me to his father, Mayor Cordosa.

The Mayor told me that on the morrow I would be formally presented to the President of the Republic of Panama. This was less than seven years after I had got my start in life by presenting myself to President Roosevelt.

If it hadn't been for Roosevelt, I would never

have been in Panama. And if it hadn't been for Roosevelt, there would have been no Panama Canal. And if it hadn't been for Roosevelt's Canal, there would have been no President of the Panama Republic to give a reception to Abe, the Newsboy.

I was ticking the right guy in the ribs when I ticked Roosevelt.

They gave me a dinner that night at the Central Hotel, headquarters of the sporting element, and Mr. Theodore McGinnis, manager of the Balboa brewery, was toastmaster. One big man after another got up and made speeches, complimenting me. You never heard anything like it in your life. I never did. Of course, I had never seen a banquet before. The first banquet I ever saw was a banquet given to me. That's a record, boys.

After they had said as many nice things about me as they could have said if I had been George Washington and the date had been the Fourth of July, the toastmaster announced that they were going to give me a gold-buckled belt with my name engraved as champion of Panama. "And now," he said, "a rising toast to Abe, the Newsboy."

They stood up and drank it off. And I supposed that was the end, as I was very tired.

But now they called on me for the speech of the evening.

Gee, fellows. What chance did I have? My brain had been pounded by this big mauler all afternoon, and it had been fried in the Tropical sun, like an omelette. And, besides, I had never been called on for a speech in all my life. The only challenges a newsboy gets are given with curses, and his only answer is a sock.

I sat there looking foolish after Mr. McGinnis called on me.

Everybody began yelling: "Get up, Abe, get up."

I had heard that cry a hundred times when I was floored and out. And I got up. And I leaned on the table while my head cleared, and I said:

"Fellows, when you offer to give me a belt, remember that I took all the belts I could stand this afternoon."

Gee, they yelled. The roar braced me again, and I said:

"I am invited to meet the President of Panama tomorrow. Now, boys, if you expect me to lick him, you have got to let me get a little sleep."

It was a riot; I ain't lying. They wrecked the place. They had all heard about me hitting the Great Teddy in the ribs; it had been printed in the Panama Journal. The sporting editor of the Journal came in and asked for a statement by me. So I told him: "I'm glad I won the championship. If that's news, you've got a scoop."

He said:

"How about being glad of the money you won. You're a Jew, Abe, have you ever thought of that?"

He had a lot of envelopes in his hand, and was laughing.

The sports who had won big on me had each

left a gold coin or two for me at the Normandie Hotel or at the Journal office. The editor handed these envelopes to me, and I put them in my pockets, too tired to open them.

The party broke up at midnight, and the Mayor's son took me back to my camp at the beach. Jollification was still going on there, with about twenty-five visitors carrying their liquor well, and waiting to talk with me. Others were "under the table."

The phonograph was playing "Alexander's Rag Time Band." That was the tune I had trained on—that and "When a Preacher Lays His Bible Down." Reader, this will carry you back to the period when it happened—when they were building the Panama Canal, and Irving Berlin, the singing waiter, composed his first world-wide hit. And when Teddy Roosevelt was an Ex-President, in good health, and my best friend.

Under the table lay a big fine colored boy. It was my trainer, Lobo. But as he lay there drunk, the other colored boys told me his full name was Prince Lobo. They insisted on the Prince. They told me he had bet the hundred dollars that was given him for saving the young lady, and had doubled his money.

"He bet it at two to one on you, Mister Abe."

"Two to one? Where did he get two to one on me? I entered the ring a favorite."

"Prince Lobo done bet you whip Mister Ortega in ten rounds."

Well, God bless his heart. I had won on a

foul in the seventh round when Ortega kicked me
to keep from getting knocked out.   Believe me,
I was proud that Lobo had mopped up on me.
When the Jamaica dingies sing "God ain't good
to the colored man," they ought to add, unless
he's under the American Flag.

That phonograph was playing:

"Come on and hear, come on and hear,
Alexander's Rag Time Band . . .
He can play a bugle call
So NATURAL
That you want to go to war.
And when you hear that Swanee River
Played in Rag Time . . ."

I had trained on that tune, and I went to war.
It's great to feel that you have battled for your
country and become a national champion. Every
patriotic song became twice as sweet to me, and
whenever I hear the U. S. Marine Band play, it
takes about four men to hold me.

The next few days were very busy. I had to
meet President Poros, and answer a cablegram
from Jamaica, where they had found another
man for me, and send a cablegram to Father
Reney of the U.S.S. Utah, thanking him for getting me started in the American Tropics. I bet
he had been reading the sporting pages to find
out what I was doing in Panama, and if he did,
he got an eyeful.

All the newspapers wanted me to furnish them
the story of my life. So I told them as follows:

"In the province of Suvalk, Russia, in the village
of Berznick, I was born in 1888. My father was

a tailor, for the reason that Jews were not allowed to own land or engage in any occupation that would give them as good a chance to make a living as the next fellow.

Pants pressing was a trade that was left open to the Jews in Russia. But the peasants in our village never had their pants pressed, so father's tailor business was never pressing. About once a year a Russian buys a new shirt, whether he needs it or not. As all the Jews in Berznick were tailors, there wasn't much work for each.

I was the last child, and my parents could not buy milk for me. Four children ahead of me, two boys and two girls, had died because of infant starvation. But I lived and was an added burden to my parents, who didn't have enough to eat themselves. An older brother, Sol, also lived. And I love him dearly. A good guy.

A notice was posted on the district police station in 1893 telling the non-owners of land to get out of the province or be fined and imprisoned. This was not aimed particularly at the Jews, as my father often told me afterwards in Connecticut. I am on the square, and I don't want to give any false statements in my autobiography. A lot of Russian bums and crooks from the growing cities of Moscow, Kiev and Odessa were circulating through the peasant country, gypping the people on skin games and robbing them with holdups and burglaries. So the Czar's police tried to clean them out, and the fact that the order to chase the non-owners of land would also drive out the poor Jews didn't worry the Czar. Every time a Russian is in trouble, he socks a Jew for luck.

We had a cousin, Max, who had travelled much. He was a strong boy and used to work as a dock heaver, carrying lumber, fish, wheat, and stuff aboard the ships, and he often shipped from port to port. This gave him a big education—like my travel on the U. S. Navy ships has given me—and he came to our family in our trouble and told father how to get out of the country.

We made our way to Manchester, England. I was then almost five years old, and there is where I went into the newspaper business, selling the Manchester Guardian and other English newspapers. So, when the English in Jamaica lost the championship to Abe, the Newsboy, I told them they had lost it to a former Englishman, and it made a hit with those sports.

John L. Sullivan, the Irish boy from Boston, lost the world's championship to James J. Corbett, another Irishman, in the old French City of New Orleans. John L. made a big hit by issuing the statement: "Thank God, an American won."

This shows that, whether you are Irish, Jew or African Negro, if you fight under the American Flag, you are an American first. Boys, it's great to be an American.

The way we came to Manchester, England, is sad. This is how it happened. Mother, Sol and I, the baby, waited in Russia while papa went to America to earn money to bring us. He had a brother in New London, Conn., and my father joined his brother in the tailor shop there.   He worked hard and saved all his money.

We got a letter from him in Russia, saying he had gone blind. He sent us enough money to go to Manchester. Father would never see his loved ones again. But we could see our father if we could get to America.

Overwork is what had made him blind, and I was cross-eyed because of malnutrition. We traveled as far as Berlin, Germany, where mother found she didn't have enough money to take us all to Manchester. She left Sol with some kind Jewish people there and took me on to Manchester. There I sold papers and mother worked in the mills until we got enough money to bring brother Sol on from Germany.   Then we all worked until we got enough money to come to the United States to see our poor blind father.

That's why I was a newsboy in New London, at the age of six. I went to school one day. But I swore at a boy, and made so much disturbance that the teacher told me not to come to school. My schooling has been the world, seen from the U. S. Navy. So they printed my autobiography in all the Panama papers.

A lot of rich aristocratic Panamanians, who traced their ancestry back to the bast Castilian families, told President Portos they would like to see me in a private exhibition. So it was arranged for me to go ten rounds with that brilliant nigger, Fitz. It was staged at an exclusive club, and everybody was in evening dress.

In the fourth round I knocked Fitz into dreamland, and he took a good long nap. It was twenty minutes before his seconds could bring him to; they thought I had killed him. He was a good guy when he had his presence of mind, but I knocked it all out of him. If they called on him for a speech, then he would have had a hard time thinking up anything funny.

I mailed a draft for six hundred dollars to my father in New London, and got a friend to write this letter: "Dear Parents and Brother Sol: Use this money to make the first payment on a house and lot in New London. I have got enough challenges from other Latin-American countries to pay out. In Russia we were not allowed to own any land because we were Jews. In America I have become a champion and am defending the colors in every country down here; and I want you to own a bit of the soil under whose Flag your son Abe is a champion and is knocking them for a goal."

CHAPTER EIGHT

WENT back to Kingston, Jamaica, where the British had developed a good welter-weight whom they called Young Joe Jeanette. The sports were very glad to see me. I still carried the Gladstone bag they had given me.

"Well, you kept your promise, didn't you?" said the editor of The Jamaica Gleaner. He seemed surprised.

"A promise is a promise," I said.

"But you were not Champion of Panama when you made that promise," the sporting editor said. He felt proud of me because I didn't take my new honors so seriously as to refuse a return fight in so small a country as British Jamaica.

"Say, kid, listen," I replied. "If I thought being Champion of Panama gave me the right to doublecross my friends, I would be so ashamed of it that I would never confess I was champion."

They gave me a dinner that night at the Myrtle Bank Hotel, and I signed articles to box their new champion for a ten-round go.

The Myrtle Bank Hotel sounds like a million dollars. I had stayed at the Marine Garden Hotel when I came to Kingston the first time. A marine garden is a lot of coral with some green sea-

weed and a goldfish in it. And a myrtle bank is
a bank of sand covered with the green myrtle
bush. In Connecticut it would have been the
bank of violets hotel. Well, I was just one of
the violets in that hotel and not one of the presidents of a bank.

But I had a good break at the Myrtle Bank.
I met a man that I had long wanted to meet.
Sitting on the verandah one afternoon, I saw a
handsome middle-aged military man smoking
one cigarette after another.

It was the face I had looked into when I
awoke from my dream fight with Ortega and
was gazing at a portrait on the wall—Colonel
Goethals.

I went over to him and said:

"We are a couple of great men and we ought
to know each other. You are the builder of the
Panama Canal, and it takes a great man to do
that. I'm Abe, the Newsboy, heavyweight champion of Panama, although I weigh only 142
pounds. It takes a great little man to do that."

He threw away his cigarette and forgot his
Canal problems while he talked with me about
my career as fighting newsboy of the Navy. How
did I get the idea of "Newsboy of the Navy"
he asked me. And I told him:

"I was selling papers in New London, and was
about seven or eight years old, when a man with
gold braid stripes around his sleeve bought a
paper from me. I grabbed his wrist and kept
looking at that insignia, cross-eyed, and said:

"Mister, are you a captain on a ship?"

I was thinking of the captain on the ship that I had come over from England on. He didn't get mad. He said:

"I am lieutenant-commander of one of the ships of the White Squadron out there in the bay."

"What's the bay?"

He pointed to the ocean and said:

"Do you see that white ship right out there? I am an officer on that ship. These other ships are called the White Squadron, and they belong to the United States Navy." He seemed to like me.

Finally he asked me if I would like to sell papers on those battleships. He said I would get five cents apiece for the papers, instead of a penny. You can guess the answer. "All right," he said, "get a big bunch of papers and meet me on the dock this afternoon at four."

When I came down to the dock, the other newskids asked me what I had such a big bunch of papers for. "Oh, look at Abie," they said, "he's going to get stuck for about twenty cents."

Twenty cents was about all a kid cleared in those days if he was a good hustler. I told the other newsies that I was going to sell this bundle of forty papers out there on that ship. And I was going to get five cents apiece for them. They yelled that I was crazy; no place in the world did men pay five cents for a newspaper. They asked me: "Who told you?"

I said a man in the uniform of the U. S. Navy told me to meet him here this aft' with a big bunch of papers and he would take me out to those ships, and I could clean up.

"He was kidding you," they yelled. "You're a fool. You're one of these bonehead foreigners. This Navy man put one over on you."

I laid down my papers and went for that kid. Gee, we had a terrible fight. He was bigger than I. We rolled in the dirt, and bit and scratched and slugged. He tore my shirt all to pieces, and I was broken-hearted. That shirt cost twenty cents, and I had a blind father. Oi yoi!

I was crying when he let me up. Then I saw the Naval uniform and yelled:

"Here he comes, now!"

The man came and picked up my papers and put them under one arm. He took me under the other arm and let me into a water front hotel and washed the blood and dirt off my face. Then we went back on the wharf and went down some steps and got into a steam launch that was waiting for the Naval Officer.

You ought to have seen those other newsies. They were pop-eyed.

And that's how I went aboard the flagship of the White Squadron and was introduced to Fighting Bob Evans . . . I told Colonel Goethals all about my whole career in the Navy, right down to the time when I won the Championship of Panama. I passed him a nice compliment, telling him that I couldn't have been the Panama Champion if he had not been successful in the building of the Canal.

Colonel Goethals patted me on the shoulder

and said:

"You're a fighting American, Abe, and absolutely artless and on the level. We need champions like you, and I hope you will always remain true blue."

A couple of negro porters, who stood watching us, said: "Dat's Abe, de Newsboy, de great American champion. Wonder who is de other guy?"

We talked a while longer, and when we parted he said that if there ever was anything he could do for me, to call on him at the Administration Building, Balboa, Canal Zone.

And so we parted good friends. And later on I did call on him for a little help. It was when I got a letter that my father was seriously ill, and I didn't want to wait for a battleship to go north, which might be months. And I didn't have enough to go on a commercial liner. Colonel Goethals gave me the "Government rate," which permits a soldier to travel for one-third the cost. The Government pays the other two-thirds afterwards.

So, Reader, if you wonder why gold could never buy Abe to do some of the things that will be described later in this book, remember that I was recognized as both a soldier and a sailor by my country. Colonel Goethals of the Army regarded me as a true soldier, and all the Admirals of the Navy regarded me as a fighting sailor, and five Presidents, who were Commanders-in-Chief of both the Army and Navy, were good enough to sign their endorsements of me, com-

Capt. Harley F. Cope   Capt. K. M. McManes   Capt. E. R. Gardner.

Capt. T. C. Aylward   Capt. G. R. Gardner.

All my good friends of the Navy.

135

To a Navy Friend
L. T. Malone Capt. USN

Captain L. T. Malone at the Naval Training Center, San Diego, who is a training officer there. He is well liked at the station and doing a great job, always trying to make the men happy there.

To: my old friend Abe the new toy whom I respect and admire

Thornton C Miller

Rear Admiral Thornton C. Miller, Chaplain of the U. S. Navy
I was very happy to hear of his promotion to Admiral. I assisted Admiral Miller in the welfare and recreation of the crew of the USS CAMDEN twenty-five years ago.

To "Abe"
Hero of a "thousand
Fights" and friend
of a million Navy men
Sincerely
Razzie Truitt

Chaplain Razzie W. Truitt, U. S. Navy
A good friend from whom I have obtained much good advice.

My good friend, Captain Warren F. Cuthrill, Navy Chaplain who has been a friend in time of need.

(Top): Your good Captain and my good friend, Capt. Henry C. Gearing, Jr., in the Naval Training Station, San Diego. (On the Bottom): Comdr. L. S. Schulten, the training officer and Comdr. M. C. Irwin, executive officer of the Naval Training Station, San Diego, and Abe, shaking hands with the Captain and between the two commanders.

Capt. Henry C. Gearing, Jr. shakings hands with Wendell Willkie in the Naval
Training Station.
Great guy and good fellow. Willkie having dinner with the sailors and my good
friend, Capt. Henry C. Gearing, Jr.

"To Abe — The Sportsman,
Lt. Com. O. B. Relyea"

To Abe — A good Effort
Capt. H. E. Richter

Lt. Comdr.   Captain
Oren B. Relyea, USNR   H. E. Richter, USN
With Athletic Excellency Trophy, April 1949.

To All with best wishes from his friends of long standing at the Naval Training Station San Diego.

26 March 1941.

Henry Gearing
Captain U.S. Navy
Commanding

These are the chiefs who have served 20 to 30 years in the Navy and have returned back on account of National emergency. They are called the Iron Men of the Navy because we used to have wooden ships and iron men. Now we have iron ships and intelligent men—a No. 1 Navy and No. 1 leaders. The bottom row is our good Captain Henry C. Gearing, Jr., and the staff of officers of the Naval Training Station, San Diego.

To Abe my
longtime friend and
advisor on boxing matters
with my regards and best
wishes. L. C. Sheelind .

One of my great Naval friends who I have known on the U.S.S. Rhode Island
many years ago. The Admiral Doctor said: "If you keep fighting you will surely
get a cauliflower ear. If you get one I will try to fix it for you." I couldn't get
in touch with him at that time. He sure is a great Doctor and
a great fellow.

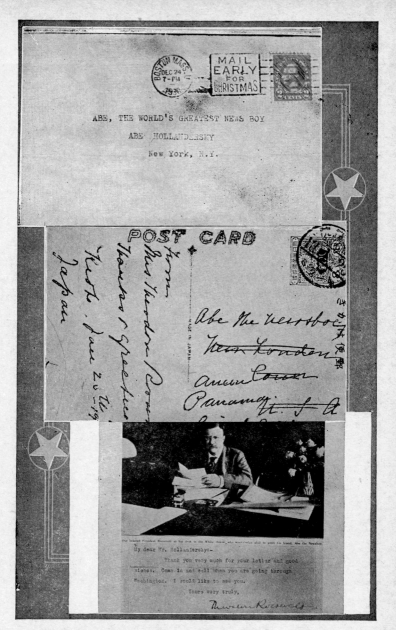

ABE, THE WORLD'S GREATEST NEWS BOY

ABE HOLLANDERSKY

New York, N.Y.

POST CARD

Abe the Newsboc

New London

Ancon Canal

Panama

From
Mrs Theodore Roose
Theodor's Greeting
Kobe June 20 '12
Japan

My dear Mr. Hollandersky:-

Thank you very much for your letter and good
wishes. Come in and call when you are going through
Washington. I would like to see you.

Yours very truly,

Theodore Roosevelt

in New York City. (Center): A post card from Mrs. Theodore Roosevelt,
sent to me from Japan. (Bottom): An invitation from the late
President Roosevelt to come to the White House at any time.

145

Three great Admirals who have passed away. (Top): Admiral Moffet; (Center): Admiral Coontz; and (Bottom): Admiral Benson.

Our fighting late president and the late Admiral Sims, whom I have known for many years.

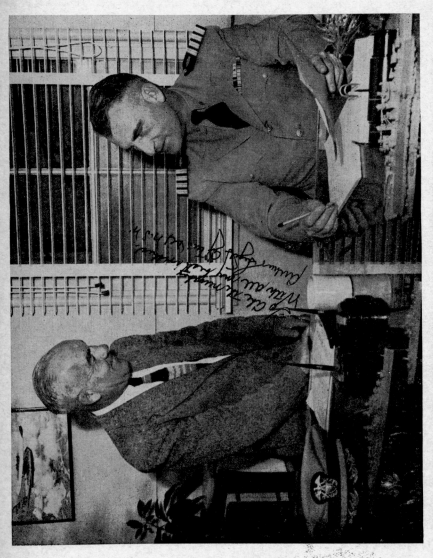

My good friend Captain Decker, Arthur Siegel, R.C., U.S.N.

Text within image, sign reads:
"THE DIFFICULT WE DO IMMEDIATELY. THE IMPOSSIBLE TAKES A LITTLE LONGER."

Handwritten inscription:
To "Abe" the Newsboy an acquaintance of many years. A loyal Navy Booster.
[signature] Captain C. U. S. Navy.

Box label reads: "OUTGOING"

Chatting about the old Navy with my good friend, Captain Albert S. Friedman whom
I have known for fifty years.

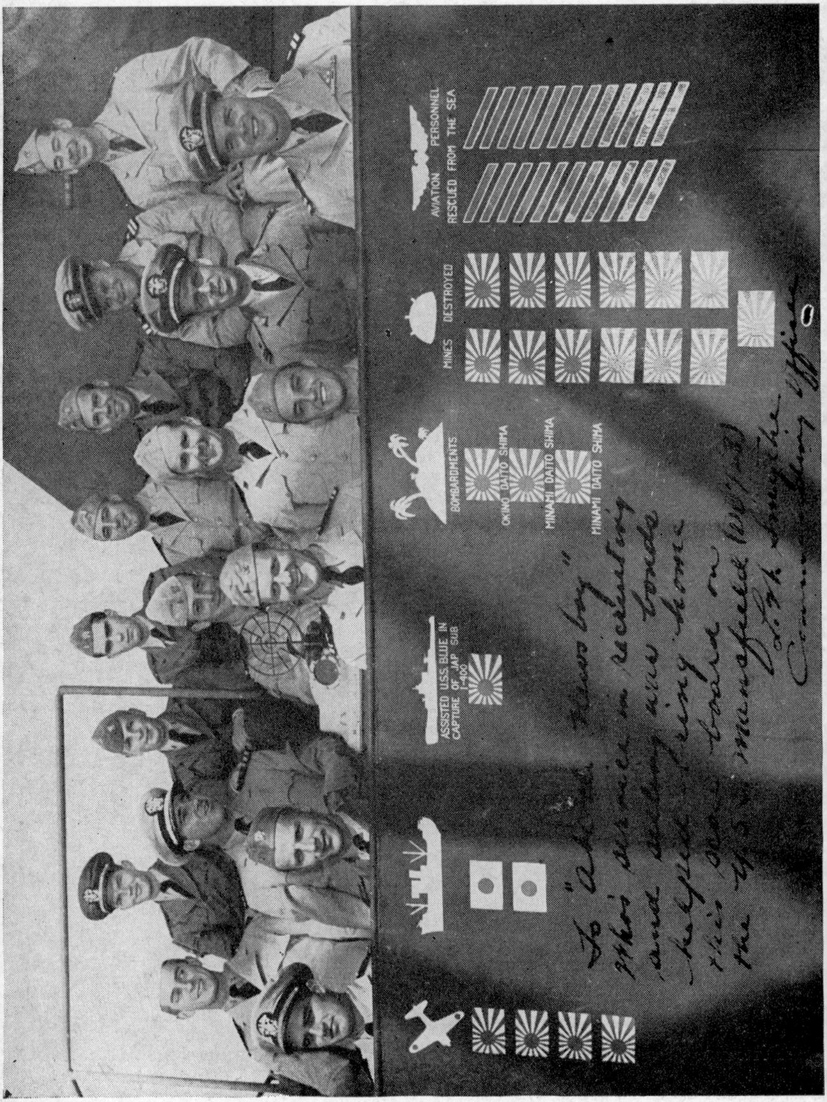

ASSISTED U.S.S. BLUE IN CAPTURE OF JAP SUB I-400
BOMBARDMENTS
OKINO DAITO SHIMA
MINAMI DAITO SHIMA
MINAMI DAITO SHIMA
MINES DESTROYED
AVIATION PERSONNEL RESCUED FROM THE SEA

missioning me to ply the newsboy trade (which
includes fighting) anywhere under the territory
of Our Flag, forever.

Well, the fight in Kingston, with Young Joe
Jeanette, came off in the open air at Central Park
arena. I had little difficulty in whipping the
colored boy. He was in the welterweight division, and didn't have anything on me in weight.
What he counted on was courage. He had lately
licked some heavier men in the British Islands
of the Western Hemisphere, and they had
brought him to Kingston to out-game me.

This made me mad. I thought of the Jamaica
negroes getting thirteen cents an hour under
Colonel Goethals, and getting thirteen cents a
day under any other flag. So I licked this darkey
so he would go to Panama to earn some good
wages and get in with a good crowd.

I returned to Panama, having received a
cabled challenge from Valparaiso, Chile. It was
telegraphed to Panama City and forwarded by
cable to Jamaica. Valparaiso has always been
a fighting point between Yankees and Chileanos.
The Chileanos are called "The Yankees of South
America." Back in President Harrison's administration, when I was a baby in Russia, a whale
of a street fight took place between the kids of
Valparaiso and the sailors of an American merchant ship. It almost led to a war between the
two countries. I heard all about it when I went
to Chile to defend my Championship.

I'll tell about this later.

But, before boxing struck the Latin-American

countries, the national sport was bull fighting. So now I want to tell you about the first bull fight I ever saw.

I went to this bull fight with a nephew of an Admiral, who was a friend of Colonel Goethals, engineer of the Canal. This lad was seventeen years old, and had come down to Panama on his school vacation and wanted to see as much as he could before returning to the States to enter college. I was asked to take him to the bull fight, because I did not drink nor smoke (being always in training to fight), and they knew I would look after the boy at all times. His name was Tom Smiley.

We took our seats in the grandstand, and they brought in the first bull. Just as it entered the ring, a guy on top of the gate, where the bull couldn't see him, jabbed a couple of steel spikes, with penants on them, into the bull's shoulders. Those Tropic bulls are small and sickly looking, not much bigger than a healthy Staten Island goat. There are so many flies and insects and ticks and diseases in the Tropics that cattle don't have half a chance for their lives. I felt sorry for that poor bull, who had to fight the climate for his life and then be abused and tormented with steel spikes in the name of sport.

This poor bull got so scared when he came out there and saw that big yelling crowd and got those steel spears in the neck, that he ran like a rabbit and jumped clear over the fence. He was out in the street, and I went out and helped chase him back into the paddock, so he wouldn't hurt anybody in the street.

They put the bull back in the ring and jabbed some more prongs into him and chased him around on horseback. He ran and ran and ran, like a mad dog, with everybody after him, and by the time they killed him he was a lather of sweat, blood and barnyard slime. He had gone round and round the ring like a garden hose full of pea soup.

They dragged him out to be cut up into Mexican steak for the poor, and the band played for the entrance of the next bull. My friend, Tom Smiley, had been getting white around the gills while they pestered the life out of that first animal. He was about ready to throw up the sponge. He said:

"I've seen enough. Let's go."

He staggered in the aisle, and I took hold of his arm and steadied him as we went for the exit. He put his hand on his stomach and yawped once, and I said: "Hold it, boy." And he fought down his nausea.

As we went through the rear exit we came out on a stairway where we looked down and saw that dead bull with the butchers cutting it up. The sight was too much for Tom. He wilted across the railing, and before I could pull him back, his dinner was descending down there on top of the butchers and the bull.

He felt awful bad about the mishap and thought he would have to go and apologize.

"Apologize nothin'," I said. "That was your sincere opinion of the national sport, and honesty never wears out. Stick with your honest opinion always. You saw what the bull's opinion of the game was."

I had challenges to fight in Guatamala, Honduras and Nicaragua, and being champion of these countries, I intended to fight in these little Central American countries and pick up enough money to go down to Chile. But then I got news that my father was sick, and if I wanted to see him alive I should come home at once.

I didn't have enough money, at the regular rate. Then it was that I asked Colonel Goethals for a favor, and he gave me the government rate. I took the next liner for home.

CHAPTER NINE

THE boxing game was at its height when I left Panama. A popular champion always makes a revival in the sport. I had become so popular with all classes, that the Panamanians were building a bigger ampitheatre and bull ring, and it was to be dedicated by a fight between me and the best man they could get—probably a return match with Jack Ortega who had challenged me again.

But when they open a new bull ring with a boxing bout instead of a bull fight, you can know I'm not stringing you when I say I had lifted boxing to a higher level than it had ever known in Panama before. When I first came to Panama an eight hundred dollar attendance was considered a mighty good house. For my second match with Ortega in the new amphitheatre, they were counting on three thousand, and offered me a thousand dollar purse.

So you see how I built up the game. I boast about this because I did it by fighting square. I want the boys who read my book to know that the square fighter will never go out of fashion, and the only way you can be great is to be square.

I fought two bouts for charity. One fight brought $1,800 for the free milk fund, and all I took out of it was a cup of coffee and a cheese sandwich. Another one brought in $2,100, and I got a glass of milk and a piece of apple pie. But Abe was proud and happy to help raise such funds for poor children. Lots of people helped Abe when he was poor.

I remember an old gentleman in New London who used to buy a paper from me every evening and he always gave me a quarter and told me to keep the change. My clothes were all rags. I went to a storekeeper and told him if he would let me have a suit, I would pay him twenty-five cents a day until I paid out.

He sold me the suit.

The man kept giving me the quarter, and I paid out. That's why I knew I could pay out on the house I was buying for my parents on my earnings in the prize ring. I had challenges from eleven different countries. And I was going to fill all those engagements. I was a big drawing card now. Just think of it, Abe the Newsboy, guaranteed a thousand dollars a fight! Because the public liked me!

Just as I was going back to the States, the flood of boxers came to Panama. Not all of them came to "get Abe," they came to get the big gate receipts where boxing was so popular. There was a ring battle every week in Colon or in Panama City, and they had forty thousand canal builders all crazy fight fans, to draw from. Money! Big money!

Reader, you know something is going to **happen now.**

Several great colored giants were developed, good tropical boxers, because the black boy was built in the tropical sunlight. He sweats and gets hot, but he doesn't get sunstruck because his skin was made to keep out the deadly sunlight. And he is a willing fighter.

Those big fellows knew little science, but they carried a wallop in both hands and were always dangerous. I once saw two black heavyweight canal builders in a battle like the Monitor and the Merrimac in the "first fight between iron gun boats." One got a sock on the jaw that knocked out two ivories. His head swung nearly to the canvas as his teeth rolled out like dice, but his feet stayed under him, and his groggy head was coming up like a tree that had been bent low in a gale. He aimed a sock and landed and knocked the other big boy out. That's fighting.

It was at this stage that the Panama ring attracted Buck Crouse, the Man Killer. When I got back to Panama, my Naval friends told me that the sports who had lost on Ortega were the ones who had imported the Man Killer to get me.

This Buck Crouse is not to be confused with Russel (Buck) Crouse who does a column of wit and poetry in the New York Evening Post. The literary Crouse got his nickname "Buck" from the Man Killer Crouse of Pittsburgh.

Buck Crouse was one of the best middleweights in the world, and he was called the Pittsburgh Man Killer because he had a terrific right which he could shoot from any angle. Pop and his opponent was dead to the world. He had scored such a vast number of instantaneous knockouts that he was world famous when he came to the Isthmus. That's why they brought him to Panama.

I am sorry to say that he left his reputation there.

Whether or not Buck was really regarded as the one man in the world who could be depended on to "take Abe," I cannot truthfully say. I give you the rumor. Because this is one of the saddest events in the story. I am telling the snuffing out of a great career. Buck Crouse's name is alive today only as the nick name of a newspaper man, and this should be a warning to all young fighters.

When the Pittsburgh Man Killer arrived in Panama, I had left the Isthmus to go to the sick bed of my father. In my absence the Killer was signed up to fight five of these negro giants who had been developed in the boxing revival then sweeping the Canal Zone.

Buck Crouse started in against these five giant negroes all of whom were so good that the Panama fans could not tell which was the best. Buck went right down the line with them. Every Sunday, in Colon or in Panama, the white boy met a colored giant in the bull ring, now converted into a boxing stadium. Sunday is different in Latin America from what it is in the North; here it is a day of quiet, but it is the feast and carnival day of the Latins.

The steel maker from Pittsburgh put away every one of those black masters of the mule kick. The Panama Journal said: "He seems to be a symbol of the steel age which is building the Panama Canal so successfully where hand labor failed a generation ago."

None of the five big fights went more than three rounds. Most of them ended in round one. Can you imagine?

The Canal was wild now for sure. Here was a white middleweight who was the master of anything they had in the Tropics, white or black. He was only 165 pounds, just one division heavier than Abe, the Newsboy.

In the midst of this excitement, I returned to Panama to keep my promises. As one man, the Panamanians and the Canal Builders, white and black demanded a match between the two men that had showed the stuff with the boxing gloves which ran the bull fight out of its own bull ring.

Charley Cantor, of the American Hotel, got hold of me when I walked down the gang plank in Colon and took me by fast train to Panama City where he introduced me to Buck Crouse. Crouse was a straight-forward friendly guy, who was glad to meet me and gave me a compliment on my great reputation in Panama. I told him that he had made a bigger reputation than I had.

Anyhow, the Isthmus was so excited that it couldn't lay straight.

(This is a gag. The Isthmus of Panama curves so much that you have to cross it to the Eastward in order to reach the Western ocean.)

I was always willing to meet the best of them. But when Buck Crouse agreed to meet me, right away, in response to the big clamor from all sides for a match between the two big shots, we found we were up against a snag. The Ortega backers had signed Buck up to meet the Mexican tough boy in a fifteen round go at the National Sporting Club. They had his contract.

They had slipped one over on the Man Killer by signing him up for Ortega while I was coming down the gang plank in Colon. Everybody knew Crouse could kill Ortega in one round if he wanted to.

Why then, did the men who brought him to Panama to take Abe, suddenly sign him up for Ortega? Well, I'll tell you.

Ortega, the bull throwing greaser, had made himself so unpopular that the Canal boys would turn out wholesale whenever Ortega was booked for a good beating. Now another great drawing card had appeared, the man-killing marvel, Crouse.

Here was a situation big enough for a Rothstein. So the Spanish racketeers got busy.

The fans thought they had a cinch to see Ortega get his head knocked off. They all bet one way.

In order to divert suspicion, the articles of the bout said that if Buck did not dispose of the Mexican inside of fifteen rounds he was not to get a penny. How fishy and suspicious that looks now, in view of what happened. But you must remember that these thousands and tens of thousands of American dollars were wagered by the Canal Builders, square guys.

I was at that fight, betting on the American, of course. But there was plenty of Ortega money in sight.

What do you know about that?

Who was betting gold on Ortega when that crooked greaser didn't have a Chinaman's chance? It turned out later that the Crouse camp was betting their shirt on Ortega and the Ortega gang were betting their shirt on Crouse.

Thus a new fable was introduced to the American sports-loving public; the story of the unpopular pug who was to fight the popular boy on his home grounds. This is the way the fable goes when read as an abstract fable without any reference to Crouse and Ortega: The unpopular pug told the popular native son:

"All your friends will bet on you as the home town favorite. There is sucker money to be taken by wise money. We'll frame the fight for you to flop. You secretly bet a thousand dollars you'll lose the fight, and you'll win the money. The money is what you want.

"I'll place your money for you. You hand me a thousand, and I'll bet it on me along with a thousand of my own money. The odds are three to one against me, so you will win three thousand dollars.

"Then we can have a return fight in my home town. All my friends will bet on me because I licked you once. I'll take a flop this time and we will trim the suckers again. The money is in the bag, kid, before we even enter the ring."

Now the way the fable ends, as you all remember, is that the unpopular pug took the popular boy's money and bet it against his own money—that the popular boy would win. Just the reverse of what he agreed to do when the popular boy agreed to flop in the fifteenth round. And when the fight started, the unpopular boy took a nose dive in the first round. And the referee began counting.

The home boy saw that he had been double-crossed. He had bet he would lose, and he was winning the fight in spite of himself. He had to do some fast thinking while the count was going on. How could he lose that fight? At the count of nine he walked over to the other man and kicked him in the ribs, thus losing the fight on a foul. That is how the fable ends.

As I said, I attended the Crouse-Ortega fight, and saw the tragic outcome of that awful frame up. In the very first round, when Crouse tapped Ortega on the chin in a pulled blow, the Mexican dived to the canvas and the referee began counting him out. I never saw such a surprised look on the face of the Man Killer. He had been used to seeing men drop when he socked them, but he was up against all new stuff when he saw a man who had not been socked, lie down and die of pneumonia from the mere breeze of a blow.

Buck strode across the ring and at the count of nine, bent over and hit him. Then he claimed he had lost on a foul.

Ortega maintained that Buck had fouled him too late, that the count was really over. When two guys each claiming they lost the fight get to fighting over who really lost it, it is time to wipe boxing out of the ring and put the bull fight back. And that's what happened.

The chief of police jumped into the ring and arrested the two fighters. Chief Pretelt of Panama City was always a square man, a great lover of boxing and of fair play. While he was holding Ortega by the ear trying to drag him bodily to jail, Buck Crouse jumped over the ropes and kept on running until he caught a boat leaving Panama, and he never came back.

Ortega got seven months in jail. All bets were declared off, and the Panama Star and Herald said:

"There was a genuine K.O. at that fight, and it is the game of boxing that has received a knock-out. The game which Abe, the Newsboy, has fought so gallantly and so honestly to uphold is now deader than a Spanish mackerel caught three days ago off Tabogga Island." They had killed the goose that laid the golden egg.

And I was buying a house for my folks on payments. I still had my newspaper business anyhow, and could keep on selling papers on the battleships.

CHAPTER TEN

FIGHTING was dead in Panama, and Ortega, the ex-champion, with whom I had been booked for a return match of forty-five rounds was in prison for killing the sport.

He was all kinds of a killer, that big cruel Mexican was. I learned that much after our big fight. I was in the cafe of the great gambling casino, the Monte Carlo of Panama, when Senor Ortega came in there, drunk and red-eyed.

He stuck a pistol in my ribs and said:

"I'm going to kill you, gringo."

He was crazy as a mad dog because I had licked him and taken the championship away. He couldn't accept defeat, he couldn't take it on the chin and smile. I saw that he was a smaller man than I even if he did outweigh me thirty-five pounds. He was yellow, and he had primed himself with liquor to get nerve enough for the cheap victory of shooting Abe, the Newsboy. The big pistol that he held against my stomach was a Smith and Wesson double action six shooter.

A double action pistol was a revolver that would cock itself when you pressed the trigger hard, and would then shoot as you continued to pull the trigger. It was the next thing to an

164

automatic, as you could shoot all six shots as fast as you could pull the trigger.

I didn't have any doubt as to whether Ortega was strong enough to pull the trigger. But I kept my head. He could not blow my brains out by sending those lead slugs through my middle.

Here's what worried me. A senorita was pressing her head against the small of my back to keep out of sight of this big drunken bruiser, and if he spilled those six slugs into my heart they would not stop there.

You think fast when you are facing death and aren't punch drunk.

Senorita Puertos, who had been drinking a soda with me, ducked her pretty face behind my back when this crazy Ortega pulled the artillery on me. There he stood scowling into my eyes and pulling on the trigger, and the girl couldn't see what was happening.

I saw the hammer jump up to half cock as he pressed the trigger, then it would go down again and bob up again. He couldn't press it hard enough to bring it to full cock after which it would have gone off and sent a bullet through my heart and into her head.

The greaser couldn't press it hard enough because he was afraid of me. Not quite mad enough. Gee, that was a ticklish situation for you.

If I said something that made him madder, he would be able to crash the bullets, bing, bing, bing, through me. If I said something that made him calmer, I could save the girl and myself.

That's when I found out I was no coward;

I was thinking of the girl instead of myself. I was calm.

"Put down that pistol, old pal," I said.

"I'm going to kill you!" he squealed.

"I know it. That's all right. That's all right. See? But we talk over the matter first."

"I have nothing to talk over with you."

"No, I know it, Senor. I make the proposition, see?"

He hadn't shot. So I knew I had saved the day. I had feared that when I opened my mouth, I would give him strength to press that trigger, and if he had pressed it just a quarter ounce harder—then blooey, good night. I was listening to hear the bang! While I was hoping to hear him say something. As soon as I heard him start arguing, I knew we were O.K. instead of K.O.

"Look here, Senor Ortega. If you shoot me you lose a return match. What the hell? You know you can lick me in the return match. Then you will be champion again, and make the big money too. But if you kill me you lose the big gate, for I am a drawing card, kid, if I ain't nothing else. It was from wise Mexican men like you that we get the saying: 'Don't kill the goose that lays the golden egg."

So I got the big bum to talking about it. I took hold of the pistol while I was talking with him, and like a pickpocket, I broke the pistol and took out the six cartridges and threw them into the fountain basin where the gold fish started at them thinking they were food. I made suckers out of those poor fish.

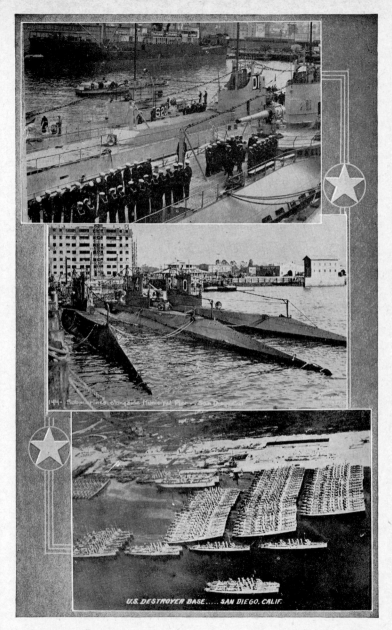

(Top): Captains' Inspection on board submarines. (Center): Submarines alongside of dock at San Diego, Cal. (Bottom): Destroyer Base, San Diego.

167

"U.S.S. PORTLAND"
KBRA CUT — PANAMA CANAL
MAY 26. 1933.

U.S.S. Houston.
"President Roosevelt
aboard."
Culebra Cut July 11th 1934.

(Top): U.S.S. Portland escorting the President. (Bottom): The "Floating White House," U.S.S. Houston, going through the Canal with President aboard.

U.S.S. Saratoga

Winstead Photo
No. 110. ©

Pacific Fleet - Long Beach Harbor

© Winstead Photo No. 99

U.S.S. HOLLAND, SUB-TENDER

Some of the ships in Los Angeles Harbor.

The Three Sister Ships.

'ive wise brothers selected a Naval career. Abe has made five new friends. Another brother
has intentions of following his brothers into the Navy as soon as he reaches the re-
quired age. The boys are all serving on the U.S.S. Pennsylvania together. Serving
on the U.S.S. Maryland are two sets of three brothers; on the same ship is a
father and son. Abe says the Navy is the best place for any young man to
serve his country in an honorable profession. This picture was autographed by Captain Russell Willson and the five brothers, for Abe.

(Top): A group of Captains from the New York Navy Yard, taken in 1905. (Bottom): Photo taken in front of Tokio Hotel, Tokio, Japan, Sept. 1908, shows officers commanding ships on Around the World Cruise. (Standing, left to right): Capt. H. Hutchins, Capt. F. E. Beatty, Capt. R. F. Nicholson, Capt. T. B. Howard, Capt. W. H. Southerland, Capt. W. C. Cowles, Capt. J. M. Bowyer, Capt. Alex. Sharp, Lt.-Comdr. C. B. McVay, Jr. (Second, left to right): Capt. H. Osterhaus, Capt. K. Niles, Capt. W. B. Potter, Capt. John Hubbard, Capt. J. B. Murdock, and Capt. C. E. Vreeland, all of U. S. Navy.

From an Admiral to a Sailor . . . getting "shell-backed" while crossing the Equator on the Panama Cruise.

Abe the Newsboy having a chat with Uncle Sam—the best
Uncle I ever had or hope to have.

Some of my Navy friends on one of our ships, and the Fleet on Parade in
San Francisco

My beloved friend, Teddy Roosevelt, sitting in the first steam shovel to break ground for the Panama Canal, which my story describes.

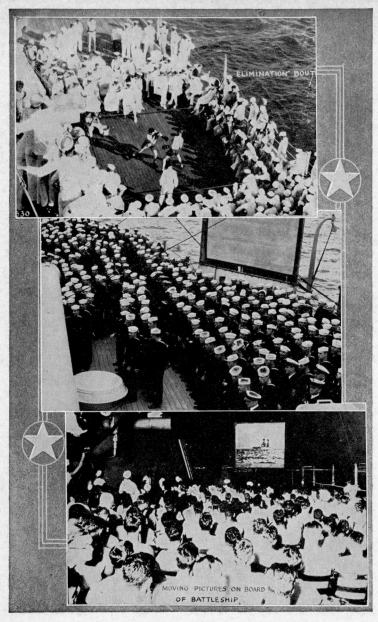

(Top): Happy hours boxing aboard a battleship. (Center): Lined up for "liberty."
(Bottom): Watching a movie.

Ships in formation. U.S.S. Northampton at top.

Discharging Torpedo 50.

War Maneuvers

(Top and bottom): Christmas on the U.S.S. Maryland, when orphan children enjoy their Christmas dinner and are then presented with a Christmas package of clothing. This good deed is carried out on all ships of the United States Navy. (Center): Father and son in the Navy—father, 25 years, and son, first cruise on same ship.

(Top): Orphans being feted and given Xmas packages. (Center): The 6th
Division on the U.S.S. Tennessee, who received first prize for the best
decorations. (Bottom): Christmas aboard U.S.S. Maryland.

This girl, Senorita Puertos, had met me at the Mayor's reception to the new champion, and told me I had the most beautiful body of any man in the world. But I told her I had been introduced often in my Navy bouts as "the homeliest man in the world." At my fight with Ortega I heard a Canal engineer's wife say to the women of the Congressional box: "Don't you think Abe, the Newsboy, is the homeliest man you ever saw?"

So I didn't know but that Senorita Puertos was kidding me. And so tonight I thought maybe she had framed me when she got me to take her into the cafe of the Casino, where this big bum came after me with his gat. Maybe she had put me on the spot!

Then I got the answer to that when she hung onto me. She was hiding behind me where she would get the full bunch of bullets if I got them. So the girl must have been right. She hadn't framed me. She was really in love with my body, for you know the gag about the kind of face that only a mother could love.

Well, reader, you know that if a champion has got a good physique—and he wouldn't be champion without it—beautiful women of the screen, the stage and the literary world will fall for him. But I couldn't afford to marry the best woman in the world now, because my poor father and mother, that struggled so hard to bring me to America, were not yet provided for. Brother Sol was starting in business for himself and could not contribute to their support at this time. It all depended on Abe.

But I knew this beautiful Spanish-American girl was all right. So I whispered to her to stroll over to the fountain and get all those cartridges and put them in my pocket while I talked with Ortega. Because I didn't know when the crazy son of a gun would change his mind and get one of those loads and plug me.

Being a gringo champion of all Latin America is no cinch job, boys, believe me.

Well, fellows, with boxing dead on the Isthmus, after Ortega put the triple-cross on Buck Crouse, the most brilliant boxer that the States could send us, I had to go to some other country for my next fight.

Chile, as I said before, is a great country down at the lower end of South America. They are called the "Yankees of the South" because they are just like the people of the United States, although they are Latins. I had received a challenge from Chile by telegraph before boxing went blooey in the Canal Zone, so now I wanted to get down there and earn a dollar or two. My parents had bought a house in Connecticut, and I had to meet the payments.

I didn't have any money to go to Chile, and I told my friends in the Navy and on the Canal. They told me that one of my big backers, a stevedore in Panama City named George, was going to Valparaiso, Chile, and had spoken about wishing Abe would go down with him on the trip. So they got in touch with George and told me to wait for him in the cafe of the Metropole

Hotel.

I went in there and stood in a corner waiting for Mr. George, the stevedore. I was feeling kind of sad and blue about the downfall of my game, and wondering how boxing could be built up again in Panama. I never wear a hat—never did; and as I stood there I looked like a forlorn fellow. My face would never be called Barnum's ten-thousand-dollar beauty, as you know. So I want to tell you what happened.

A bunch of American canal mechanics were at the bar drinking with a salesman representing some machine company in the States. He was a big brown-eyed fellow, a little too fat for his age, because his collar pulled in a puffy jowl, though he was in his twenties.

He was doing all the ordering, not letting them buy in turn, and I watched him out of the corner of my cross eye and didn't fall heavily for him, because he reminded me some way of Senor Ortega. He would hold up a handful of money and say:

"Bartender, a little service, please. What will it be, gentlemen?"

They didn't seem to like his ways, for they knew that the Latin Americans didn't have these bull-throwing manners and yet were good guys. Finally the show-off saw me, and said:

"Yes, and we will buy the bum a drink. Bartender, ask the bum what he wants."

Before I could say anything, one of the American riveters said:

"You would drink with a bum, wouldn't you?

Well, I wouldn't. So that lets me out. I won't drink with a man who will drink with bums."

Nobody in the party knew me, that's what made it so funny.

The good guy, who wouldn't drink with the four-flushing guy any longer, turned his back on him. And the rest quit his party, too. Then the riveter walked over to me, but before he got to me he said to the big guy:

"However, this gentleman is no bum, and I am going to have a drink with him."

Then he said to me:

"Old man, are you temporarily broke?"

And I said:

"No, I'm just waiting here for a friend. It's all right, bozo. Go back and kid that big bull-thrower along."

Just then Stevedore George came in and introduced me to the crowd as the Champion of all Latin America. That big Babbitt, who had been trying to sell himself heavily to the Canal boys, lost all his starch and crumpled up like a paper napkin in the soup.

"Who's a bum now?" they yelled as he slunk out the door.

But it was all his own fault. He had made a bum of himself. It is four-flushers like that who give Americans a bad name wherever they travel.

The trip down the west coast of South America was a pleasant one, and Mr. George and myself enjoyed it very much. The purser on the boat was the best boxer in the company, so he and I put on an exhibition bout.

When we got to Valparaiso, my friend George said to me:

"The local newspaper men will be down to the dock to meet the Champion. I won't tell them who you are. They'll be looking for a big heavy-weight. See if you can get by without being recognized."

So I went off the boat carrying my bag in one hand and my overcoat in the other. As I passed through the waiting groups on the pier I noticed three white men and a black one. The black boy looked like a gorilla, but I spotted the white boys as newspaper men.

They noticed my cauliflower, and stopped me to inquire:

"Do you know Abe, the Newsboy?"

"Yes, he is my sparring partner," I answered in Spanish.

"Where is he?"

"He's on the boat. He'll be off pretty soon."

They swarmed about me and asked all kinds of questions. They wanted to know how big he was, and I told them he was about six feet high. They kept popping questions at me, and I soon realized that this gorilla-chinned black boy was the champion that had challenged me. So I began sizing him up, while I answered their questions. Everything I told them about Abe's size, shape and style of fighting was all wrong, of course, because I wasn't handing out the right information. They were there to learn what they could from me, and I was there to learn from them. I guess I got the better of the bargain.

The newspapermen soon checked on me and found my statements didn't talley. If Abe was six feet high he wouldn't have a sparring partner my height. They decided I was a bum who had never seen Abe, the Newsboy, and they told me so.

"I'm his secretary," I replied, and reached in my overcoat pocket and pulled out a bunch of letters addressed to Abe. "I am carrying his overcoat and bag; he'll be off the boat any minute now."

That convinced them, and soon there was a crowd of about fifty sports waiting to greet the visiting Champion. But he didn't come off the boat, and they made inquiries and found out all passengers were now ashore.

Then they began cursing me with that peculiar word which, in our language, only means apple-sauce, but which, in Spanish countries, is as vile an insult as our fighting word about canine ancestry.

So then I told them that I was Abe, the Newsboy.

"You Abe, the Newsboy?" they cried. "A little fellow like you? Impossible."

I opened my bag and showed them my clippings and photographs. The newspaper men saw at once that I was the guy. It disconcerted the negro champion; his name was William Daly.

"But you have to fight me. You're a little man. I am a big man. You can't fight me. I am too big a man."

I took him by the wrist and turned him clear

around, looking him over back and front. I brushed my palm across his wide shoulders and felt of his arm muscles.

"You're not too big, William," I said, and picked up my bag. "I have licked lots of bigger men than you."

And I had the poor fellow licked right there.

CHAPTER ELEVEN

 LOST the fight with the negro, Bill Daly, after all. The psychology of it was all right; I really had him licked before we started. But I lost on a foul.

You remember that the Americanos are not popular in Chile. A bunch of merchant sailors put on a big rough house in Valparaiso back in the nineties, and several street boys were killed. The Chileanos protested to the American Minister, and he told them they were lucky that the Americans didn't mop up the whole tribe of them, and he recommended to Washington that the United States declare war on Chile.

It was like a giant offering to fight a midget, and the Chileanos, naturally, were still sore about it when I arrived down there in 1914 to fight their heavyweight champion. I intended to show them that they had got the wrong impression of America through the mistake of that hot-headed Minister. I would show them that Americans don't always pick on somebody smaller than they are.

They had my picture in all the papers the morning after my arrival, and as I was going down the street a little newskid said in Spanish:

"Senor, your picture is in the paper."

He was a cute little kid—a combination of Spanish and Irish blood, which is so common in Chile. When I looked into those sweet eyes, I wanted to do something for that newsie.

I went back into the hotel and asked Stevedore George to lend me a hundred dollars. I told him I had my fight won in advance, and was sure of the big end of the gate, and I wanted to fix up the newsboy.

I went back and bought all the papers that cute little kid had, and then I took him to a clothing store and bought him a decent suit of clothes. Then I went home with him. He had two little sisters and a dear mother. His father was a longshoreman, working hard for little pay, like my Cousin Max did before he was able to get away from Russia.

I told his mother I used to be a poor newsboy like her nice kid, in New London, Conn., and one day a man named Doctor Appleton of Back Bay, Boston, who spent his summers in New London, came along and bought a paper and gave me a quarter for it. And I used that quarter to make the first payment on a suit. And when he saw me in new clothes, he asked me about it, and when I told him a merchant had sold me the clothes on my promise to pay him every quarter the good customer gave me, Doctor Appleton said he wanted to meet that merchant. I told him the merchant's name was Mr. Fisher. So I took him to the store, and Doctor Appleton bought two more suits for me.

Of course, a suit of clothes for a little boy

cost only about four dollars in those days. But I could not have saved four dollars in a year.

The Chileano boy was tickled to death, and his mother thanked me and wished me good fortune in my battle. I then gave her a twenty-dollar American bill, equal to a hundred in their country, for the difference in dollars is five to one in that country.

Then I went back downtown and got a twenty-dollar bill changed in Chile money in what we would call nickels and pennies. I started on a stroll through the principal business streets and soon I had a lot of newsboys saying, in Spanish:

"There he goes, that's Abe, the Newsboy."

I took out a handful of coin and threw it among them. What a scramble.

I walked along, throwing a handful of money from time to time. The tone of the kids' voices, in saying Abe, the Newsboy, changed after that first shower of coin. And more newskids joined us at every block.

"Abe, the Newsboy, Abe, the Newsboy!"

Their cries filled the city like a Hallelujah chorus. Abe, the Newsboy, has come. Abe, the Newsboy, is king of the ring. He is champion of champions. He is mightier than the mightiest. Hurrah for the greatest newsboy that the world has ever known! That was the line those Chileano kids fed me, and it was certainly worth the money. Because, what the hell is twenty dollars? You know . . .

The big fight was set for one week from the

day I arrived. I always keep in training, so one week was enough for me to polish up to perfect condition.

I got a telegram from Senorita Puertos telling me that Ortega had served out his jail term for faking in the Crouse-Ortega frameup, and asking me to come back to Panama and knock his head off for her sake. Her sake was all right with Abe, but I intended to knock that guy's head off for my own sake.

In the old days, champions used to have a pretty lady to fight for. But I was fighting for the old U. S. Navy and for Roosevelt, who gave me my chance, and for all the boys who backed me and believed that square fighting is the best fighting, and that it will win.

The poem says:

I live for those who love me,
Whose hearts are kind and true;
For the heaven that smiles above me,
And the good that I can do.

And I was fighting for the lads that love me, and the Stars and Stripes above me, and the damage I could do to the other guy.

When I entered the ring in Valparaiso to fight the champion of Chile, the newsboys were all for me, but outside of them I had about as many friends as the Fourth of July would have trying to tour England as a road show.

The referee of the fight turned out to be an Englishman. He had once been the favorite jockey of King Edward the Seventh, and had made a fortune in the nitrate fields of Chile. He was a multi-millionaire.

He said to us, in giving us our instructions:

"Noo whin you books, you are to bryke clean."

"What kind of book language is this?" I asked. "Is that English or Chileano? I came down here to fight. I know nothing about books."

"You kyme here to boox this man."

"Books, hell, he can't read nor write any more than I can. I came here to knock his illiterate head off, and I'll do it."

"Ow, ow," the referee said. "Quite jolly 'ow. You count hit in the bryke a-wye."

Well, we went to it.

The big colored brother was scared of me. He had every chance to lick me except that he wasn't heavy on the think stuff. The referee talked "books," but he wasn't referring to Dr. Elliot's six-foot book shelf education. This six-foot jungle darky had a jaw sticking out like the jaw of the Egyptian Sphynx, but he wasn't as wise as that.

What he did do, boys, I've got to give him credit for. In the fifth round of a twenty-round go, he caught me with the hock of his glove and cut my nose in two. What a cut that was. What a nose I've got now; it scares women. Jack-o'-Lantern has nothing on me. Holy mackerel; he not only smashed the bridge of my Jewish nose, but he cut it down level with my cheeks. The lower gristle part of my nose was cut free of the smashed upper part.

How the blood spurted now. It was like wine out of a broken bottle.

The black champion's eyes lit up; hope flamed in those jungle eyes; he thought he had me. The bell rang, and I backed into my corner and sat down, trying to wipe that flow of claret away with my glove, so I could breathe. You know, like this—puff, puff—blowing like this and shaking my head, and wiping it with my gloves— you know how a fighter does trying to get his wind in the rest between rounds.

The band played "Take Me Back to New York Town." Just a few strains of that, and then "Home Sweet Home." They thought I was gone. But, reader, you know I wasn't, or I wouldn't remember what they played. They couldn't kid Abe. I knew that I would not die from loss of blood; I have often given a pint of it for charity in blood transfusions at the hospital. Why should a pint kill me now, when it was for the cause of Old Glory? Gee, I like to fight. I like to fight!

The next round, he came out eager; he was on fire with victory.

And O, boy, how I laced into him. Fighting is wine to me. They are wrong who think a Jew won't fight. I am what the Georgia Southerners call a fighting po' fool. A fight to me is like a flight to Lindbergh. I feel carried away with patriotism. I feel romantic toward all the women in the world when I'm in the center of the rosined canvas, with the claret splattering and the old fists going sock, sock, sock. I could have kissed Senorita Puertos then if she had been handed to

me on a boxing glove. The old flag was waving
back and forth before my eyes, and I could no
more have done anything small or crooked than
I could have flown.

And then I fouled him and lost the fight.

I had stung him so hard amidships that his
head came down, and as I jerked my head up to
see how he was taking it, my thick skull caught
that protruding jaw. I had bunted him. You
know what a bunt of one head on another will
do. It cut his massive chin from ear to ear. It
looked like his throat was cut with a guillotine.
He bled like a stuck pig. Both of us were drench-
ing each other in blood. The ring was so slippery
we almost fell down. They had built the stage
slanting; I don't know why. Maybe to get the
advantage of me, because I was short, and they
wanted me to have an uphill fight. But I kept
him retreating uphill and was winning all the
way—so why should I foul him intentionally?
I had him licked. It was an accident.

When I entered the ring, the crowd had booed
me. I was wearing black tights from hips to heel
and had an American flag around my waist line.
The crowd yelled for me to take off the black
tights.

They kept yelling and yelling for me to take
off the black tights.

I don't know why. But I took off the black
tights and borrowed a pair of white gymnasium
pants. Then they kept yelling for me to take off
the American colors from my belt.

I wouldn't do that.

I told them they could cancel the fight, but I

would not lay down the American colors.

"What kind of a frame-up is this?" I yelled at that mob. "Do you think I am hoodooing the nigger by wearing black tights?" Well, I took off the black, and didn't ask him to take off his black. Now I won't take off the red, white and blue. What chance have I got against a combination like this? Here I am fighting in Chile against a big African, with an Englishman for referee, and I am an American Jew from Connecticut. What chance?

But, when we got to fighting, everything went all right. The Englishman was a fair referee, and I was licking Mistah William Daly in fine shape when the accident happened, and I lost the fight on a foul.

When the newspapermen swarmed in on me for a statement about the fight, I had to be very careful not to stir up any bad feeling by what I said. The fight had been such a bloody affair, and both of us were so terribly disfigured that the crowd's nerves had been drawn up to a dangerous tension.

I tried to ease the tension with a little humor. I told the sporting editors:

"This was a regular bear fight. It is the second bear fight I have been in, and it ended disastrously, like the first."

They asked when I was in a bear fight. I told them back in New York City. They said, impossible. They didn't believe it; they thought I was kidding them again, as I did when I came off the boat. So I told them the story:

"**One day I was going along Fourteenth**

Street, when I passed Huber's Museum, where they had a big sign out announcing the Wrestling Bear, and they would pay a dollar a minute for any man to wrestle him. The artist had pictured in lurid colors, a big bear wrestling with a giant Zulu, who looked very much like your black champion, Daly.

"A dollar a minute looked like fast money to me, as I had to sell papers all day to make a dollar or less. I went in and arranged with the management to wrestle the beast at the afternoon performance.

"I went on down the street to Tom Sharkey's saloon. Tom Sharkey was the heavyweight of the Navy, who whipped them all but the champion, and gave World Champion Jim Jeffries the hardest fight of his life. Tom would have been Champion if Jim Jeffries hadn't been such a bear.

"Tom Sharkey and his friends tried to laugh me out of the idea. But I insisted I was going against the Wrestling Bruin, and that Tom had to come and be the referee. I had faith in Tom for a square deal, and I believed I could throw the bear if I had a fair referee.

"Word went out that they had gotten Abe, the Newsboy, to wrestle the man-killing bear, and that Sailor Sharkey would referee, and it was no fake.

"The theatre was packed with Tammany politicians and their wives, because it was a chance in a life-time to see a real contest between a man and a brute. Most such contests are mere stage play.

"They dressed me in a heavy padded canvas

(Top): U.S.S. Nevada. (Center): Lt. English shaking hands with Abe. (Bottom).
Distinguished Service Medal being presented by Admiral Willam D. Leahy,
on board the U.S.S. Nevada, to Lt. Robert A. J. English, for distinguished
service in the Antarctic Expedition with Admiral Richard Byrd.

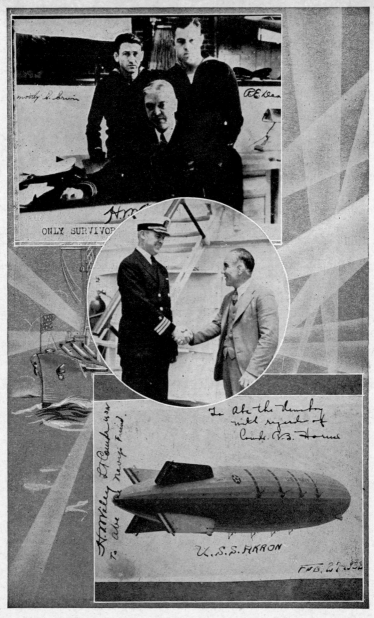

(Top): The only three survivors of the U.S.S. Akron disaster. (Center): Comdr. H. N. Wiley and friend Abe on the U.S.S. Pensacola. (Bottom): The U.S.S. Akron.

Views of the boys in the San Diego Training Station. I want to thank and give credit for this and other pictures, to Mr. Waterman. Mr. Waterman and his son have photographed more Navy men than anyone else in the United States

Autographing the first edition of my book with Waterman's great pen. Not only a good pen, but he is a good fellow.

U. S. S. San Francisco
San Diego, 10 April 1934
To Cdr. The Newberry.
R. E. Ingersoll
Captain. U. S. Navy.

U.S.S. CALIFORNIA.

(Top): New U.S.S. San Francisco. (Center): Old U.S.S. San Francisco
(Bottom): U.S.S. California

It just shows you how we love our country and we want to do our share. The father and his seven sons are in the Navy serving Uncle Sam on the U.S.S. Nevada. The name is the Patton Family. Abe, the Newsboy, the "Pal of the Navy" is shaking hands with the father. The men are shown on top of the guns.

(Top): U.S.S. Los Angeles crossing the Fleet. (Center): U.S.S. Los Angeles in a night scene. (Bottom): U.S.S. Macon crossing Manhattan.

Navy Aeroplanes leaving North Island.

Planes crossing Alaska.

S.S. ROBISON
ADMIRAL USA
COMMANDER-IN-CHIEF
BATTLE FLEET

ADMIRAL
R.E. COONTZ USA
COMMANDING
UNITED STATES
BATTLE FLEETS

My late friend Admiral Coontz, who gave me permission to sell to the entire fleet newspapers on the Australian cruise in 1925.

My good friend S. S. Robinson, Admiral U.S.N., retired President of the Admiral Farragut Academy who always admired me for my boxing. He is a great sport and always loved fights. He was loved by everyone on the U.S.S. Calif. while he was Captain.

To all friends for kind wishes,
the master of the Washington
signals X.O.R. — thanks

To: My News paper friend
Abe the News Boy

My hero friend, Captain George Fried, who was once in the Navy. The Captain who saved so many lives—that's what our good Navy did for him.

USS. Arizona — WINSTEAD Photo No. 351

USS West Virginia — WINSTEAD Photo No. 215

U.S.S. OKLAHOMA — ©WINSTEAD 3.A

Some of the ships on which I have sold a lot of orders for my book.

(Center): Old U.S.S. Tennessee.

U.S.S. Chicago (top) in the Hawaiian Islands, and the Saratoga and Lexington in Honolulu.

(Top to bottom): U.S.S. Delaware, U.S.S. Chesapeake (later called the Severn), U.S.S. Hartford.

214

coat, that came up around my ears, like armor, to keep the bear from clawing my neck. He was muzzled, to keep him from eating my head off. When I saw that long, flat pink tongue that came sliding out like a snake, and licked all around the bars of his muzzle, I felt creepy. His teeth were clean and white when he lifted his lip, like a grinning dog.

"His breath smelled like a clean butcher shop; you know, that smell of fresh raw beef. He was a nice, well-kept bear.

"Before introducing me and the bear, the stage manager recited part of a poem by Kipling about the Bear That Walks Like a Man. It was a Russian bear named Adam Zad, and he tore the eyes out of the hunter who had let him get too close:

"I have looked no more on women,
    I have looked no more on the snow,
    Since I went hunting Adam Zad,
    Forty summers ago.
"He tottered near and nearer,
    I saw his shoulders sway . . .
    From brow to jaw his steel clad paw
    It ripped my face away!"

"I didn't know they opened a bear fight with poetry. And I've never had any use for poetry since."

CHAPTER TWELVE

BOYS and girls, this is a hard-boiled world. The manager of that wrestling bear knew he had a big feature event, and so did that packed audience. But when he curdled my blood by reciting Kipling's bear poem, I lost what little belief in Santa Claus I had. I wish he had recited "The Night Before Christmas," instead.

Then they introduced the bear, as "Custer."

When they introduced me, they said:

"Take a last look at Abe, the Newsboy."

We sparred around for position. Then I closed in and dived for his legs, but the bear put his right paw on my head and pushed it down almost into my hip bones. I groaned in agony, and felt as if my spine was telescoped. I have never seen the picture of a bear since, without feeling a terrible pain in my neck.

I wriggled free, and just as Custer was reaching out to repeat this stunt of shoving my head into my heels, I went wild. I forgot I was wrestling and thought I was in the ring with a big black giant. Instinctively I warded off his paw with my left hand, and with my right I gave him the old socko punch right on the nose.

The bear rolled in agony off the stage. He fell on a bass viol worth $150, and it was worth nothing. He kicked a grand piano full of holes. The audience was in a near-panic. The manager came rushing forward, and the bear's owner charged into the ring. I drove them back like a wild man, and stood in the middle of the stage shouting to the audience that there weren't enough men and beasts in the world to take Abie.

Sailor Tom Sharkey had to calm me down. When he got me quieted and took off the padded coat, he wanted to take me home.

"But I want to get my money first," I protested. "I stayed one minute with that bear, and I want my dollar."

The manager was as mad as a wet hen.

"Pay you a dollar, heh? Hell! You broke up two hundred dollars worth of furniture."

"Pay me my dollar now, and then sue me for the two hundred."

Somebody slipped me a dollar and they hustled me out of there.

A Y.M.C.A. secretary, where they taught me scientific boxing, once said to me: "Abe, when money is at stake, the sport always becomes corrupted. So do not fight for money, Abe. Always fight for medals." I saw now that there was much truth in his advice. If I had wrestled that bear for a medal instead of a dollar a minute, I would not have got into all that squabble about the money.

This is the story I told the Valparaiso newspapers after being disqualified for accidentally fouling my opponent in the big fight. They played up the bear story in a good-natured way, and it had the effect I intended.

The newsboys were so excited about me fighting a bear up in North America, that they didn't
feel disappointed about my losing out in the local
fight, and Abe, the Newsboy, was a bigger hero
than ever.

I challenged William Daly to another bout,
and he accepted. I also received invitations from
half a dozen other cities to come and meet the
local champions.

As soon as my nose got well I started on my
tour of Chile to meet these lesser fighters and
see the country. Chile is a beautiful country,
very much like California.

In Santiago, the capital, I got into a contest
that beat anything I had ever gone against yet.
I tackled a Japanese champion in a Jiu Jitsu fight.

Everybody has heard of this Oriental method
by which the smallest Jap can conquer the biggest
bruiser that ever pushed leather. It is a secret
system of doing terrible damage to an opponent
before he knows what you are doing to him.
They dislocate your joints, break certain bones,
or press your pneumogastric nerve until you become unconscious. They classify it as wrestling,
and the Western mind classifies it as "a myster-
ious murder" done before your eyes. The mystery
is not Who did it? but How?

A troupe of six Japanese champions were on
a world tour, and I crossed their path in Santiago.
I had seen them before in Panama when I was
training for Jack Ortega. They issued a standing offer of five hundred dollars for any man

who could stand up with one of them in five
rounds of Jiu Jitsu.

I needed that money.

I once boxed a kangaroo in Australia for an
offer of a hundred dollars for every round I boxed
him in which he didn't knock me down. His
arms were so short and weak I knew he couldn't
put me down like that wrestling bear. But the
kangaroo was smart. He hit me a kidney punch
with his tail and knocked me clear out of the
ring. They had to help me get up. Oh, boy!

I decided to go against these Japanese Jiu
Jitzers if I could make a good, hole-proof contract with them. When you fight these unknown
monsters, they spring something that you didn't
know was in the contract.

I would be willing to fight the world for experience, if the other guy is fighting for the experience. But if he's getting paid, I ought to
get in on the money, too. I owe it to myself.

Well, the wrestling bear and the boxing kangaroo and these Japanese athletes were taking in
big money at the box office, and so Abe, the
Newsboy, was entitled to perform for compen-
sation without losing his amateur standing.

Not taking any money for a fight makes you
an amateur, but taking a medal is all right. I
was still an amateur in my battles with the
beasts, as I had never got anything out of any
of those man-against-animal fights, not even a
medal.

I went to the manager of the Japanese troupe
at the theatre where they were performing and

told him I had a proposition to make.

"Your men are well versed in the American style of 'catch-as-catch-can' wrestling as well as Jiu Jitsu. I am an American. Now, in place of your offer of $500 for staying five frames of the Jap style of wrestling, I've got a mixed program to offer. One frame Jap style, one frame American style, and the final frame to be in the style of the nationality of the winner of the previous frames."

The Japanese gentleman considered it seriously.

One thing he knew, when you can get an international contest on, it will draw a packed house. That's why world wars always have a popular start.

The manager consulted the Chileano sport editors. They told him I was a boxing champion, not a wrestler. So he took up my proposition, and the papers came out announcing that the Americano would meet one of the sons of the Mikado.

Count Saka, one of the best men in the troupe, who had wrestled American style, accepted my challenge.

On the night of the performance we had a tremendous house. Half the blood in Chile is Irish, their national liberator having been an Irish hero named O'Higgins. So they are great sports and would rather see a good grueling fight for a little money than to win a million dollars on a fake fight. John L. Sullivan's name is still remembered there with reverence.

The announcer stepped out to the center of the stage and said:

"The contest tonight is part American style and part Japanese style, between Count Saka of Japan and Abe, the Newsboy, from the United States of North America.

"The first round will be Japanese style. The second round will be American style. The man who gets the quicker fall in these two rounds, will name the style in which the final round is contested. Best two out of three wins.

"The offer of $500 is suspended in this contest. In its place the men will wrestle for a side bet of $200."

The audience began betting among themselves, as the Jap and I made our bows and went to the mat.

We had tossed a coin to determine which style we would wrestle first, and I had won the toss. I chose Jiu Jitsu. I suppose if the Jap had won, he would have chosen Jiu Jitsu also. But you can't tell; they are very clever, very smart. He might have chosen "catch-as-catch-can," so as to go against his hardest game while he was fresh.

That's why I chose Jiu Jitsu. While I was fresh and clear-headed I would have my best chance to keep him from getting the clamps on me. I knew more about Jiu Jitsu than about bear fighting and kangaroo boxing, believe me, or I wouldn't have had a look-in. I had received a lot of instruction in the Jap method of grappling from Mr. George Bothner of New York City. A willing kid always gets plenty of free help in the sports world.

I'll never forget that Jiu Jitsu bout; it was one of the greatest struggles in my ring career. You have to dress for the job in something like the straight jacket you put on when you cross noses with a wrestling bear.

They furnished me a big felt coat and a pair of felt trousers. Then a big felt belt was wound around my middle. They do this to fix you so they can't kill you. I must have looked like the Sultan of Turkey. All I needed was a red fez and a tassel, and I would have thought I was going to the harem instead of to the mat.

And they didn't have a mat. We wrestled on the bare wooden floor.

I soon saw why they didn't have any mat for a Jiu Jitsu bout. The same reason they don't have any cloth for a butcher's block. After the day's work, the butcher takes a carpenter's plane and trims off splinters, blood, meat and everything from on top of the block and is all set for the next day's business.

We proceeded to do war on the bare floor.

My business was to keep him from getting his hands on me; I knew better than to try to throw him with what little "jits" I knew, because he was a master of it, like the bear was master of pushing a man's head through his shoe soles. Every man to his own game.

We crashed into the scenery and ran around on the piano top, like a goat on the edge of a cliff with a grizzly bear chasing him. We stepped on the audience and fell in their laps. It seemed to me I had stood him off for half an hour before he got a grip on me.

He got hold of my Adam's apple.

Talk about a cider press! He was choking the life out of me, killing me as I lay there and couldn't say, "I surrender." I hadn't thought about that. I was fast becoming unconscious, not only from the pain, but because I couldn't breathe. And probably that terrible Manchu would be holding my corpse by the neck until it was cold. He had $200 in the pot.

Finally I rapped three times on the floor to signify my defeat. When he let go of my wind pipe, it was glad thrilling news to me, the kind of news the whole world got on Armistice Day.

The time of the fall was sixteen minutes. After a ten-minute rest we hopped to it again. This time the style was to be catch-as-catch-can. It was up to me to drop the Jap inside of sixteen minutes.

And listen, boys and girls—I did it.

It took me all of fourteen minutes, though, and it began to look like I had wrestled another bear. My legs and shoulders were all full of splinters from that first round of Jiu Jitsu; it is some sport they have in Japan. But I finally got him with a toe hold, and he went down with two minutes to spare.

And so the final was to be American style. He would have to throw me to win that $200. He stood to lose $200 and also lose the winner's percentage on the house, which was sixty per cent. When those Japs made that contract with me they never dreamed I had a chance.

The Jap struggled nobly, and he actually lasted six minutes in the final bout.

And so I romped away with all the money.

I sent my parents another payment on the house they were buying and told them how well I was getting along. I didn't tell them what an ugly nose William Daily had put on me; there was no use of me sticking my nose into their affairs.

And now came some more good news. The white champion of Chile was in Paris, where George Carpentier had set the French wild for boxing. His name was Arburto Roges, and he was the pride of South America. They draw the color line in Chile, so the man I fought was the black champion. Now the white champion, the beautiful Arburto Roges, was coming back from Paris to meet Abe, the Newsboy.

CHAPTER THIRTEEN

 DID not get a chance to fight Arburto Roges, the handsome white champion of Chile, for a strange reason. It was not his fault nor mine. He had returned from Paris because the people in Chile were clamoring to see him and Abe, the Newsboy, in one ring, and I had signed articles and started training for the battle.

But the fight was prevented by four men on horseback.

You probably think I am lying when I say that four strange men came riding over everything and stopped this fight. But you have seen these four men pictured in the movies as riding through the skies in the film that made Rudolph Valentino famous.

Yes, the Four Horsemen of the Apocolypse rode through the skies of South America and stopped the championship fight between me and **Arburto Roges. For Chile** had officially declared herself in on the European War, and the Government told the American consuls to give all traveling Americans their passports.

So I went back to Panama, because the four horsemen, named War, Rapine, Pestilence and

Famine, were taking the Europeans for a ride.

And when I got back to Panama I met the lady that all champions meet. She has many names, but they all spell love. Some call her Venus.

Boxing was on its feet again in the Canal Zone, when I returned to fulfill the request of Senorita Puertos and try to whip Senor Ortega again. Boxing had been dead for over a year after the blow dealt it by Ortega and Buck Crouse. After that frame-up, the Panama National Assembly had got busy and passed a law. The purpose of the law was to keep dishonesty out of the ring.

Every promoter had to deposit the sum of five hundred dollars in gold or United States currency with the state before he could stage a bout. And if the Congress of that Republic decided the bout wasn't strictly on the level, Congress kept the five hundred dollars.

This is the best law I ever heard of to prohibit anything, and shows that the Latin-American legislators are smart. If the United States Congress should pass a law that every bootlegger had to deposit a thousand dollars with a Congressman before engaging in the selling of liquor and, furthermore, if the Congressman didn't think his liquor was the real thing when he tasted it, the Congressman could keep the thousand dollars and the liquor too, that would be a prohibition law that would put the bootlegger on the bum.

The five-hundred-dollar law against funny

fights in Panama put an end to boxing there. For it is needless to say that no promoter fooled with the leather-pushing game during the life of this law.

Realizing that the forty thousand Americans employed on the Isthmus must have some form of public amusement at least once a week, now that boxing was dead, the leading Panamanian citizens decided to do something for the sport-lovers. They decided to build a palatial bull ring with an amphitheatre into which any American would not be ashamed to go and take his lady. They contributed thousands of dollars and started building the great Bella Vista Bull Ring near the site where I trained for my first battle with Ortega.

I wonder now if the gentlemen who risked their money in this investment considered, at the time, the principal part Abe, the Newsboy, would play in the role of main money-getter to the box office at that arena, which was built with the express purpose of holding bull fights?

When I got back to Panama, this magnificent ring was in the process of construction.

But something had happened which took the Panamanians' minds off bull fighting and got them back to boxing. Jack Johnson, World Champion, had staged a battle in the Tropics. And Jess Willard, the white farmer from Kansas, had whipped the black boy in the Tropical battle. This bout, as you remember, took place at Havana.

That got the Americans crazy for some local

fighting again, and a glove artist of renown came over from Havana and camped among them. It was Eddie Ryan. Eddie was gifted with about everything a successful boxer needs. He had science, speed, ring generalship, and terrific hitting ability.

When this great American boxer came to Panama, the Congress repealed their law, and the square-shooting Eddie Ryan soon built boxing up to where it had been when I first took the championship from Ortega.

For my second bout with Ortega, I pitched my training camp on a beautiful island out in the Pacific, about fifteen miles from Panama City, called Taboga Island. And here is where the love idyl began.

Senorita Puertos took a cottage on the island for the month that I would be training there, and she introduced me to the Spanish people living on that little piece of Paradise. They were old-fashioned people, and were very polite to me. Senor Pancho Arias, one of Panama's greatest sportsmen, assured the people that I was a square fighter.

"We will burn a candle for you, Senor Abe," they said.

And they pointed to the church on the hill.

It was a beautiful little church, three hundred years old. And that is where they lit the candle for me. I did not know what it meant, but Senorita Puertos told me it was the custom of those honest people to light a candle at the shrine of the Virgin Mother to bring her blessing on

any boy they were praying for.   These good
people of Taboga were all praying that I might
win my second battle with Ortega, which was
to go forty-five rounds.

Day and night they kept that candle burning.
When one candle came to its end, they lit another
candle from it, and so kept the light burning all
the time I was training on the island, and they
would keep it lit until I entered the ring.

I wonder if any other prize fighter ever had a
kind and loving congregation, belonging to a
different church than his, keep a candle burning
before the Virgin, for his success.

Things like that make a boy feel the greatness
of his destiny. I was a fighter, but they did not
fear me. I was a foreigner who had come and
conquered the champion of their own blood. And
now they were burning a candle in their church
because Abe, the Conqueror, had landed on their
shore.   But they were not burning it to implore
the help of Heaven to defeat Abe.   They were
burning it as a prayer to the saints to help Abe
win his battle because they believed in his honesty.

If prayers could lick that rascal Ortega, I had
him beaten. You remember, in my first fight I
had the prayers of the young lady whom Prince
Lobo helped when her horse threw her.

Prince was in my camp as trainer again. He
was now called Battling Prince, having made a
great reputation fighting the big black boys in
the ring when the Canal developed its string of
colored giants. And a better trainer than Batt-

ling Prince no fighter ever had. Another of my
trainers was Sam, a brown boy, half negro and
half Hawaiian, very handsome, like Battling
Prince.

Senorita Puertos called us the Three Bears.
You know the fairy tale about the Three Bears.
There was the Big Bear, the Little Bear, and the
Middle-sized Bear. I was the Little Bear, she
told me.

I did not know anything about the ways of
women, so what happened later was a surprise
to me.

I was soon boxing eight or ten rounds a day,
and taking a mile run on the beach. Once a day,
at high tide, we went into the surf for an hour
or so. At one point on the beach there was a
shoal, about a quarter of a mile out, and the way
the incoming tide dashed over this shoal was
like a great big fountain.

One afternoon the tide was right for bathing
at about sundown. I and my two sparring partners put on our bathing suits and plunged into
the surf. As usual, we started swimming all the
way out to the shoal. It was our custom to go
out to the shoal and be tossed about in the crazy
surf there.

But, this evening, as we approached the shoal,
we saw that other swimmers were there ahead of
us. As we got closer we saw that they were
women. Suddenly Battling Prince said to me:

"I gone!"

He turned and dived under. Sam said:

"Us all two both gone!"

My old friend Jack Dempsey trying to poke me in the nose. I said no because he hits too hard.

Instead of that I told him to read my book. He said I have a great book.

All the Stars Came To NTC in Wartime

The Naval Training Center, during the war, was a busy place. With the crowds came the Hollywood stars to entertain and build morale.

The Center's proximity to Los Angeles made it one of the most frequently visited of the Military establishments. Hardly a week passed but there were shows in the boxing arena, Luce Auditorium, or the R-2 building, in which famous stage and screen stars participated.

NTC was the scene of many wartime broadcasts, for which, a radio control booth was built backstage at Luce.

The Hoist this week looks back to those years and from its photo files obtains the group of pictures appearing elsewhere on this page. If you haven't tried to identify

HOW MANY CAN YOU RECOGNIZE?—The pictures above are o famous and not-so-famous stars who have appeared in shows on th Training Center, mostly during the war. The answers to the numbere pictures can be found in the story

them, take a try before reading the identities as listed below:

The performers are: 1, Broderick Crawford; 2, Marilyn Maxwell; 3, Henry Fonda; 4, Kay Kyser; 5, Lynn Bari; 6, Franchot Tone; 7, Betty Grable (in auxiliary uniform); 8, Harpo Marx; 9, Gene Kelly (in NTC's barber shop as a recruit); 10, Jimmy Durante a Abe The Newsboy; 11, Jinx Faul enburg, and Groucho Marx; 12, T Andrews Sisters; 13, Pat O'Brie 14, Tyrone Power; 15, Rose Mu phy; 16, John Payne; 17, Ge Krupa; 18, Ilona Massey; 19, P Silvers; 20, Joe Louis and, 2 Sophie Tucker.

Some of the people I worked in the movies with some time ago.

Working out with the boys on some of the ships . . . And, believe me, they can fight!

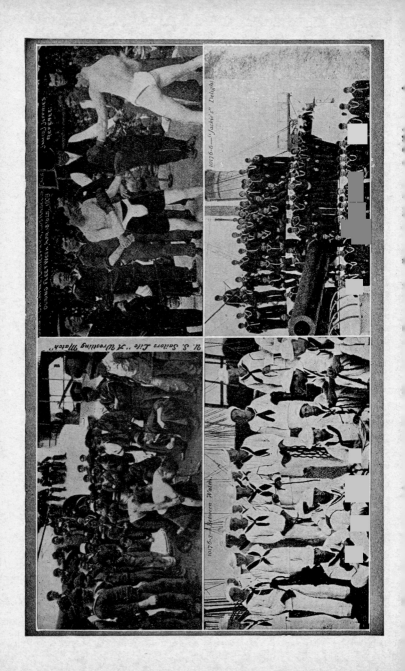

U. S. Sailors Life. "A Wrestling Match."

10176-6—"Yacks" Delight

10176-3—Between Watch

Catholic Church 300 yrs. old Taboga Island, Panama

(Top): The late Chaplain Reney, who was loved by everybody in the Navy. He was always willing to do something for Abe. (Bottom): Where candles were burned for Abe, the Newsboy before his 42-round boxing match with Jack Ortega. Abe won the fight, in Panama City, in 18 rounds.

235

(Top, left to right: John Murphy, Abe the Newsboy, Jack Kennedy, Tommy
MacAllister, Jimmy Woodruff, John Murphy, Jr.—all friends of mine. (Center):
U.S.S. Tennessee, the rebel ship. (Left to right): Mike Hector, All-Navy Champ,
Jake Shugrue, Tennessee's outstanding athlete, and Abe, the Newsboy. (Bottom,
left to right): Paddy Ryan, who said I was going to be a great fighter, about
30 years ago, while he was in the Navy; Larry White, manager of Young Corbett;
Young Corbett, and my great friend, Moose Taussic.

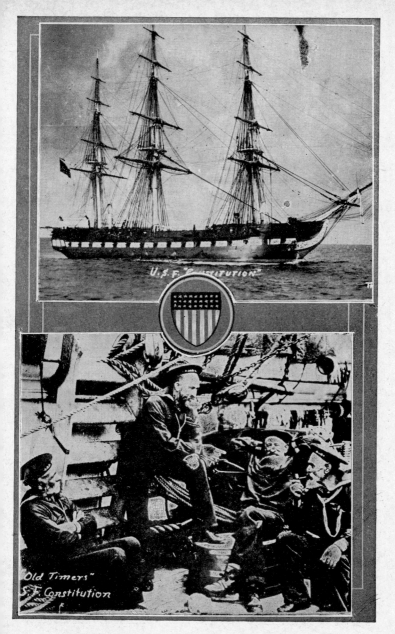

David Ireland, Gilbert Purdy, John T. Griffin, John King.

BLUEJACKET
1841

CAPTAIN U.S.N. 1812
SPECIAL FULL DRESS

MARINE OFFICER 1812

MARINE PRIVATE 1812

Uniforms of the old Navy officers.

The oldest Marine in the Corps—also carries two hash marks in his pocket, because he hasn't room for them all on his sleeve.

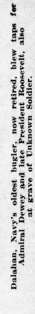

Dalahan, Navy's oldest bugler, now retired, blew taps for Admiral Dewey and late President Roosevelt, also at grave of Unknown Soldier.

Human flags made of Sailors.

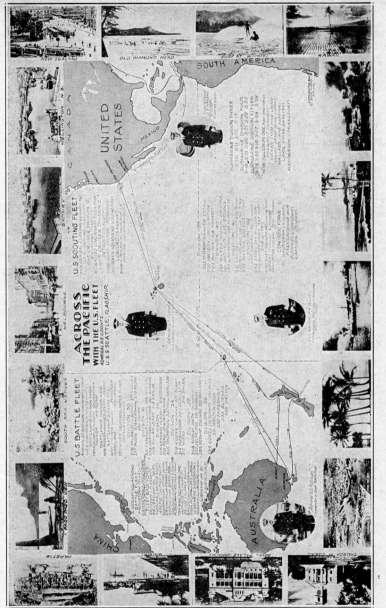

Places of interest, where the Navy stopped on their Australian cruise in 1925.

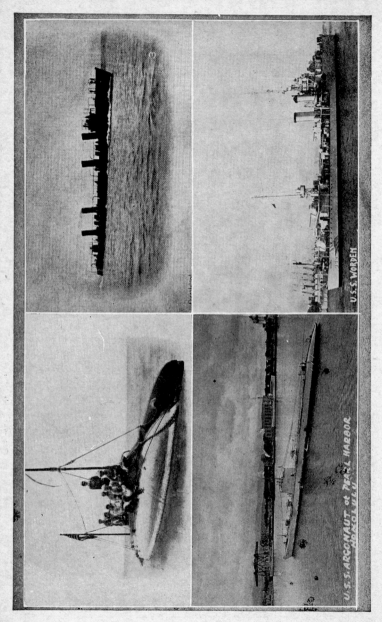

U.S.S. ARGONAUT at PEARL HARBOR

U.S.S. WORDEN

The smallest and the largest U. S. submarines (left) an d (right) the smallest and the largest U. S. destroyers.

Scenes of sailor boys coming to aid the stricken area of the Long Beach earthquake in 1933. Lower right-hand photo shows Comdr. Benson, Abe, and the late Capt. Smith, who had charge of aiding the earthquake sufferers.

Illumination by

FLEET SEARCHLIGHTS AT SAN PEDRO, CALIF.

Beautiful illuminated scenes of Battleships in the harbor.

(Top to bottom): U.S.S. Holland and crew; U.S.S. Holland;
U.S.S. Holland and submarines.

Having a heck of a good time on a hospital ship.

And he turned back and followed Battling Prince. I knew what "all two both" meant. It is Jamaica negro dialect. But why they suddenly turned back, I did not know until I swam on and recognized who the bathers were on the shoal.

Carlotta Puertos was there with two other girls. One of them was Nita Corboda. I had been introduced to her by Lotta. The third one was a smaller and darker girl that they introduced to me in the swirl of the shoal surf, but whose name I have forgotten. She was brown-skinned.

Just what was the matter with the bathing costumes on this social occasion is something I don't like to say. In different lands there are different customs in the book of ettiquette. In some Latin countries it is the custom for the women to enter the surf wearing long robes, which they cast aside as they plunge into the waves.

Senoritas Puertos and Corboda were of mixed French and Panamanian blood, and they had been educated in a girls' school somewhere in New England. They spoke English perfectly.

I was not embarrassed, as I had traveled all over the world on the Fleet and had been in London, Paris and Rome, as well as China and Japan.

I did not understand why my trainers, Prince and Sam, became panic-stricken when they saw me meeting the girls in the surf. They had turned and beat it, as if they were hoodooed.

It was the custom of the washerwomen in Panama and other Central American countries to discard their clothing when they entered the river to wash the laundry, and they would stand there, waist deep, hours at a time, washing the linen, and nobody paid any attention to their attire.

But, when I returned to camp, my training partners told me why they had become so excited and had run away from me.

"Mistah Abe, we advises you to run away from dem women too."

"I don't run away from any man or animal. I ain't afraid of anything that lives. How could those women hurt me?"

"Dem women in love wit' you, Abe."

"No, they're not. They're just friends of mine. They were educated in the States, and like to talk with boys from the North."

"Women don't have to be educated anywhere. Dey born knowin' enough to ruin any man."

"Did women ever ruin you, Prince?" I asked.

"Sure enough did."

I looked him in the eye. The big handsome fellow faced my gaze; he meant what he said.

"And dat's why I ain't black heavyweight champion of Panama today."

He told me how he got going good after my victory over Ortega. The Canal Zone had become a boxer's paradise. That hundred dollars given him for saving the Spanish girl had been the beginning of his fortune. He fought several fights and won by the quick knock-out route. They called him Battling Prince, and he was looming up as the probable champion.

He was matched with the mighty Buck Crouse in a headliner that filled the old bull ring to capacity. But his rise to fame and fortune had got the women after him. A polite man can't say no. The attentions of these admiring sirens interfered with his training duties. The night before the big fight he didn't get any sleep at all.

He was tired and logy when he entered the ring. The Pittsburgh Man-Killer found an easy mark for his white lightning. And Prince was licked and busted. With his fame and his money gone, he was abandoned by the women, too. They wouldn't wade into the stream and wash clothes to support the man who had been so generous with them. He got the idea that all women are bad, not knowing that there are three classes of women: good, bad and indifferent; but most of them are good. When I got back to Panama to train for this fight, I found Battling Prince broke flatter than a pancake, and with no clothes except his shirt and dungarees. I bought him a swell outfit the first thing before establishing a training camp.

"I'll stay away from these Senoritas, all right," I said. "Now don't you worry about that, Prince."

But he was blue about it. He didn't believe it was possible for me to keep my resolve. He thought my fight was as good as lost already. He said that no man, white or black, was strong enough to resist the lure of women. "For, why should a man resist?" was Prince's argument. A man wins fame and money only for the purpose of getting women. What other purpose did I have in life?

I told him that I carried the hopes and the confidence of forty thousand backers in the Canal Zone. Their money was up on me. And I had the loving trust of these Spanish people on Taboga Island, who believed that clean sport is possible and that Abe, the Newsboy, will stay clean.

I pointed to the old Spanish church on the hilltop where the candle for Abe was burning before the Virgin's altar.

CHAPTER FOURTEEN

THE ladies used to come to my camp every day and watch me at my training exercises. We now called them the Three Bears, the name they had first given to us. The smallest one of the three, whose name I do not remember, spoke only Spanish. I will call her Little One.

One day the Little One made a remark that I got a big kick out of.

I was skipping rope, and Senoritas Carlotta Puertos and Nita Corboda were admiring my muscles.

"What a magnificent animal he is. Look at the muscles of that broad chest," said Carlotta.

"And his neck," said Nita. "Did you ever see a neck bulging with muscle like that, except on a young bull?"

"And he's even got muscles in his ears," said the Little One, in Spanish.

Gee, I got a big kick out of that. I laughed so hard I almost fell over myself. Muscles in my ears. The kid thought those cauliflowers were muscles.

We had lots of men visitors too. There was a big convalescent hospital maintained by the Canal Commission on Taboga Island called the

Aspinwall Hotel. It was named after Colonel Aspinwall, the American engineer, who built the Panama Railroad long before the Americans had to build the Canal. My girl-friend, Carlotta, knew all about the history of the American railroad and the French canal, for she was the grand-daughter of a French engineer who died of Chagres fever. I will tell more about the Chagres fever, which prevented the French from building the canal, but that will be in a later chapter.

The Americans licked the Chagres fever, or you wouldn't have any Panama Canal today. Whenever a Canal employee had a fever stroke, they rushed him to a hospital close at hand. As soon as he got well enough to be discharged from the emergency hospital, Uncle Sam gave him two weeks rest in the great Aspinwall Hotel on Taboga Island. He got full pay during the free vacation.

So, you can see, Uncle Sam treated his Canal diggers right. What happened when the French tried to build the Canal, without knowing how to lick Chagres fever, is one of the great horrors of history. I will tell about that later.

Now I want to tell you about three visitors I had the second Sunday at my camp. These three visitors, and the trick they tried to pull on me, made me ashamed of the human race. As I said in a previous chapter, I felt no embarrassment when the sirens flirted with me out on the moonlit shoal.

But, when these three men stripped bare the baseness of their souls before me, I felt different about it than when the senoritas were wooing my favor.

These three sporting characters were known to me as the big-shot gamblers of Panama. And, as you know, a big shot is always a sure-thing gambler. Here is the way they opened up the conversation:

"Abe, you know you only weigh a hundred and forty-five pounds. You can't expect to hold the heavyweight championship long at that weight. When do you expect to be defeated?"

"When I meet a better man in the ring."

"Don't you know that we are going to bring some of the best heavies in the world here and get you?"

"Well, when you get me, you will have me. What's the big idea?"

"Your chance to cop the money will be over then."

"I can still sell papers for a living."

They thought I was talking wise money to them. So they looked at each other, nodded, and said:

"We get you, kid. Let's take a walk."

I went with them, and we walked for about two miles without mentioning the object they had in view. We finally stopped in a big pineapple plantation, where there was nobody around but lizards and sand fleas.

One of the gamblers opened a leather bag he had been carrying and pulled out a green velvet bag. He loosened the puckering strings of this bag and opened its contents to my view. It was bright yellow coin.

"How much have you got there?" I asked.

"Three thousand dollars."

It looked awfully pretty, that yellow gold against the green velvet bag. They had made it look as sweet to me as they could. I may be a fool, but I knew that I was up against wise old-timers. It was the first time I had ever been offered a bribe, and they had dressed it up to look as ravishing as they could.

I thought of the sirens dropping their drapes to reveal their attractive figures to the eye.

Three thousand dollars would pay out on that house I was buying in Connecticut. My mother and my blind father would be relieved of anxiety. I could make their home secure for life with the bag of gold.

It was in 1921 that my mother died suddenly when I was away on a cruise. The letter from my brother, which told of her brief illness and death, gave me her last words. After saying her final prayers, as is the custom in our religion, she composed herself for the end. Turning her eyes to my brother, her last words were:

"Don't forget I owe the grocer a bill of sixty-eight cents for eggs."

To the great and rich men of this earth it may seem small and simple to be so honest. But, to me, it was the last lesson that my mother's lips could teach me. She did not have enough milk to give me when I was a baby, and yet I had become a strong man. I had always followed her teachings.

It was because of Russia that she had been milkless for her babies. But, under the Flag in the American Navy, I had been nourished and developed into an athlete.

Boys, if you think Abe would sell out that Flag for three thousand dollars, you haven't guessed my price yet.

I ran my hands through the gold coin and felt of the soft velvet bag.

I said:

"Three thousand dollars isn't very much money for what you ask me to do."

They said:

"Your guarantee for the fight is one thousand. With this three thousand, you will have four thousand. You take this four thousand and bet it on Ortega. Ortega wins because you take a flop, and you come out eight thousand dollars to the good. More money than you ever saw before."

"That isn't enough," I said.

They argued that it was all they could afford and all I needed. They said I could explain my sudden wealth by saying I got into a heavy gambling game and won the money. They assured me they would corroborate my story of winning it at the gaming table.

I told them they would have to offer me more inducement.

"How much do you want to throw this fight? We've named our figure, now you name yours."

"A million dollars."

"You're foolish. You are an ignorant newsboy. There is not a million dollars in the gambling game in Panama."

"Gambling game?" I said. "Do you guys call yourselves gamblers?"

"What do you suppose we are?"

"Cheap skates. Sure-thing con men. You're not gamblers, because to gamble means to take a chance. When I said it would take a million dollars for you to buy me, I wanted to show you that I was over your heads. I am a gambler myself."

"What do you mean, you're gambler?"

"I bet my life every time I enter the ring. You don't risk nothing. If the game isn't in the bag for you frame-up artists, you don't bet. You are pikers. And you call yourselves gamblers. I'll tell you who the gamblers of Panama are. They are the square guys who bet their shirts on Abe, because they trust in his honesty."

"Do you bet on yourself?" they sneered. "We never heard of you putting up a side-bet. It was the sailors who covered Ortega's side bet, not you. You don't bet anything."

"Listen," I said. "I don't bet anything, eh? I go into the ring against the biggest bruisers you've got in Latin America. I can't read and write. All I have got is stored up in my nut, see. If these big heavies ever land one of their sledge-hammer wallops on my skull, they will put me out of business forever. Look at what Ad Wolgast and Battling Nelson did to each other in their last fight. Beat each other's brains out, and both of them have been goofy ever since. When my

ring days are over, I have to sell newspapers,
and I can't do that if I get my bean cracked and
go around goofy ever after, thinking I'm Na-
poleon Bonaparte."

They got me then. They saw I was betting
my life against their lousy attempts to buy me.
They couldn't fool me. The proverb says: "If
you sleep with the tramps, don't be surprised
when you wake up lousy yourself."

So I told these gentlemen, with the green bag,
just where they got off.

They said:

"Well, you're a damn fool. Ortega can lick
hell out of you anyhow. You have got all swelled
up because he didn't take you the first time.
Listen, Jew, he lost to you on a foul, because he's
got more brains than you have. The Canal
suckers are now wild to bet on you. That's what
we all want, kid. Your Uncle Sam is paying
laborers seventy cents an hour, and engineers
seventy dollars a day, so the whole damn tribe
of gringoes down here are feathered with money.
And we're going to take it off them now, see?"

"How are you going to take it from them?"

"We just told you, you dumbbell. We've
worked it so that they are all betting their shirts
on you to lick big Jack Ortega, and you little
shrimp, you couldn't lick Ortega the best day
you ever lived. The checks are drawn now. Your
gringo friends are now going to lose a million
dollars, and you will get your head knocked off
in the bargain."

I told them that I had recently heard that

there wasn't a million dollars in the betting game in all Panama.

"Well, you can't believe all you hear," they said.

"I damn well can't believe what you tell me," I said. "Gentlemen, good day."

They went away sore as a sick bull in the ring. And that was the one ray of hope they gave me. If they were really sure that the Spanish champion could lick me in forty-five rounds, why did they try to bribe me to take a dive?

I lay awake a long time that night thinking about it, before I could go to sleep.

CHAPTER FIFTEEN

AS my month of training drew to its close, Carlotta and Nita grew more romantic all the time. They were very beautiful women, and the little Spanish-Indian maid that lived in their cottage was not so bad looking, either.

This was one of the loveliest periods of my life. Two wealthy and educated girls daily visited me to cheer me on in my training, and every afternoon, when I plunged into the sea, they swam with me.

No longer did I hear the remarks that I always used to hear as I entered the ring, when officers' wives were in the boxes. Those wives would laugh and say:

"I think Abe has the ugliest face in the world."

But Senoritas Nita and Carlotta were always saying:

"I think Abe has got the most beautiful body I ever saw."

We all like to hear compliments, boys. I ain't lying. A newsboy has to smile and pretend he likes insults better than compliments, but don't let me fool you.

I was very happy. Great bouquets of flowers were sent to my quarters every day by the people of Taboga. I had been plugging all my life, a poor boy, plugging hard and fighting his way up from the bottom. Now suddenly I seemed to be at the top peak of fame and fortune. I was in a Paradise of the Pacific, welcomed by the people and their priest, and wooed by their beautiful and ambitious daughters. I felt like Little Nemo in Slumberland; it all seemed like a boy's dream.

I asked Senor Pancho Arias:

"How did this all come about? Why are you good people making so much of me, a poor fighting newsboy?"

"The last shall be first, and the first, last. You have heard that, haven't you?" he said.

"No, I never heard it," I replied.

"It is the principle that our church is based on," he replied, pointing to the chapel where the candle was burning for me. And he went on to say that their religion teaches them that the humble, honest man, who has nothing but his good name to recommend him, may live to find himself exalted by the nation, while the proud and corrupt leaders are cast down. Senor Arias thought it was strange that I had never heard this principle, although it came from the Bible.

"Oh, I recognize it now," I said. "The way I heard it was: A good name is rather to be chosen than great riches."

So I told him about the big-shot gamblers offering me three thousand dollars in gold coin, and because square-shooters like him and the Yanks on the Canal were betting on my good name, I was not to be tempted.

"You know, a Jew is a good bargainer," I said. "And if a good name is worth more than big money, what a fool I would be to sell and lose money on the goods."

People understand each other in this world if they are patient enough to talk it over till they learn each other's language. I made up my mind then that, if I licked Ortega, I would write my autobiography (I would have to hire scribes, like the kings of old), to tell the world that Abe, the Conqueror, won more with his good name than he ever won with his fists.

And boys, I afterwards won eighty thousand dollars with my fists, and I am now worth three million dollars. One million dollars is my health, one million dollars is the value of my nerve, and one million dollars is what the love of my girl is worth—but wait, I'm getting ahead of the story.

I had two girls while I was training on Taboga. Lotta Puertos was almost a blonde. Nita Corboda was the full-blooded Spanish type. The little mestizo that I call the Little One was not really interested in me. I think she favored Sam, the Hawaiian, rather than Battling Prince.

I asked Battling Prince, one morning, before any visitors came to our camp:

"What about these two beauties that are being so nice to me. Are they kidding me? Or what's their game?"

"Why do you inquire of me, Mistah Abe?"

"On the level, Prince. I'm not stringing you. I want to know what you think about it. You're the guy that told me to run from them. What's their game?"

"Do you t'ink dey fooling, Boss?"

"They're not fooling me. Nobody fools me. But you've been around women, as the necktie said to the corset."

"I done told you what de women done to me."

"Yes, they bulled you out of the championship by complimenting you so much before the big fight. Do you think those women were hired by the other camp to put you on the fritz before the battle?"

"No, sah, Mistah Abe. No, sah, no, sah!"

I wish I had a phonograph of the way he said it. He meant it. Prince wasn't casting any reflections on those Spanish-Indian beauties who ran him ragged before the big fight.

"But, Mistah Abe," he said. "De women folks can't resist a handsome man."

"I'm not handsome. Do you call this cross-eyed ugly mug of mine handsome?"

"De ladies nevah look at you face when you is stripped for action. De serpent ain't got no purty face. But, oh, dem coiling muscles. Eve couldn't resist de muscles of de serpent."

The negroes are wonderful philosophers. But I was glad that Battling Prince didn't think Nita and Lotta were hired by Ortega and the sure-thing gamblers.

"But even if the sure-thing big-shots put the girls after me," I said, "they'll find it is no sure thing that Abe falls for them."

"No, no, no, sah. No, sah, indeedy, deedy, deed, no, sah," said Prince. "Dem ladies not paid to love you, Boss. Dem high-born ladies, and dey **jes'** can't help loving you because you got a well-

U.S.S. North Carolina—Official Photo of U. S. Navy
U.S.S. Washington

U.S.S. Arkansas, good old lady, who did a big job in the war, never to be forgotten.

7 Cruisers Awarded NUC for Heroic Action

USS St. Louis (CL 49)

USS Philadelphia (CL 41)

USS Honolulu (CL 48)

USS Columbia (CL 56)

USS Montpelier (CL 57)

USS Cleveland (CL 55)

USS Denver (CL 58)

NAVY CROSS

Congratulations, to you all—Officers and Men—for getting the Navy Cross.
You have done a great job in the war, from your old friend Abe the Newsboy.

Here is one of the Aircraft Carriers who was crippled in the war—limped back one of the Navy yards, was repaired, and went back to fight.

U.S.S. Prairie, mother ship of the destroyers.

Having exercises on an aircraft carrier every morning, to have them fit.

Destroyers throwing smoke screens.

(Top): The old U.S.S. Texas, later called St. Marcus. (Center): City and State—
U.S.S. Houston. (Bottom): U.S.S. Texas.

U.S.S. BOISE

Hoffman Phote Studio

U.S.S. San Francisco
San Diego, 10 April 1934
To Ace, the newsboy
R. E. Ingersoll
Captain U.S. Navy

U.S.S. Cruiser Marblehead, 1935

Three Navy heroes
that beat hell out of
the Japs. U.S.S. Boise,
U.S.S. San Francisco,
and U.S.S. Marble-
head. Still carrying
on in Japanese wat-
ers, God bless them.

(Top): U.S.S. Richmond; (center): U.S.S. Bushnell; (bottom): U.S.S. Chester

290 — U. S. ARMORED CRUISER "NEW YORK." 500 OFFICERS AND MEN. LENGTH 380 FEET. MAIN BATTERY 14 GUNS.

U. S. S. New York

U. S. S. Nevada

U. S. S. Nevada

Old and New Ships

Our Marines—Always first and ready. In 1914—Vera Cruz, Revolution; in 1917—World War . . . now Shanghai. And, believe me, not only Good Fighters, but Good Fellows. They are always first.

Capt. Jack Kennedy, the most honest referee in the boxing game. Will never be forgotten by the civilians and officers and men of the U. S. Navy.

New and Old Ships. (Bottom, left): U.S.S. Oregon

Ships of the Old and New Navy. (Top, left): Old U.S.S. Marblehead. (Top, right): Old U.S.S. Denver. (Bottom, right): U.S.S. Massachusetts.

U.S.S. CINCINNATI

U.S.S. Indianapolis
in Culebra Cut
Panama Canal
3-1-33

Best wishes
to Alec the
Landlord,
J. Lawrence,
Captain, U.S.N.

Old and New Ships. (Bottom): U.S.S. Indiana and U.S.S. Ohio.

built body and you lick de champion."

As I said before, I was glad to know that they had no crooked interest in me, like the birds with the green bag of gold coin. The eyes these girls cast on me were more like the glass eyes of the wrestler I slept with, that kept open all night—watching me for no mercenary motive.

But I was getting the lucky break, Battling Prince told me, in having two beauties trying to rush me at once.

"If two different serpents had tried to make Eve at one time, dey would done fought themselves to death in a duel, and de lady go home to Papa Adam a good wife, and nobody could say a word against her without having to fight Mistah Adam, too."

"Now listen, kid," I said, "you darkies are wonderful in your talk. But you never come right out and say anything plain. I get you, all right. But I'm going to take this matter up with the ladies and talk cold turkey to them."

"Yes, you are, Mistah Abe. You can't fool me. You can't talk cold turkey to de lovin' women. You'll be duck soup."

Reports came from Panama that it was a sell-out at the National Stadium. The Canal boys were slapping the bets down behind every bar in Panama City. The odds were on Abe, the News-boy, although Ortega had trained himself into perfect form. It was forecast that the odds would be two to one on me before ring time, and it was good news to me. I was overloaded with con-fidence. I felt that I was in the best condition of my ring career. And I was going to stay in that condition. Senorita Puertos would have to talk fast to argue me out of that resolution. Other fighters might lose their head when pretty women vamped them. Not Abe.

There is a time to love and a time to keep out of love. And the time to keep out of love is when you have important business to do. The way to keep your mind off women at that time is to keep your mind on your duty.

My duty was to fool those gamblers who claimed I would get licked anyway. They said Ortega laid down to me in the first fight in order to lure the Gringo suckers on to lose a million in the second fight.

Well, they had worked their trick on poor Buck Crouse, and if all bets hadn't been declared off by the referee, the Canal boys would have been gypped good and proper.

I kept my mind on this, when Senorita Puertos played her card.

The way it happened was this. I pulled away my canopy one night to get into bed, and I found somebody sitting on my bed. If you don't know what a canopy in the Tropics is, I will tell you. It is a cloth netting to keep out mosquitoes. If you let the mosquitoes bite you in Panama, you are exposing yourself to Chagres fever.

Carlotta told me all about the French, and how they were defeated by Chagres fever when they tried to build the Canal. It was because they didn't have any mosquito screens.

When I pulled my mosquito netting aside and

saw Carlotta sitting there, I said to myself:
"Here is a mosquito as big as any I ever saw in
Panama, but I don't intend to get stung."

She was wearing a lovely evening gown of
blue and gold, with a red flower in her corsage.

I backed out and put on the old bath robe in
which I had approached a hundred battles.

"Come on, Senorita, I am going to take you
home."

It was nearly a mile down the beach to her
cottage, and we had time to do a lot of talking.

"Why were you sitting on the bed that I have
to sleep on?" I asked.

She answered in a cooing and kidding way.
Her voice was soft and her face looked wonderful
in the moonlight. If I had listened to her line, I
would have thought I was Rudolph Valentino
and the Four Horsemen and part of the horses.
Probably their manes. I asked where her pal,
Juanita, was. And she said Nita had been called
back to Panama on family matters.

And I said to myself: "You probably framed
it to get Nita called back and give you a clear
field for one night. There are more ways to kill
a cat than choking it to death on butter."

It was just as Prince said. The only thing
that had saved me from the women, up till now,
was because there were two of them after me at
the same time. It is easier to fight off two Greta
Garbos than one.

"Now I know why you called me and my
trainers the Three Bears," I told her. "You were
planning to do your Little Curley Locks stuff

the first time you got a chance."

She wanted us to go to the Padre and get married.

"Listen, Baby," I said, "they're not burning that candle for a great lover; they are burning it for a great fighter."

"But I love you, Abie dear, and you know it. You will fight all the better for love of me."

I told her Battling Prince said she was in love with my body, and that she never looked at my battered face."

"No, no, it is your intelligence I love. Your personality. Your brains."

"If I get mixed up with the ladies now, I'll get my brains knocked out. Then you wouldn't love me any more."

She put her arms around me and clinched. Such sweet talk you never heard. Her shoulders were covered with that French perfume that makes strong men grow weak. "Oh, promise me." That's what she was cooing. She couldn't let me go until I promised to marry her. I told her I couldn't talk about love till after the fight.

She wasn't fighting fair, I thought. Like a crooked boxer who puts ammonia on his shoulders to blind the other guy, she had put that subtle perfume on her shoulders to blind me to my duty and get me crazy. She held my head close, and I could hear her heart beating. These people had been very kind to me, and this girl had been nicest of all. If she had been a pugilist, I could have wrestled out of the clinch, or broke it up with blows to the ribs.

CHAPTER SIXTEEN

OF course I got out of the clinch with pretty Carlotta Puertos, but not without damage to myself, as I learned the next morning when I started for Panama. Senorita Puertos informed the whole island that I had promised to marry her after the fight.

She was a smart girl. But, if I got my head knocked off in the fight, she would not hold me to my promise. I knew that much. And, furthermore, I hadn't promised her any such thing.

All I said was that I couldn't talk about those things when I had the big fight on my mind.

The people of Taboga turned out that Saturday morning like a Christmas pageant, to see me off for Panama. They carried palm leaves and flowers. The Little One, that pretty Indian girl, placed a wreath on my head, made of bright green and red feather from Tropical birds.

Gee, fellows, I was made an Indian chief, just like the Tammany leaders on Fourteenth Street.

The Arias family sent me a huge bunch of white flowers and a message of good luck. Senor Pancho Arias assured me that he had reserved a ringside box and would be there on the morrow to cheer me on to victory.

I was indeed a happy fellow as I went aboard

the launch and it started steaming across the tossing green waters toward the capital of the Panama Republic. The only thing I had to worry about was if I won the fight, there would be another battle between Nita and Lotta to marry me. I thought of the body of the dead bull from the bull ring, which was carved up as free meat for the poor. If I won in the boxing ring, my body would become meat for those loving girls to fight over.

The launch docked at Panama City, and I was met by cheering crowds. A big automobile, driven by the Mayor's son, was again waiting for me to take me to the arena.

When we arrived there, my first act was to inspect the ring. I was looking for trap doors. Believe me, fellows, after what I had learned about the crookedness of big gamblers, I was taking a terrible gamble myself. In one of my fights in South America, way up on the Chilean desert in the copper country, I was the only American within a hundred miles, and they determined to beat me. I would have got knocked out, either with the gloves or with knock-out drops, if it hadn't been for a couple of engineers employed by the Guggenheims.

One was an Englishman and the other a German construction boss, and they tipped me off not to drink any water between rounds nor even wash out my mouth with the bottle the seconds would furnish.

I fought fifteen rounds without daring to gargle my throat. When you fight in a hot, dry air, like this desert, you can imagine how your throat cracks. The Englishman had a ringside seat at my corner, and he and the Dutch friend had their pockets full of oranges peeled and quartered. Between each round they would slip me a quarter of an orange, and I would wet my cracked throat with the juice. If I had taken a sip from the water bottle prepared by my seconds, I would have strangled on carbolic acid.

The man that fights alone in strange lands hasn't got a Chinaman's chance, unless he picks up local friends as he goes. The Navy boys used to sing when I entered a bout:

> "Good Ol' Abe, the Newsboy!
> Watch him take a fall;
> He isn't very pretty,
> But he's got a lot of gall."

And whenever they introduced me to some important person, they always said:

"Don't judge by his looks. But he's got a wonderful personality."

But being big-hearted and having a winning personality won't save you if you ever step on a trap-door and the crooks dump you into the river. So I looked that ring all over with a wise eye. The ring floor had been covered with a new canvas, and that was good, because the rainy season was on, and the old canvas was moss-grown and slippery. But I tested every inch of that canvas-covered floor. It was O. K.

For the next few hours I was kept busy shaking hands. Delegations came from Colon and other towns. A big contingent of sailor boys came in, accompanied by Mr. James Daly and his party of sporting business men.

"How is your condition, Abe?" Mr. Daly asked in my ear, indicating that if anything was wrong, I must not fail to let my friends know.

"I'm in grand shape," I replied. "I could lick my weight in wild-cats. This Mexican is no wild cat; he's a bull."

"Can you lick your weight in bulls?"

"If I didn't believe I could lick this big thug, Mr. Daly, I would tell you. I don't forget that you were the first sport to back me when I landed on the Isthmus."

"The kid's all right," Mr. Daly told the crowd. "Now let's leave him alone to rest until the fight."

So the long reception ended, and I retired to my room in the Normandie Hotel while the crowd thronged to the cafes to eat and drink and have a lot of fun on the eve of the great fight, like the crowds on Broadway celebrating New Year's eve.

Mr. James Daly, relying on my word that I could take this big boy in forty-five rounds, laid down a wager at the Balboa bar that Abe, the Newsboy, would win by a knock-out. He staked a thousand dollars in gold, even money.

That is quite a load to carry, boys. At 148 pounds I had to knock out a heavyweight who had trained down to 184 pounds. Ortega meant business when he trained like this. His final statement to the newspapers was that he had been under-trained when he fought me the first time. Now he was properly trained to go 45 rounds in the Tropic heat and would kill me long before he got half the distance.

At nine o'clock I hit the hay, and as I lay there dozing off I could hear the hum of revelry in the bar and the conversation in the hotel lobby, all about the coming fight.

The little newsboy of the Navy was still hot stuff in the great Panama Canal Zone. At the completion of that Canal the world was to break into war for the mastery of the seas. This prize fight I am describing took place in 1913, before the completion of the Canal.

I arose the morning of the fight and took a brisk walk on Bella Vista Beach. On returning, I looked into all the cantinas, as they call the saloons, and on every back bar were stacks of gold coins, most of it in twenty-dollar gold pieces, the wagers on the boxing contest.

On re-entering my hotel I was stopped by an excited man who said:

"Abe, I won the lottery's grand prize today. I got three thousand dollars. I have placed every nickel of it on you. If you win this fight, I am going to split fifty-fifty. Abe, old boy, you get fifteen hundred dollars from me if you win. That's more than your guarantee from the promoter."

If I won the fight, do you suppose this man would pay what he promised? You never can tell.

Mr. Daly reported to me that he had found out that it was the ex-champion's money that covered his thousand-dollar bet. This might have unnerved some fighters, but Daly knew it wouldn't unnerve me. He told me about it because he knew it would spur me up to do my damnedest for him.

He further reported that Ortega was in absolutely first-class shape. All right, t' hell with him.

The weather turned out splendid. Just before noon a rain set in and lasted until one o'clock, cooling the air. At this hour Senor Pancho Arias visited me with a delegation of aristocratic Latin-Americans and told me that the candle in the church was renewed to last until the fight was over. The main bout was scheduled for four o'clock.

I thought of the days when I was a prelim. fighter, and how us pork-and-beaners used to sit around the gymnasium of the fight clubs waiting a chance to go on. You know, they schedule enough preliminary bouts to last until the hour set for the main event. These prelims are from four rounds to six rounds. If a knock-out ends a prelim in the first or second round, they have to throw in another bout to take up the time. Many times a pork-and-beaner doesn't get a chance to fight and earn a couple of dollars because the prelims all go the full distance.

Probably I was a sentimental fool to be thinking about these things instead of my main fight. Some say that when you get up in the world you should forget about the boys who are still at the bottom struggling upward. But Theodore Roosevelt, President of the United States and creator of the Panama Canal, didn't forget that he was once a spindling, unknown, four-eyed boy, and he gave Abe a friendly pat on the back when he saw me starting from the bottom.

Enormous crowds were packing into the National Sporting Club stadium, and you can imagine my delight as I saw that slow-moving line of humanity fighting its way to the box office. It was another fight fiesta day for the folks of the Isthmus. The mood was joy and gallantry. I was proud to think that the great country of the Yankees had been given this slice of Central America, so that when the Atlantic and Pacific Oceans joined waters, the Latin-Americans and the North Americans joined hands too.

Here were Spanish gentlemen and U. S. Naval officers pouring into the gate, side by side, together with private soldiers and sailors and Panamanian workers and Canal diggers. Some crowd!

Soft drink venders and beer sellers and what we would call in the States, "peanut, candy and chewing gum" men, were doing a land office business. Everybody had plenty of money and seemed eager to spend it. For a minute I was sorry that I was a champion ring performer instead of a vender down in that crowd that was buying everything that was shoved at them. I wanted to grab a bunch of papers and get busy.

I will be a newsboy as long as I live.

The hope of selling my autobiography some day, as the last venture of my newsboy career, had already formed itself in my mind. It all depended on whether I could really lick this heavy champion, now that he was in condition to make his best fight.

At exactly three forty-five the solemn face of Battling Prince, which always smiled at his own troubles, appeared in my room and said that the semi-windup was on.

"Cheer up, Bat," I said. "This is a laughing matter. This is no funeral. At least it isn't your funeral, so grin, kid, grin."

He peeled his white ivories in obedience to my request, but not in any joyful humor. He thought I had been secretly married during my training period, as he later told me.

Turning to my seconds, I said:

"Let's go."

And I grabbed my bath robe, and we all ran for the waiting motor car. Five minutes later we had been pushed inside the club by Panamanian cops, and the first man I saw was Ortega himself. He was slender and nervous, evidently in the prime of condition. Boys, when a fighter is trained down to the "pink" he is nervous, and trembles all the time, like a thoroughbred race horse or a highly trained deer hound. Senor Ortega was quivering that way.

Maybe I was too. About as much as a wooden nutmeg from Connecticut. For I am really one of the toughest kids that ever lived.

It was an accident that Ortega and me both came together as we entered the building to go to our dressing rooms. I walked up to him and offered to shake hands.

He refused.

The crowd hissed him. That was a bad break

for him, but it was his own fault. One time Jim Corbett met Bob Fitzsimmons by accident when they were training for the big fight. They happened to come together when they were doing road work. The Australian offered to shake hands, but Gentleman Jim refused. His purpose was to throw a scare into Bob. But it only made Bob fight the harder, and he won. Corbett always said, afterwards, that he made a bad move in the "chess game of strategy," and gave Bob full credit for winning. And Ortega lost in the strategy game when he let the crowd hiss him.

But, of course, hissing doesn't win any fights. If it did, the goose would be the bird champion instead of the eagle.

CHAPTER SEVENTEEN

 GLANCED around at the faces near the ring-side. There were my old Chinese friends and the fruit selling Turk. They were smiling confidently. Why did I inspire such enthusiasm in men of all nationalities? They say that Jews are internationalists. And this friendship for Abe, the Newsboy, by men and women of every race and nationality seemed to prove it.

I saw lots of pretty women in the audience, for the women were out in bigger numbers than were ever seen at a prize-fight before. I know it was not my matinee idol's face that attracted them, for I heard the usual remarks among the fair sex:

"Abe has got a face that would stop a freight train," one laughed.

"He looks like an accident going somewhere to happen," said an officer's wife.

But they couldn't get my goat. If they didn't want to see me, they didn't have to come there. And I knew that I was the card that had drawn this mammoth crowd.

We were called to the center of the ring for our instructions. Ortega was not sneering at me this time. But he was utterly confident, and acted at ease. He wasn't trying to bluff me, but he was going to lick me.

Out of the corner of my eye I saw the Mayor's son, Dave Cardoza, trying to stop a Spanish young man from offering to place a bet on Ortega.

Then I spotted the three big-shots that had tried to bribe me. One of them held up his hand and said:

"Five hundred on Ortega."

The sailors that rushed to cover the bet almost trampled the crooks underfoot. I retired to my corner to await the bell. As my chief second, I had one of the best boxing advisors on the Isthmus, a German American named Jack Steiner. During his earlier years, Mr. Steiner had earned the reputation in California of being one of the best referees the Coast ever produced. He knew the boxing game from every angle, as it had been developed by that great innovator, James J. Corbett, and I felt mighty comfortable with Steiner as my chief advisor. If I could ever give the big boy a lacing, it would be under a fair referee and with a second like Steiner. The referee was Soldier Kearns.

Joe Engleberg, the announcer, said:

"The main event this afternoon is Abe, the Newsboy, of New London, Connecticut, heavyweight boxing champion of the Isthmus, weighing one hundred forty-eight pounds, against Jack Ortega, of Mexico, one hundred and eighty-four pounds. In this corner, Jack Ortega, in this corner, Abe, the Newsboy."

A hush fell over the crowd. For a second only. Then the bell rang. And we went to it.

Only boxing took place in the first three rounds of this battle. Ortega feared me and I feared him, and we kept feeling each other out. Never once did I let the big fellow clinch. The crowd found these rounds slow and uninteresting, and probably began to think it was a frame-up. But I realized the contest might go forty-five rounds, and Ortega was just as careful and calculating as I was. That meant a real fight was coming.

I didn't want it to go forty-five rounds if I could stop the other guy short of that. But if I couldn't, I was going to protect that half million dollars that was bet on me.

This sounds nice and cool as I sit here in a cool room in New York dictating the story. But can you imagine fighting half a hundred rounds under the Tropical sun? Remember that Gene Tunney and Jack Dempsey twice contested the World's Heavyweight Championship in bouts limited to ten rounds. And they were both big, strong heavyweights in a cool climate.

I was a heavyweight in name only, and I undertook to lick a real hot country heavyweight in a fight whose limit was four and a half times the distance that they went in Philadelphia when the heavyweight crown changed hands without a knockout. I don't say a ten-round bout is not big enough for a championship, but I say a forty-five-round battle in the Tropics certainly is, and I don't mean maybe.

Lightweights and featherweights in the States will quibble over a pound. Here I was conceding thirty-two pounds. But I had my battle planned.

U.S.S. DETROIT

U.S. BATTLESHIP "GEORGIA." 812 OFFICERS AND MEN.
LENGTH 435 FEET. MAIN BATTERY 24 GUNS.

U.S.S. MICHIGAN

New and Old Ships. (Bottom): U.S.S. Georgia and U.S.S. Michigan

295

PRESIDENT ROOSEVELT

"UNCLE SAM"

"ABE THE NEWSBOY"
HERO OF A THOUSAND FIGHTS

BY A FRIEND ED. PRANG U.S.N.

ABE SAYS "GO OUT THERE AND WIN THE WORLD'S TITLE" WITH PRESIDENT ROOSEVELT BACKING OUR BIG NAVY, WE CAN'T LOSE

Winner and still world's champion.

"God bless the Navy for a job well done."

San Pedro, California,
28 June, 1935.

Abe, The World's Greatest Newsboy:

Abe, the Newsboy, deserves his title.
I have known him for over thirty years.

J. M. REEVES,
Admiral, U.S. Navy.

My dear friend, Adm. J. M. Reeves, whom I have known since his Midshipman days, and sold many newspapers to him.

O — U. S. BATTLESHIP "LOUISIANA." 881 OFFICERS AND MEN.
LENGTH 450 FEET. MAIN BATTERY 24 GUNS.

Ships of the Old and New Navy.   Bottom right, U.S.S. Minnesota.

Ships of the Old and New Navy. (Top left): U.S.S. Louisville, the Hero of the Navy, having saved 575 lives. (Bottom left): U.S.S. Kentucky. (Top right): U.S.S. Tuscaloosa, first in gunnery, first in engineering, 2 years in commission. (Bottom right): Old U.S.S. Alabama.

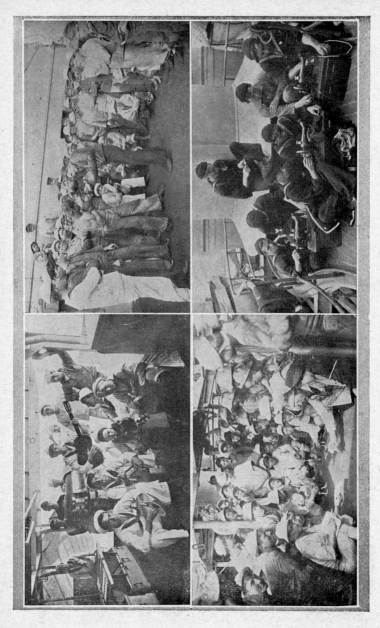

Happy Hours in the Old Navy. (Top): Sailors Band and Sailors Boxing.
(Bottom): Having a Cock Fight and Mending Their Clothes.

Views of Interior of "Old Ironsides."

(Top): Old U.S.S. Philadelphia.   (Center): Old U.S.S. Pennsylvania.

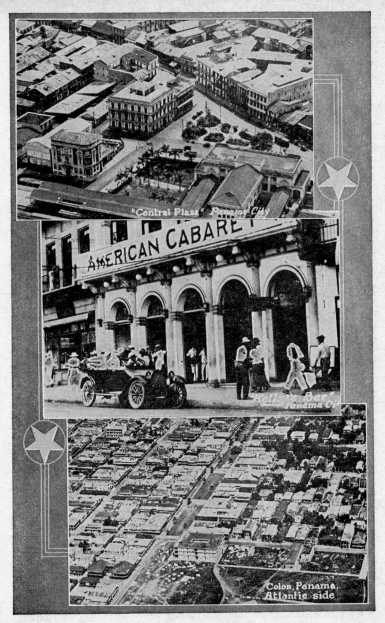

"Central Plaza," Panama City

AMERICAN CABARET

Kelly's Bar, Panama City

Colon, Panama, Atlantic side

Scenes in Panama.

"HONOLULU SUGAR MILL" HAWAII.

HAWAIIAN GRASS HOUSE.

CRATER OF HALEAKALA, "MAIN ISLAND" HAWAII.

Scenes in Hawaii.

Panama City....Pacific

Bull Fight
"Panama City"

Bull Ring....Panama City

Scenes in Panama City.

War scenes in China.

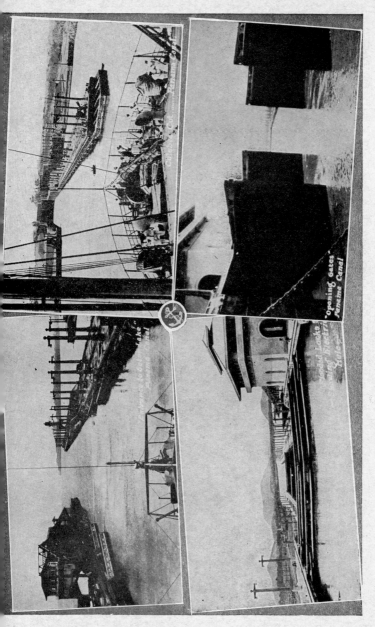

The Locks of Our Great Panama Canal.

Scenes in Panama City, and the Locks of the Canal.

MINOR TACTICS
SHANGHAI, CHINA

MARINES READY FOR PEKIN PARTY, CHINA

HORSEBACK RIDING AT PANAMA

MARKET AT GUANTANAMO BAY

103

(Top): Scenes in Shanghai and Pekin, China. (Bottom): Scenes in Quantanama Bay and Panama.

On the March from Port Melbourne to the City of Melbourne Aug. 31, 1908.

Sailors' Parade at the Flower Festival, Santa Barbara, Calif., April 28, 1908.

(Top left): Sailors' Parade at Honolulu in 1908. (Top right): Sailors enjoying a barbecue in Los Angeles. (Bottom left): On the March from Port Melbourne to the City of Melbourne in 1908. Bottom right): Sailors

I will not pretend, like a stage magician, to be surprised at my own tricks. My tricks were in the bag before the show started.

So, what the spectators lost in the line of excitement during those slow, cautious early rounds, they got fully repaid for later on. When the fourth round opened, Ortega was ready to trade wallops with me. And I was a ready customer for him. It was a fight now, and we began a fast exchange. During the first minute of this session he handed me a beautiful right-hand sock, which the papers said afterward "had all the ear-marks of a knockout."

I always thought that was a good line about the "ear-marks," for it was an old American expression coming from the custom of farmers to notch the ears of their hogs to show who owned them.

This punch made me dizzy, but I recovered from it before he could plant a real knockout. I have the ear-marks of a hundred knockouts on me, but I didn't get all those knockouts, I only got the ear-marks.

I sailed into Ortega and landed a left hook to the stomach that made him clinch, and we did fully a minute of infighting. We were out of it and boxing when the bell rang.

I returned to my corner and got a severe bawling out by my chief advisor.

"Don't you know better," said Jack Steiner, "than to clinch with a man so much heavier than you? The engineer in your brain must be a dead cockroach. You want your clock stopped, don't you? The next time you clinch with him, I hope he gives you the works."

This was not much encouragement for my own plan, so I decided to take my chief's advice. Box and tire out the big fellow.

On came the fifth round. I was to box him? How could I, when he kept tearing in like a wild bull. It was like me trying to box the kangaroo that knocked me hump-backed with his unexpected tail. Ortega wouldn't box. He was bent on rushing, slugging and clinching. It was clinch, clinch, clinch, and fight me in the clinches. He put all his weight on me for his own advantage.

I can't even hope to tell you how often this big veteran punched me in the kidneys, pounding and pounding and pounding at that vital point while we were locked in a close-up. Before the end of that desperate round was over I realized that it was a much better man I had in front of me now than the Ortega I licked the first time.

It is all right to fight an opponent the way your seconds tell you, but maybe he won't fight that way. When the Civil War started, the Southerns said they could lick the Northern boys with corn stalks. And after the war ended they were asked what was the matter, that they didn't lick the Yankees with corn stalks, and the answer was:

"The Yankees wouldn't fight that way."

When I returned to my corner badly used up, Steiner did not scold me. He saw I couldn't make the big fellow box when he didn't want to. I think my backers mentally kissed me good-bye.

In the sixth round I got some better breaks. I planted a wicked left to his stomach that caused

him considerable trouble. His face looked like
my friend did when he vomited over the dead
bull. I later crossed a right to the jaw, and he
winced like a guy with a toothache.

This was good drama for the crowd, which,
up till now, had been silent. And I could hear
the hum of their rising excitement. Just then he
missed a hay-maker aimed at my face, and I
staggered him with a left to his heart.

A man arose in the audience and shouted:

"If you put him away, Abe, before the tenth
I'll give you a thousand dollars."

This was some inducement, boys. Because it
was not an offer to lay down. I couldn't tell who
the man was, but his voice sounded like Jim
Snappy.

So, when I came to my corner and received
the encouragement of Jack Steiner, I said, between puffs, as I fought for a deep breath while
the seconds massaged my arms and chest:

"I'm still—here—ain't I? Well, let me—fight
him my own style—and I'll lick him anyway."

Instead of holding me to his plan, he said:

"Go to it, Abe. But be careful he don't sneak
in a low one in a clinch."

That round was fireworks, and so were the
next three. The audience was up on their toes
now, watching the big-time stuff. Every time
the big fellow wanted to clinch, I clinched with
him. Like a Broadway baby clinching with a
"sugar papa."

I played on his heart all the time. Twice I had
seen that man's eyes go glassy from heart blows,
so I found out his fond heart was his weak point.

I sent valentine after valentine to him while the big boy was trying to bear me down with his brute strength and ruin my kidneys with his attentions.

If there is anybody in the world who thinks I did not earnestly try to put him away inside the ten-round limit, he ought to have been at the ring-side and watched my work. A thousand dollars is a thousand dollars, and I don't want my readers to get the idea that money means nothing to me. Ford and other rich men can say that money means nothing to them, but those who are poor want money. So I went after that thousand-dollar offer, and tried hard to put him away before the bell in the tenth. But Fate and the big fellow stood in my way.

In the eleventh I was still pounding him in the heart and stomach, and taking an occasional shot at his jaw for good luck. His good condition had enabled him to weather the storm so far.

One thing was certain now, he could never go the full distance. The men around the ring were yelling:

"Three to one on the newsboy."

And no takers. But Jack was game, and the crowd realized it. He was taking terrible punishment and still rising at each bell for another hopeless round. There is something kind of sad in seeing a brave man take a licking, even if he is a mean guy. But I had to give it to him.

In the thirteenth round, after six clinches in which he could make no progress to stem the tide, he whispered in my ear:

"Take a flop and I will give you two thousand dollars."

My reply was:

"Fight, fight."

His breathing was heavy and he had lost all his skill. As he panted and fought for breath I wondered if the candle was flickering that they lit for me on Tabogga at the Virgin's shrine. My breathing was easy; I had my man.

Near the close of the sixteenth, as he rushed blindly at me, I hooked a right to his heart. His eyes went glassy. This was the third time I had seen that awful look; it was like the eyes of the bull that had been run to death in the ring. The bell saved him, but I knew the finish was at hand.

To make it brief and painless as possible, I will tell only the last few moves. As he rushed me I caught him hard in the stomach. He tried to clinch, but I evaded him and snapped him on the jaw to tell him that I was dictating what we did from now on.

He backed away, leered at me, and then deliberately raised his leg and kicked me in the belly.

No wonder the Spaniards, with their belief in gallantry, wanted me to knock the rascal out. He wouldn't take it on the chin, as the code of good sport teaches us to.

I was still champion. And again the crowd carried me on their shoulders, and there was high celebration all that afternoon and far into the night.

Senoritas Nita and Carlotta sent messages to me, but they could not get a chance to draw me away from the crowd of merry-making sportsmen who had me in tow.

The over-excited stranger who had promised me half of the three thousand dollars he won on me, never showed up. I never heard from him again.

CHAPTER EIGHTEEN

"THE real stature of Abe is now seen," said an editorial in the Panama Journal. "The sawed-off, hammered-down, little, old, cross-eyed son-of-a-gun is a colossus that doth bestride our narrow world like Caesar in Rome."

I asked my Naval friends what a colossus is. They told me that in ancient days, a little old seaport named Rhodes, built a big statue of a man whose wide-spread legs formed an arch over the entrance to their harbor.

This Colossus of Rhodes was one of the wonders of the world in its time. And when Julius Caesar became boss of Rome, someone said he was a "colossus that doth bestride our narrow world."

So the gag in the Panama Journal was a good one, if you get it. See? Because the Isthmus is the narrowest part of the two American continents. And Abe, the Newsboy, was the modern Wonder of the World who was champion of the Isthmus.

The marvel of the sporting world is what I mean, of course, because the real wonder of the world in Panama was the Canal. This engineering effort was so much bigger than anything ever done by man before, that my accomplishment in whipping several two-hundred-pound boxers, when I weighed a hundred and forty-five, is not to be compared with it.

The Isthmus of Panama was a giant, and the only man who could have licked it was the army engineer, Colonel Goethals. And he could not have done it if he had not been so ably seconded by that great sanitary engineer, Major Gorgas. They had a little champion to lick. The Chagres river mosquito was then champion of Panama.

Let me tell you what these two American engineers went up against. It was Chagres fever. You remember I mentioned Chagres fever, the terrible scourge which Senorita Puertos described to me. This disease came from the Chagres river, but what it was and how it came was more than the French could understand. It took the Americans to find out it was the mosquito.

Out of every seven hundred men the French put on the job, six hundred died of fever. Lotta Puertos was the granddaughter of a French engineer who married a lady of Colon, when the French first came to Panama. Two weeks after their marriage, the Frenchman was buried in Monkey Hill Cemetery.

The men of the French Canal, when the work was at its height, were dying at the rate of ten thousand a year. Most of the workers were negroes from Jamaica. The black men were dying at the rate of seven hundred a month.

"My grandmother told me," said Lotta, "that it was no uncommon thing to see a negro pushing a wheelbarrow full of earth, fall down between the handles and die there on the dump. Chagres fever works fast. The next negro who came along would dump the wheelbarrow of earth on the poor fellow who died before he could dump it himself. And that was his burial.

"The French engineers and their ladies, and the Panamanian families, rich and poor alike, died just as helplessly when the fever struck them. The old Spanish city of Colon was almost wiped out in 1886," Carlotta continued. "When grandmother went up the mountain-side to Monkey Hill cemetery, to decorate her husband's grave, four years after his death, she saw a whole trainload of other people buried.

"The people were dying so fast in that year that two long trains of flat cars, piled high with wooden boxes full of corpses, came to that one cemetery every day. Long trenches were dug, as in war time, and the bodies were dumped out of the boxes into the trench, and the boxes were shipped back to be refilled with people who had died while that train-load was being buried."

When Lotta told me these terrible things I realized how brave and yet how blind are all races of people. The pogroms which we Jewish people suffered in Russia were no more cruel and unnecessary than the slaughter of the engineers and laborers who tried to build the French Canal.

People have often asked me:

"Why did you poor Russian Jews try to survive when you knew the Russian government despised you and wanted to wipe you out?"

I never knew how to answer that argument until I heard, from the lips of a woman who loved me, this story of her ancestors, the French in Panama. They tried to survive in the face of a pestilence that seemed to be the anger of God.

What were the French doing here? And why did they keep trying and trying to finish their canal while the unknown plague took vengeance on them without any reason, and was slaughtering them like the Four Horsemen of the Apocolypse?

"The French had a great engineer, Count Ferdinand de Lesseps," Lotta said. "He built the Suez Canal. That gave England and the rest of Europe a short route to India."

"Yes, I've been through that Canal," I said.

"Then you know that Columbus was seeking a short route to India when he went bang up against the American continents tied together with this Isthmus."

"Yes. But where do the French come in?"

"The French had an engineer big enough to tackle the job of dividing the continents—to unite the nations."

"What do you mean, unite the nations?"

"The sea is the great highway that brings all nations together."

I saw it was true. I had gone all over the world on the Fleet and had found friends in every land, including Australia, where the boxing kangaroo outsmarted me by hitting me with his tail. But I am not sore at kangaroos; they just plan their fight differently from mine, that's all. But if it hadn't been for the Fleet on the high seas, I would never have known where the kangaroo totes his wallop.

And where does the little old mosquito tote

his wallop? The little old Chagres River wiggle-
tail—how does he wiggle his tail so as to knock
out the French engineers in Panama?

That's the big point in the story Lotta told
me.

In the intestine of the Chagres River mosquito
there is a microbe that lives and breeds there and
doesn't bother the mosquito any more than lice
bother a Russian peasant. But when a Chagres
River mosquito bites a man, whether he is a Latin
American, a North American or a Tropical negro,
the microbes from the mosquito get into the
man's blood and kill him. That's Chagres fever.
In New Orleans and Charleston, S. C., it is known
as Yellow Fever, because the white man's corpse
turns yellow. When it kills the black man, of
course, it cannot turn him yellow.

What surprised me was that the whites and
blacks working on the French Canal did not get
scared when they found this awful death rate
cutting them down. At that time they didn't
know what caused it, but they faced it blindly,
hoping to win.

But why did they try to survive and put
through the canal that would unite the nations?
Because men are born to be godlike, that's all.

Senorita Lotta told me about the conditions
in the negro barracks when the French were
bossing the blacks. When they started work,
they brought five thousand laborers from Trinidad. Every one of these black fellows died, and
none went home to tell the story. Then they
brought thousands and tens of thousands from

Jamaica.   And the fever licked the Jamaicans next.

This was just the reverse of my experience. The first negro champion I licked was the Jamaican called "Young Jack Johnson." And the second champion the British dug up to go against me was "Babe Jeanette," a negro from Trinidad.

They were up against a mere man. But what the colored boys were up against in digging the French Canal when they went against the mosquito is something else again. I quote the diary of Carlotta's relative, which was republished in the Panama Journal the day they let the water into the American Canal.

"Without bedding or pillows the poor black fellows slept naked, like a row of clothes pins laid out on a bench. It may have been no place for a lady to go, but I had a heart of pity for all human beings and I wanted to do what I could for them. So I examined their barracks.

"The bench they lay on was tilted so their heads were higher than their feet. It ran the entire length of the long wooden building, which was usually 100 to 200 feet long. Without mattresses or any other cloth, the negro laborers lay side by side on this hard bed. The lower side touched the floor, and their heels rested on the floor and kept them from sliding out of bed. The higher side of this sloping bed served for a pillow.

"There were no chairs for the men to sit on while undressing. A long bench running the full length of the barracks on the side opposite the slanting bed served for chairs. The only other furniture supplied the darkies was a peg in the wall for each of them to hang his clothing on.

"As the men wore only two garments, shirt and pants, that was plenty of peg to hang them on. Each laborer sat on his share of the bench, took off his garments and hung them on the peg, and then lay down on his share of the long wooden bed to sleep, or perhaps to die.

"If he woke up alive, he went back to work, no matter if the sickness was upon him. He was entitled to sick leave of one dollar a day, a rule the company had made in Paris, not knowing that all the laborers on the job would be sick before many months had passed, and all would be dead before the end of a year.

"But the contractors on the job soon found that all the laborers were sure to perish, and that if a man got sick one day he would be dead in three days at the most. So, whenever a man reported sick, they discharged him, and a few days later he was thrown into a nameless grave.

"That is why the negroes never reported sick, but went to their work and fell dead at the wheelbarrows."

That is a sad and terrible story. No wonder the French failed to dig the Canal. They wore themselves out digging trenches to bury their dead.

I thought of the Jamaica darkey who sang me his song:

"God not good to black man,
God not good to black man.
Let he get thirteen cents the hour,
American man get seventy."

If I could have seen that British negro again I would have told him that God was good to the black man when the Americans came to build the canal where the French had failed because of Chagres Fever.

Because no black man died of Chagres Fever building the American Canal, and ten thousand of them died on the French job, the first thing the American did was to find out what this fever was and how you caught it. They suspected it came from the Chagres river mosquito. Two Army doctors volunteered to let the mosquito bite them and give them the fever. They got it and died of it.

But, as the result of their experiment, the Army learned how to lick the mosquito that had said no nation shall ever build this canal.

Lots of people have told me:

"Abe, you're a fool. You will go against anything. You have fought bulls, bears, kangaroos and two-hundred-pound boxers. And look what a face you have got on you now."

But the French were willing to go against anything when they tried to build the canal without any health precautions nor, in fact, any modern steam shovels big enough to dig it. And the Army doctors who died to learn the secret of the poisonous Chagres mosquito were willing to go against anything. And they are in their graves. But they won the canal and that is their monument.

That was the conclusion I came to when I talked all this matter over with the pretty Senorita Puertos.

"If there is anything you are afraid to go against," I said, "you are not a real man."

She put her arms around my neck and almost choked me to death.

"Marry me, my darling Abe," she cooed. "You're not afraid of me, are you?"

CHAPTER NINETEEN

WAS not afraid of Carlotta Puertos. She was a beautiful woman and well to do. I did not doubt she was sincerely in love with me. But it was my physical being she loved, for I had no education, like her. She was cultured and polished in all the things that I knew nothing about.

When you marry, you must marry someone of your own faith, your own mental equipment; some girl who, when she gets tired of your style, will have to be tired of her own style too, because you are both the same style.

I have seen melodramas where an English lord married a pretty girl from the music halls, and after he got tired of her, about ten years later, and gave her the air, she said:

"You took the best years of my life, and now you cast me aside like an old glove."

So I knew that this Latin-American beauty would love me as long as I was a winning champion. But when I got beaten down and my physical power was gone, she would cast me aside like an old boxing glove.

Besides, I had fallen in love with a girl in New London when I was a ten-year-old kid selling paper. Her name was Rose Kahn, and it was

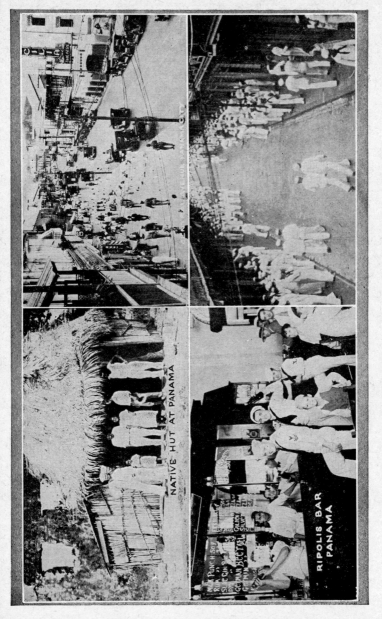

NATIVE HUT AT PANAMA

RIPOLIS BAR
PANAMA

Scenes of Panama and Colon, where the boys are having a great time.

Beautiful scenes in the Hawaiian Islands.

TURNING BACK. THE SPORT PAGES. Wallace Beery and a group of oldtime fighters appearing with him in a forthcoming movie include, left to right: Al McCoy, former world middleweight champion; Jim Flynn, Phil Blum, Frank Moran, Joe Glick, and Abe.

(Top, left). Movie scene from "Roadhouse Nights," with Fred Kohler. (Bottom, left): My good fighting friend, Spike Robison. (Top, right): A scene of the old Bowery, with Wallace Beery and the old fighters, Al McCoy, Jim Flynn, Phil Blum, Frank Moran, Joe Glick, and Abe. (Bottom, right): Scene from "Across the Pacific," with Monte Blue and Myrna Loy.

(Left, top and bottom): Abe in the movies with Mary Astor and Edmund Lowe in the picture, "Dressed to Kill." (Top, right): Scene from "Roadhouse Nights," with Fred Kohler. (Bottom, right): "Across the Pacific," with Monte Blue.

Capt. Jack Kennedy, who retired twice out of the Navy. A farewell party given by all his old friends. He refereed many of my fights. Was loved by everyone, and all will miss him.

A party given to my sailor friends after my wedding.

A selection of my life-time collections of autographed pictures and clippings that are in my great book.

Some of the movie stars with whom I have worked in pictures. (Top, left):
Mary Pickford. (Top, right): Mary Astor. (Bottom, left): Ameli Galli-Curci.
(Bottom, right). May McAvoy.

334

HILO HARBOR – HAWAII

SUNRISE AT PUNA BEACH – HILO HAWAII

Beautiful scenes in the Hawaiian Islands.

(Top, left): Douglas Fairbanks. (Top, right): Fred Kohler. (Bottom, left): Victor McLaglen. (Bottom, right): George O'Brien. Some of the movie stars with whom I worked in pictures.

(Top, left): Irving Berlin. (Top, right): Abe himself. (Bottom, left): Rube Goldberg. (Bottom, right): Monte Blue—some of the friends I have met.

(Top): Abe with some championship belts. (Bottom): My friend, Rudy Vallee, and (right) Abe in a movie scene.

(Above): Victor Varconi and Joseph Schildkraut, two stars with whom I worked in the movies. (Bottom): Abe and his friends in the movies.

(Top): Abe as Champion and (Right) shaking hands with Jack Sharkey's manager, Mr. Buckley. (Bottom, left): Barney Williams, Jack Sharkey, Battling Levinsky, and Abe the Newsboy. (Right): Max Baer, Champion.

Abe the Newsboy in the prime of his boxing day. Champion of Panama and
South America.

U.S.S. MARYLAND

The U. S. S. Baltimore

all right for her to play with me when we were kids. But when she got older, her folks being rich, she went away to school, and they never would let me get in touch with her again.

I carried the image of Rose in my heart. I would not give her up, and I could not marry anybody else.

Then America entered the World War. My country was at war! I must give up all this boxing and join the naval ranks as a fighter.

The first thing I would have to do would be to get my cross eyes straightened if possible. For cross-eyed men cannot be accepted for enlistment in the Navy.

So I left Panama to go home to New London.

I had seen the Panama Canal when it was half built and I had bummed across the Isthmus on the work trains. Later, when I was boxing champion of the Isthmus, I had seen the water let into the big ditch. What a ditch that is, boys. They cut through mountains, they dammed rivers to make great lakes to sail through, and they built locks as tall as skyscrapers to equalize the different levels of these various waters.

When the Lord divided the waters of the Red Sea to let His chosen people through, it was a great miracle, like what the Americans did when they divided these continents to let the people of all nations through.

I had seen the first ships go through the canal. And I had the honor to go through on one of the ships. With Captain Campbell on the U.S.S. Charleston, and Commander C. W. Cross, I broke the world's record in selling newspapers.

When I went aboard on the Pacific side of the Isthmus, I carried a thousand papers. Five hundred of them were stamped thus:

"This paper was bought from Abe, the Newsboy, on the Pacific Ocean . . . . (date)."

They sold like hotcakes, because the sailors like to send home souvenirs.

Eight hours later, this Naval vessel was in the Atlantic Ocean, and I sold five hundred more papers stamped: "This paper was sold by Abe on the same date, in the Atlantic Ocean." The boys bought me out because it took both papers to make the souvenir complete, one paper bought on the Atlantic and the other on the Pacific, the same day.

That's where I proved that I was the world's greatest newsboy.

What other newsboy or circulation manager himself, on any paper in the world, can go out and get the public to buy another copy of a paper they have already bought?

Lots of people say I never was a world champion. Well, beat that record and I am not a world's champion.

That is why I always had them introduce me in the ring as Abe, the Newsboy. For I am a great fighter, I will admit, but I am the greatest newsboy that ever lived.

And so I left Panama with this record behind me: I had fought everything that came along. My bout with the great Eddie Ryan, ending in a drawn verdict, filled the new Bella Vista Bull

Ring on its opening day, a record for all time.
For, as I said, it was built by public-spirit Panamanians to furnish high class bull fights to the
canal diggers after boxing had been killed there
by Buck Crouse and Ortega. But Eddie Ryan
and I rehabilitated boxing, and were selected to
open the bull ring, and we filled it to capacity.
I quote from Mr. J. P. Greening, sporting editor
of the Panama Star and Herald:

"The battleground selected was the Bella
Vista Arena, built for bull fights only. The mob
came in jitneys, in horse cabs and on foot. For
over an hour I sat at the ringside and saw that
mammoth structure fill to capacity! And again
the thought came into my mind: What confidence the public will place in men whom they
believe to be on the square!"

Many a reputation has been lost in Panama.
Buck Crouse, the Pittsburgh Man Killer, was one
of the last of them. The great French engineer,
Count Ferdinand de Lesseps, who made a world-
wide reputation in Suez, lost it in Panama. He
ended in jail in Paris, as Buck Crouse would have
finished in jail in Panama if he had not jumped
through the ropes after his fake fight and outran
the Panama police.

But it was not a fake fight that the French
engineers had made against the Giant of the
Isthmus. But they had miscalculated on the
awful slaughter from Chagres fever. And Count
de Lesseps had not figured on the landslides in
Culebra Cut.

He had figured that 127 million dollars would

dig a sea-level canal. He formed a company that raised that sum from 200,000 stockholders in France. De Lesseps was eighty years old and had a young bride of twenty, Carlotta told me, when he visited the canal in 1886. He thought to find the canal about finished, but when he arrived he found it wasn't half done. And all the money was gone. Much of it had been gambled away in the casinos of the Spanish towns, for Panama has always been the toughest gambling center in the western hemisphere.

The landslides in Culebra Cut had used up the rest of the money. The old engineer decided he would have to raise another 127 million to finish the canal. He went back to Paris and tried to keep the news from leaking out that the canal had failed. The canal company bribed legislators and bought up newspapers to keep the scandal from breaking out.

But when it did break out, the people who had invested became enraged at the loss of their money. They had the old Count put in jail for life, and they had no pity for his young wife, who had borne him a child. They claimed that the Count was not the father of the child, that he was too old. And so the old man died, crushed by disgrace. The great reputation he had made in the eastern hemisphere was sunk in the Isthmus of the West.

I was unknown when I landed in Panama, and had no reputation to lose. You can imagine how my home town of New London was surprised when they saw Associated Press dispatches saying that Abe, the Newsboy, was heavyweight champion of the Isthmus, and to the sport-lovers was a colossus that did bestride that narrow world!

The gamblers who tried to destroy my reputation as they destroyed de Lessep's, had told me that Ortega would whip me anyhow, and they would then spread the report I had been bought and laid down on my backers.

But they couldn't accuse me of laying down when I licked the big bruiser again. You can't lick a man lying down. I fought the clever Eddie Ryan to a draw. I stood up and slugged twenty-five gruelling rounds with the great Kid Norfolk, who afterwards licked Battling Siki and other world-famous heavies. I fought Steamboat Bill Scott to a draw in fifteen rounds. And later licked him in six rounds.

The way I came to fight Norfolk before I fought Bill Scott was this: Bill Scott had trained Jack Johnson for his fight in Havana, where Willard restored the championship to the white race. Scott then went to the Canal Zone and in several fights showed remarkable ability. The great Kid Norfolk then came to Panama, and the fans demanded a match between them.

But Steamboat Bill Scott would not sign up to fight the colored wonder.

I was in Chile at the time. The promoters told Bill Scott that he was afraid of Kid Norfolk.

Just at that time, I landed back in Panama, and the promoters said:

"We'll get Abe, the Newsboy. He'll fight

either one of you."

I was at the Hotel Metropole when a match-maker telephoned from the National Sporting Club:

"Abe, I've got a fight for you. You can have either Kid Norfolk or Steamboat Bill Scott."

I took on the mighty Kid Norfolk first.

There was much money bet that I could not stay ten rounds with the black master. One of my friends at the ring-side bet a thousand dollars I would. I did.

At the end of the tenth, I hollered to him:

"Better bet another thousand that I go the distance."

And I did. In the eighteenth round I was in a bad way. I didn't believe I could come through, but my will-power saved me. I took an awful beating in that fight, but I managed to stand toe-to-toe with him and slug it out for twenty-five rounds. The decision was for Norfolk, and I was no longer heavyweight champion.

After that, Bill Scott had to face Kid Norfolk, and Norfolk knocked him out in the ninth round. And, as I said, I later licked Bill Scott.

So I was leaving Panama with a clean record.

I told Senorita Puertos that, while I was very fond of her, I had sense enough to know that our love affair was merely a passing incident.

"Panama is now full of American pugilists since they can get a thousand dollars for an evening. You will have a chance to pick out a real

'U.S. Naval Academy,

Annapolis, Maryland,

October 20, 1909.

To whom it may concern:--

"Abe the Newsboy" was in charge of the Bum Boat during the Summer Practice Cruise of 1909 and was most faithful in attendance on the Squadron. When in Gardiner's Bay and on the drill grounds in the Sound he never missed a trip, in spite of fog and bad weather.

He was also most useful in bringing off the mail and packages.

He is energetic and honest.

Captain, U.S. Navy,

Commandant of Midshipmen,

Late Squadron Commander,

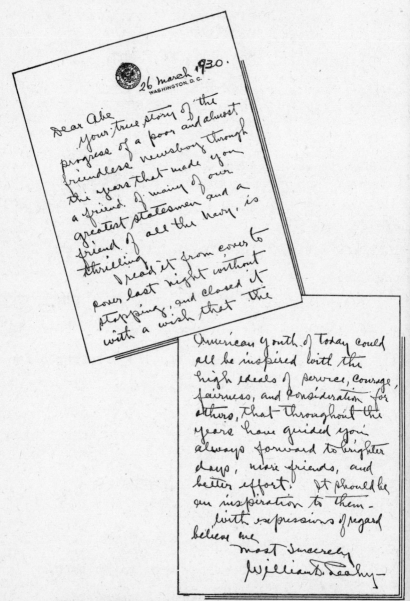

26 march 1930.
WASHINGTON, D. C.

Dear Abe

Your true story of the progress of a poor and almost friendless newsboy through the years that made you a friend of many of our greatest statesmen and a friend of all the navy, is thrilling.

I read it from cover to cover last night without stopping, and closed it with a wish that the

American Youth of today could all be inspired with the high ideals of service, courage, fairness, and consideration for others, that throughout the years have guided you always forward to brighter days, more friends, and better effort. It should be an inspiration to them.

With expressions of regard believe me

most sincerely

William D. Leahy—

Letter to Abe from William D. Leahy, Chief of Naval Operations.

Apollo now. One who is not cross-eyed. But the Navy is in the Big War now, and I am going with the Navy."

CHAPTER TWENTY

RETURNING to New York, I went to the Manhattan Eye and Ear Hospital and had them operate on my eye. It didn't cost much. They just took a knife and cut a certain muscle. My eye ached like a toothache the first night, but the pain was much less the second day and soon wore off.

And so I had a new face. Two eyes looking straight ahead instead of one eye watching the other.

But I had lost my chance ever to be a pretty man—a he-doll for the movies. For, when my features were shapely and handsome, my cross eyes spoiled the picture, and when I finally got my two lovely brown eyes, the rest of my features had been pounded to a pulp.

With my new eyes, I went to the Submarine Base in New London to enlist. I talked to my friends, Admiral Decker and Captain Edgar. They told me my cauliflower ears would be a bar to my enlistment.

"I'll have my ears fixed by a surgeon," I replied.

They said, no. I must not have my ears tampered with. They said I had done enough fighting for my country and must not make any more sacrifices.

It finally came out why they didn't want me to enlist. My friends among the sailors told me. You have to have the equivalent of a high school education to enlist in the new Navy; the old Navy, in the days of Fighting Bob Evans, took on anybody, whether he could read or not.

"I'll go to high school," I said, "and fit myself to pass muster."

"And by that time the war would be over, Abe, and you would have the reputation of a slacker."

They had a better job for me. They made me boxing instructor for the Naval station where five thousand recruits to the Naval Reserve were encamped on the great pier. Of course, I had the privilege of selling newspapers to these five thousand men, and they were all millionaires.

So here, again, I proved myself to be the world's greatest newsboy. What other newsboy ever had the exclusive right to sell papers to five thousand millionaires? If any other newsboy had come on that pier to sell a paper, he would have been arrested by secret service agents. Abe had a monopoly on those five thousand millionaires; they were all in the bag.

They loved their country so well that they wanted to fight for her on the sea. This pier jutted out to sea, so they spent the period of the World War on it.

And they did some fighting, too. I was their boxing instructor and I made them fight.

This pier was called the Million Dollar Pier long before it became to the home of a host of young millionaires. It was built by the state and the municipality at a cost of a million dollars. Mayor B. F. Mahan was a leader in the pier project.

One day a strange man on the pier bought a paper from me. He asked for the New York Times, and gave me a dollar for it. After glancing at the paper, he said:

"What's the name of that ship out there?" He pointed to a camouflaged Naval vessel.

"I don't know," I said.

"Are they making any ammunition here?" he asked.

"I don't know."

"What do they make here?"

"I don't know what they make."

"How many men are there here?"

"I don't know anything about it."

"You sell papers here, don't you?"

"Yes, I sell papers. All the news that's fit to print is in that paper you just bought."

The man opened his coat and said:

"Kid, you're all right."

He showed me the badge of the secret service.

Now it can be told what the boys were making on that pier. They were manufacturing nets to catch submarines. They strung these net traps all up and down Long Island Sound.

Before we entered the war a German submarine had bobbed up at New London at the State Pier. It was the famous Deutchland that visited America with a cargo of merchandise. I went aboard that submarine and sold newspapers.

After we entered the war, no German submarine could have bobbed up at our own submarine base, New London. For the millionaire boys made nets and laid them all along the coast.

They were eager to fight, and soon they got their chance. After they had made these steel nets and laid them, they began manning the submarine chasers which the Government was then turning out in quantity. Which shows that rich and poor were alike in the war. These chasers were small boats, swift as birds and with a wide cruising radius. They had to patrol the war zone looking for the German shark boats. Life aboard these little speeders was terrible. They tossed all the time, like the back of a pacing camel, thus making it impossible for the crew to be comfortable any time. And they were in constant danger of being sunk without a trace.

Every week I saw a boatload of my millionaires embark for the war zone on one of those terrible little submarine chasers, and I was rather envious of their heroism.

I didn't get a chance to risk my own life on those death-infested seas. And I forever revere the brave boys who did it. "The Navy took them over, and the Navy brought them back."

As I look over my clippings, recounting over 1,100 ring battles, I am unable to produce any accounts of service at sea in the war. I didn't get to sea, but my millionaire friends did. And I would have given a million dollars to be in their shoes.

The only clippings I have which do not deal
with wrestling and boxing are the accounts of
several rescues I made, two of them on sea and
one on land. The land adventure I will reprint
first. This is from a New London paper in 1906,
the year I met President Roosevelt and chucked
him in the ribs as he twisted my cauliflower ear:

"Young Abraham Hollandersky, more com-
monly known as Abe, the Newsboy, who has a
penchant for helping people out when they are
in trouble, added another good deed to his list
yesterday afternoon. He rescued a woman and
her small son from a runaway accident, thus
appearing in a new role. Previously he has saved
three persons who were drowning in the bay, and
one woman who was drifting out to sea in a
helpless launch. Now he has become a hero on
land.

"Abe is training for a wrestling bout, and part
of his daily exercise consists of a walk from
Groton Ferry to Eastern Point and return. As
Abe was walking past the Point he saw a horse
attached to a light wagon, coming down the road
toward him at race horse gait. He saw a woman
tugging at the reins and a small boy clinging to
the bouncing seat beside her.

"Abe doesn't know much about farm horses,
but he realized that the horse had got beyond
the woman's control and was running away.

"He tried to stop the horse by standing in the
animal's path. But the horse swerved around
him. Which was probably lucky for Abe, as the

little fellow could not possibly stop a plunging horse with his shoulders.

"The newsboy gave chase and lunged and caught the horse's bridle at the bit-ring. The horse reared and lifted Abe off his feet, but he hung on, dragging the horse's head down. The hoofs of the animal barely missed Abe's head, as Abe was dragged along on the ground. But he brought the animal to a standstill.

"The woman thanked him profusely. She did not know why the old family horse had run away with her. Abe examined the animal's mouth and found a big cockle burr sticking into the tissues. The animal had taken fright from the pain of this burr in its mouth.

"When the burr was removed, the horse went along as gently as usual."

That's the story the editor wrote, and it has a nice little lesson in it to horses. Not to get afraid of pain. But, of course, you can't teach a horse to meet an unexpected pain without panic. But, boys, you can learn not to be afraid of pain. It is a lesson that has been taught by the patriarchs from the most ancient times.

Physical pain is nothing to get excited about. If you ever want to be a great man, you must be superior to pain. Of course, if I had never felt any pain, I would not be the right man to tell you to take it on the chin. When my friend Gene Tunney studied Shakespeare, he found where Shakespeare said: "The man that never felt a pain thinks it's funny when the other guy groans." That's not the book words; they are:

"He jests at scars who never felt a wound." That means the kid who has never had a wound thinks the other guy's cauliflower ears came easy, and are a joke.

But I can talk as one who knows, fellows. These cauliflower ears were given to me in agony. And I was born cross-eyed, so everybody said: "Look at that poor child." And I never got an education, but had to support my blind father, knowing how he was suffering without complaint against his hard fate. Then I had to fight a thousand battles and lick men far bigger and more famous than me, to show I had any class. And I was kidded because I was a Jew, and they tried to poison me in South America because I was a Yankee. And I was licked and almost killed by a bear because he had super-human strength, and I was knocked humpbacked by a kangaroo because he had a tail and I didn't. And I was made a monkey of by smart New York fight promoters—but still didn't have a tail.

Let me tell you that story.

Listen, boys, one time I was commissioned to supply preliminary fighters for three bouts. After the fights were over, the promoter counted out our money in five-dollar bills, put it in an envelope and handed it to me, saying:

"You see the boys when they get dressed and give them their divvy."

I put the envelope in my breast pocket, and took the other five fighters to a restaurant and ordered a dinner for six. After we had eaten, I said:

(Top): Boxing squad of the U.S.S. Tennessee for 1934-1935. (Center): The Arizona 1935 Cutter Champions. (Bottom). Champion wrestlers of the U.S.S. Nevada.

Wedding reception of Abe and his bride at the Synagogue of the Hebrew Sheltering Home for the Aged.

(Top): Wedding pictures of Abe, the Newsboy and his bride, taken on the steps of the Hebrew Sheltering Home for the Aged, with his Navy friends and the C. C. of the United States Navy and his staff, on June 7th, 1931. (Left to right): The late Lt. Comdr. Skelton, Rear Admiral W. T. Cluverius, and Admiral Jehu V. Chase. (Bottom): Abe and his bride.

H. M. (Spike) Webb, athletic instructor at Annapolis Naval Academy.

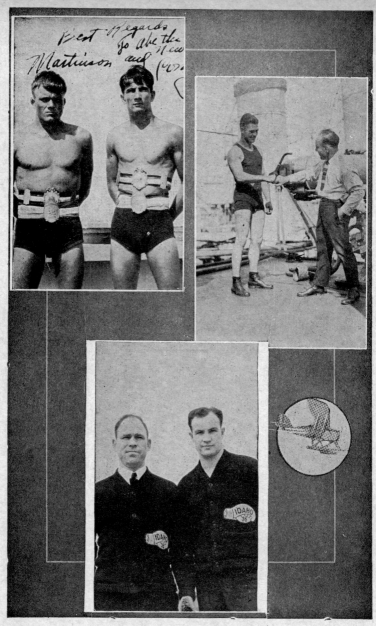

(Top, left): Navy Champion Wrestlers Martinson and Conley. (Right): Jeff Brittenbeck (All-Navy Champion boxer), and Abe. (Bottom): Terria, champion boxer and trainer, and Bill Boyd, heavyweight champion of the Navy.

(Top, left): Abe the Newsboy and a group of his friends on the U.S.S. New Mexico. (Top, right): Two wrestling champions of the Navy. Mack Simpson, welterweight; K. R. Houghtling, middleweight. (Bottom, left). Captain and race boat crew of the U.S.S. Utah, winning the Bathenberg Cup. (Bottom, right): Bobbie Smith, All-Navy champion and "Joke" Shugrue, on the Rebel ship U.S.S. Tennessee

(Top): George Blake, a prince of managers, and his champ, Fidel LaBarba, Abe, and Jack Dempsey. (Center): Gene Tunney, Abe, and Larry Williams. (Bottom): Abe and Benny Leonard—all retired champions.

(Top): One of the toughest fights I ever had in my career (in Colon, Panama), with Kid Norfolk, once the contender for the light heavyweight championship of the world, who outweighed me 30 pounds. I received $250 ($10 per round) for 25 of the most gruelling rounds, but my sailor friends gave me $1700 of their winnings. (Bottom): Winning the championship of Central and South America from Jack Ortega, in 18 rounds of a 45-round battle. Ortega outweighed me 40 pounds. Fight took place in Panama City.

Abe, the Newsboy, as a wrestler. It was at this period of his physical development that he began giving the blood of his vigorous body, for transfusion, to save the lives of weakened children.

368

Poses of Abe in his early boxing days.

Abe, the Newsboy, Author Wants to Get Married
Book Needs Profits
His Fiancee Is Waiting

By Damon Runyon

No Shrinking Violet

Between You and Me!

Abe, the Newsboy, Writes a Book, Hoping Profits Will Allow Him to Get Married

By Damon Runyon.

Continued from Page 2.

He's a Champion?

1929 Ring Battles

My great friend, Damon Runyon, was not only the best sports writer, but also the best good fellow, for whose great story about my first book I am very grateful.

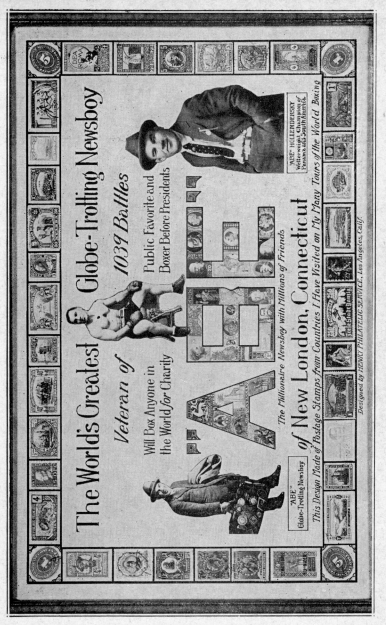

Stamps from all over the world, of places that Abe visited.

A wealth of newspaper clippings from all over the world.

A photo given me,
while Champion
Wrestler of the
World. A good fellow.

Sammy Stein

Abe, The Newsboy,
Champion of Panama
and South America.
Hero of a 1000 fights.

A photo given to me
while Champion of
the World. A good
fighter and also a
good fellow.

Max Baer

Abe signing in one of the 1700 recruits for the war.
Abe also helped sell millions of dollars of bonds in the Naval Tr. Center, San Diego.

"Now we'll divide up the money."

I took the envelope out of my pocket, opened it and flashed the bills. They were not the bills the promoter had showed me when he put them in the envelope. What I had was a bunch of cigar store coupons.

The five fighters thought I was kidding them and had embezzled their money. So I faced the situation of having to stand off five infuriated prize fighters in one after-dinner speech.

Unaccustomed as I am to public speaking, believe me, I made the most eloquent speech you ever heard. I finally convinced them that it was not I who was cheating them, but the promoter was the smart guy who had put Abe in the position where he would be murdered. And dead men tell no tales. If that speech had been recorded on a movietone, there would be something they could write a whole drama around in Hollywood.

How I got out of that restaurant alive I am not going to tell until I get this book copyrighted. It is too valuable an incident to be tossed around where somebody could steal it, the way that smart promoter stole the services of me and five other willing sluggers for his knockout show.

CHAPTER TWENTY-ONE

UT I started out to quote clippings about life-saving I have had an opportunity to do. I made three different rescues at sea. The first one was a beautiful young woman of the upper classes. But she must have been awfully dumb, because she was in an open launch, without gasoline, drifting out to sea and didn't know it. I quote from the New London paper:

"Abe, the Newsboy appeared in a chivalric role yesterday. Abe has stopped runaway horses, rescued children from drowning and accomplished other feats of daring. But yesterday's deed was slightly different and didn't require any great exertion of courage, merely good sense.

"Abe has a little boat, presented to him by Admiral Evans, in which he visits the war ships and yachts in the harbor, selling newspapers and magazines. About six-thirty, yesterday evening, he was rowing in from the cruiser Newark at the Pequot, a hotel and wharf, when he noticed a gasoline launch drifting about helplessly off the lighthouse.

"Abe went to the rescue and found the sole occupant of the launch was an aristocratic young woman. She did not appear frightened at her predicament, but seemed to think Abe had some ulterior motive.   Abe looks like a seventeenth century pirate.

"The Newsboy asked if she was in trouble. And she replied that her engine wouldn't run, but she would drift in all right."

"Abe saw she didn't realize her predicament. The tide was running out, and she was drifting toward Fishers Island. So Abe decided he better take a hand.

"He climbed into the launch and endeavored to start the engine. His efforts were fruitless, and when he examined the gas tank he found it empty.

"Abe then told her what she was up against. She was dismayed, but not the doughty newsboy. He got back into his rowboat and passed a line to the launch, and bucking the tide with his strong muscles, he rowed all the way in, towing the lady's launch to the Hotel Griswold dock.

"She thanked him cordially, telling him she was accustomed to going out daily alone in her launch. She is evidently a summer resident at this resort, but she ought never to forget our famous newsboy, whose wit and gallantry have been demonstrated on so many occasions."

After quoting that clipping, I bow and accept the nomination. Now I quote the one, printed in 1907, in which I saved a man and woman who were actually drowning. Here it is:

ABE, THE NEWSBOY
SAVES TWO PEOPLE

NEW LONDON STRONG LAD
IS REAL HERO

Last evening as Abe, the Newsboy, was returning from the warship Nevada in his natty little craft, he was attracted by cries for help. Turning, he saw a man and woman struggling in the water near the Pequot. He rowed swiftly to the assistance of the couple whose boat had been overturned.

Abe reached out and caught the woman by the hair and held her head above the water, while the man was able to grasp the gunwale of the Newsboy's boat. Abe's small craft was so loaded with merchandise that there was no room aboard for anybody in addition to the hero.

So Abe yelled lustily for assistance. The monitor, Florida, was within hailing distance, and when they heard the voice of the newsboy in distress, they manned a launch and put out with all haste.

The rescued couple were taken to the Pequot dock, both much exhausted from their struggle in the water.

Abe got all that was coming to him in the way of thanks, but, like the modest young fellow that he is, he merely remarked: "Glad I was here, that's all. I would have done the same for anybody."

A naval officer said:

"You mean anybody would have done the same for these people?"

Abe blushed in embarrassment, then he laughed and said:

"I no spika English. What my naval friend says is right."

Then he got in his boat and proceeded on his journey to sell his papers.

The man and woman refused to give their names for publication. But they were extremely fortunate that assistance was near at hand, and that it was a strong fellow like our Abe. Abe is being hailed as a hero by his friends today, but he modestly says: "Don't use my name if they don't use theirs."

Abe is not to be outdone in modesty by anybody.

* * * *

The editor that wrote that piece was a good friend of mine, and I think he was kidding somebody in a good-natured way. But you can't blame those well-bred people for withholding their names. Who wants to tell the world they have been intimately mauled around by a cross-eyed newsboy?

Later in this book I am going to publish a picture of the dear girl who is engaged to marry me. Lots of people will say it is in bad taste. But I want my friends to look at her picture and say whether my taste is bad or not.

Now for another rescue:

ABE AGAIN IS
A LIFE-SAVER

PULLED ITALIAN OUT OF WATER
NEAR PEQUOT HOUSE
YESTERDAY

Abe Hollandersky, better known as Abe, the Newsboy, performed another rescue at the Pequot yesterday.

Abe had been selling newspapers and magazines to the ships anchored off the Pequot, and was returning to shore when he saw an Italian, who had been fishing on the deck, lose his balance and tumble into the water.

The newsboy quickly rowed to the spot, and when he got there he found the Italian clinging to the slippery piling and almost exhausted in his struggle to keep the tide from carrying him away. He could not swim.

Abe shouted encouragement to him, and getting close enough, he grabbed the helpless man by his coat collar and pulled him aboard his rowboat.

This was no easy task, and Abe's boat was nearly capsized in the effort. The lad was undaunted, however, and stuck to his task until he had landed the man safely aboard. The boat was almost full of water by this time, but it did not capsize, and Abe carried his man ashore.

The Italian was taken to the emergency hospital and we did not learn his name. But we predict a great career for Abe, the Newsboy.

*   *   *   *

Since the days when the newspaper editors began to say nice things about me I have indeed had a great career. To have been the darling of the Navy and heavyweight champion of Panama while they were building the canal, is a great career. I whipped all Latin America before the rise of Firpo. After each of my great victories, the sailor boys used to ride me on their shoulders, shouting:

"He is some baby!"

That was the slang of the period before the World War. It means, this is the most remarkable one in his class.

And if I ever have a tombstone with anything written on it, that's what I want it to be: "Here lies Abe, the Newsboy, who sold papers on the battleships." The verdict of the Navy is: "He was some baby."

I have been subjected to every defeat and every handicap and humiliation that can come to a poor boy. Yet I have risen above my handicaps to victory, and the verdict of my country is for me. So I should worry.

One time I broke the prohibition law. Not the law against drinking liquor, but a law against prize fighting. A bunch of hot sports matched me to fight a colored pugilist, and because of the aforesaid law, the fight had to take place in secret. The sports assembled after dark in a big old-fashioned farm barn. Each of them carried a wax candle, which they lighted when we got inside, and closed all doors and vent holes.

It had to be in the dark to keep the constables from spotting that barn and raiding the illicit bout.

Candles don't give much light. Just about as much as a negro's eyes give in the dark. This was the first time candles had ever been lit for me before a fight, but they were not placed at a shrine to pray for my success. These candles almost caused me to get an undeserved beating.

For I couldn't see my black opponent in the semi-dark.

His dark skin made him totally invisible. I had to fight him by ear, and what I could see of the whites of his eyes. But I couldn't tell his eyes from the candle lights.

But my white ghost-like body loomed up before him as a constant target and an easy mark.

He could have hit me at will.

But the ghost-like part of it is what licked him. He got scared stiff, and when I managed to connect with a cruel punch in the third round, he curled up and quit.

One time I was boxing a preliminary with Jimmy Carter at a New York club, and we were promised five dollars apiece for the fight. The referee was the great trainer, James De Forrest, who later conditioned Wild Bull Firpo for the Dempsey fight. I landed a hard sock on Jimmy Carter's ear in the first round and it began to puff up like a fast-growing pink toadstool.

"Oh, boy," I cried. "You're going to have a nice cauliflower ear, like mine."

He began shielding the ear with his elbow, and wouldn't box, but only cover up.

"Come on and fight!" I yelled. "We're hired to fight."

The referee, Mr. De Forrest, also told him he must fight or get out of the ring.

"Fight, hell," he replied. "I'll get five dollars for the fight and it will cost me ten dollars to have my ear doctored."

He quit, and took off the gloves.

The promoter docked me four dollars on that fight and said I would have to fight another man if I expected to earn the full five dollars.

"Give me another man," I said. "I need the money."

They put in a big negro named Young Peter Jackson, and I knocked him out in one round.

Thus I had made the record of whipping two

men in one ring in one evening for the promised
sum of five dollars. They docked me again for
knocking out the second man too soon, so all I
got was two dollars for licking two men.

There is money to be made in prize fighting
if you can lick enough men. The old saying of
the working man is:

"A dollar a day for a hundred days is a hundred dollars."

CHAPTER TWENTY-TWO

Y last professional battle took place three years ago in Honolulu when I boxed before Governor Farrington, the Administrator of the Hawaiian Islands. I won the fight, but if it had gone any great distance I would have lost it, for my legs tired under me. Once or twice my knees sagged.

So I knew my ring career was over after fighting more than 1,100 fights. For years I had fought every night if I could get a bout during the boxing season, and sometimes twice a night.

And I sold papers all day. The day I went twenty-five rounds with the great Kid Norfolk, I had been on my feet continuously from six o'clock in the morning until I entered the ring at four in the afternoon.

I quote from the writings of Mr. J. P. Greening, sporting editor of the Star and Herald, Panama City, 1914-1920:

"I saw the little fellow from New London stand toe-to-toe with Kid Norfolk for twenty-five gruelling rounds. On this memorable Sunday afternoon in the City of Colon, the newsboy entered the ring weighing 148 pounds as against Norfolk's 180. The odds were five to one that Norfolk would finish him inside of ten rounds. On the day of the contest the arena was packed from ring to rafters, and hundreds were refused admission. The battle was scheduled for twenty-five rounds. And it went the distance.

"The referee's decision was for Norfolk. He outpointed the newsboy in fifteen of the twenty-five rounds. Abe was defeated, but what a glorious defeat it was.

"And what a handicap he fought under, not in weight alone. For from eleven until two o'clock on the day of the battle, Abe was delivering newspapers and magazines on the U.S.S. Minnesota, which had arrived in Colon harbor at six that morning. The Minnesota was carrying marines to Mexico, America having entered the World War.

"Duty to the sailor boys brought the newsboy aboard the big ship. He did not want the boys to leave for a foreign post without plenty of American reading matter.

"A little incident happened after the Norfolk fight. The big colored fellow wanted the boxing gloves used in the fight to keep as a souvenir. But Abe wanted them more than the Kid. To decide which one should have the gloves, Abe suggested that they set to outside the ring, the winner to receive the gloves used in the official battle. However, Norfolk gracefully declined this fight and let Abe retain the historic souvenirs.

"Abe took the eight o'clock train back to Panama City and walked into the American Hotel and, shaking hands with Mrs. Charles Cantor, he shouted: 'Hurrah! I stayed twenty-five rounds with Norfolk, and if the bout had gone five more rounds I would have knocked him out!'

"For many hours he was kept busy telling hundreds of Panama City people the details of the battle in Colon.

"Kid Norfolk was in his prime at that time, and since his meeting with the Newsboy, he has succeeded in beating Billy Miske, Battling Siki and other world-famous fistic stars. After Abe's fight, the audience, to a man, stormed the ring and carried the little fellow on their shoulders. No hero in a world's series ever won the hearts of the fans as Abe, the Newsboy, did on that Sunday afternoon in the City of Colon.

"I think it is a wonderful thing for the fight game that it can boast such fellows as Abe, the Newsboy. He was never a world's champion.

"But tell me of any world's champion the little fellow would not meet in the ring. If fortune had ever willed it that this lad was to be a world's title holder, unheard of purses would have been offered to see him in action, and crowds such as no amphitheatre could accommodate, would have striven to get within seeing distance of the remarkable fighter.

"There are hundreds of interesting incidents I could record of what happened to Abe during his stay in the Tropics. But I feel sure he will relate all of them in his forthcoming book."

That's about as nice a send-off as the Panama folks could give a retired pugilist. I thank the sporting editor for those kind words. But what a struggle I have had to get my book written and published.

Three years ago I said farewell to the professional ring, as I told you, in Honolulu. Then I took ship for San Francisco, returning to the States to get my book out. Before leaving Honolulu, the sailor boys tossed me, as a sign of their good wishes. Many of them ordered my book and paid for it in advance.

When the commercial liner on which I was returning approached the Golden Gate of San Francisco, a fog held us up, and the boat cast anchor and waited. A young woman passenger came fluttering out of her stateroom, half dressed and greatly excited, thinking the ship was sinking because the engines had stopped and nothing could be seen through the fog. The fog horn kept blowing like a demon howling for help.

The woman ran into me and asked:

"What's the matter? What's the matter?"

"Nothing much, lady. Calm yourself," I answered. "We have reached the Golden Gate harbor, and the skipper has lost the key to the gate. He dropped it overboard when he pulled it out of his hip pocket. They have sent a diver down, and as the water is shallow he will soon recover the key."

The young woman returned to her stateroom entirely satisfied.

When we got into San Francisco, I called on my friend, Mayor Rolf, four times elected to that office. He advised me to go to Hollywood before proceeding East, as he thought I would be wanted in the movies.

When I got to Los Angeles I received a welcome. Bull Montana, who looks as tough as I do, only he is bigger, was very cordial to me. He asked me if I needed any money to go East and finance my book.

I told him the sailors were helping me finance it by ordering it in advance, but I had very little money of my own. And what do you suppose Bull did? He offered to give me a thousand dollars if I would go right on to New London, Conn., and get my book in shape right away.

That was very generous of Bull Montana. Who would have thought the old battle-scarred wrestler was so devoted to literature?

But I couldn't accept his donation.

I wish now I had. I mean, if I had taken his thousand dollars and put it into my book, as he advised, I would have got out the book that much quicker. It would have been a good bargain. For I never caused Bull Montana a thousand dollars worth of competition in the movies—not even a dollar's worth. The reason why I will tell later.

But I am glad I didn't take Bull's advice, because, if I had, I would never have met the little lady who is going to be my wife.

But before I tell you about Freda, I must tell you about my first film; for I have appeared in dozens of them, though never as a star like Bull Montana.

I went to the office of a casting director whom I had known in the East long before. When he saw me he said:

"Good for you, Abe. We can use you next week. Stick around."

They said they wanted me to act as an underworld character. I stocked up with papers and magazines and went aboard a warship in Los Angeles harbor. Two weeks later they found me selling papers on the ship.

"We've been hunting all over for you," they said, "Now get back to the lot as quick as you can." When I came into the studio, the director exclaimed, in disappointment:

"Great scott, you won't do at all, Abe, you're too short."

They had cast me for a taxi driver. But they all agreed that a man of my short stature could not be used on the screen. I was greatly disappointed, and I cried out in mock despair:

"I am too light for heavy work and too heavy for light work; I was too good for the welterweight division and not good enough for the heavyweights; I am too old to fight and too young for a pension; I have stayed too long in Los Angeles to be told I am too short for Hollywood. What do you expect of me, anyway?"

They fixed me up with some high-heeled boots that made me taller, and told me I was to be a taxi driver. When they put me in the taxi and told me where to drive, I had to tell them I couldn't drive a car.

Then they had another fit and cursed me out again.

It reminded me of the time when I was to be awarded the Carnegie medal and cash prize of five hundred dollars for saving the lives of the boat capsized in the bay. When the authorities tried to learn the names of these three persons, there was no way of locating them. So I didn't get any prize.

But I got a prize in Los Angeles, as I hinted before. I won the sweetest girl in the world, and this is how it happened:

I went into a stationery store to buy some envelopes to send my brother Sol some clippings from the Los Angeles papers telling about the murder of my friend Director Taylor by a wild woman.

A sweet little girl waited on me and sold me the envelopes. Right away I fell in love. She reminded me of Rosie Kahn, the girl I had played with when I was an eight-year-old in New London. I asked her to address one of the envelopes for me, and she did.

"I told her I was mailing the story of the wild actress that shot William Desmond Taylor."

"Did you know that woman?" she asked.

I said I didn't know her personally, but they're all alike. If you know one woman you know them all.

This made the girlie sore.

"Who do you think you're talking to?" she asked.

"I am talking in general. I never saw you before and you never saw me before."

"No, I never saw you before and I never want to see you again," she said.

I apologized, and she wouldn't listen.

The owner of the store said:

(Top) Mascot of the Old Main, 40 years ago. (Center): Jiggs, the Mascot of the Marines. (Bottom): Another one of the ship's mascots.

My treasure of Liberty Card Passes, permitting me to visit the ships with my great book. Any citizen who finds one of the Liberty Cards, please drop into a U. S. mail box, for the good of the sailors.

SUPPLEMENTARY
PICTURE
SECTION

—— and ——

REPRODUCTIONS OF LETTERS FROM

SOME OF MY FAMOUS FRIENDS

Abe wishes to thank the following for their kindness in
furnishing photographs, etc.:

"OUR NAVY," (Brooklyn, N.Y.)
U. S. NAVY MAGAZINE, (San Diego, Calif.)
NAVY RECRUITING OFFICE (New York, N.Y.)
BUNNELL PHOTO SHOP (1033 Sixth Ave., San Diego, Calif.)

UNITED STATES FLEET

HEADQUARTERS OF THE COMMANDER IN CHIEF
NAVY DEPARTMENT, WASHINGTON, D. C.

November 16, 1942

Abe the Newsboy,
  715 West Seaside Blvd.,
    Long Beach, California

Dear Abe:

        I have your letter of November 13th - and am in sympathy with the good work that you are doing on behalf of the Navy.

    You are at liberty to show this letter as you wish in pursuance of your work for the good of the Navy and of the armed forces generally.

    I suggest that you paste your photograph on this letter as a ready means of checking your identification.

    With all good wishes, as always, I am

Faithfully yours,

Admiral, U. S. Navy.

A letter received from Admiral King in 1942.

U. S. NAVAL TRAINING STATION
SAN DIEGO. CALIFORNIA

June 12th, 1943

Dear Abe:

It gave me great pleasure to see you again in my office. Your splendid record as a pal of the Navy and your excellent book serve as an inspiration for the young bluejackets of the present day.

I am happy to know that you are still actively telling people what the Navy stands for and how well our young American boys are serving the colors.

The work you have done in the interests of the Navy Relief Society will always be appreciated by Navy men and civilian friends of the naval Service.

With best wishes and warmest personal regards, I am

Yours very sincerely,

W. A. MAGUIRE
Captain (ChC) USN

Mr. Abe Hollandersky
715 West Seaside Blvd.
Long Beach, California.

The Chaplain's Book, "Rig For Church," is a masterpiece. Read it.

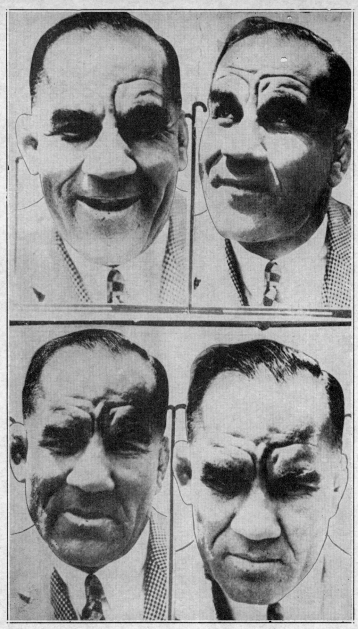

Character studies of Abe in the movies. Abe is very grateful to the directors
and their assistants, with whom he has worked. He says they
always take care of the old-timers.

(Top): A few critics on Abe's book. (Bottom). My friend, Lt. Jack Kennedy, the most honest referee in the boxing game.

(Left): My brother Sol, who you will read about in this book. (Left): Abe.

lieve It or Not
—BY RIPLEY

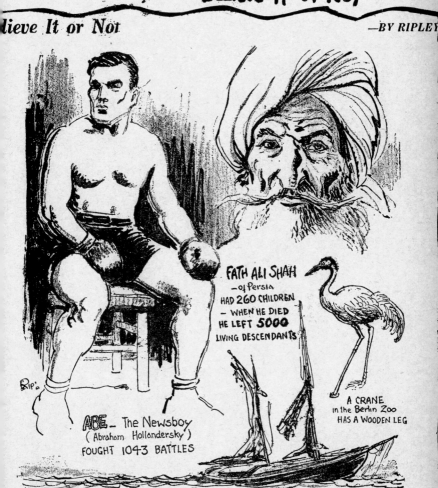

FATH ALI SHAH
– of Persia
HAD 260 CHILDREN
– WHEN HE DIED
HE LEFT 5000
LIVING DESCENDANTS

ABE – The Newsboy
(Abraham Hollandersky)
FOUGHT 1043 BATTLES

A CRANE
in the Berlin Zoo
HAS A WOODEN LEG

THE SEA GHOST – THE SUNKEN FISHING SHIP "COLUMBIA" CAME TO THE SURFACE FOR 10 MINUTES
– AND THEN SANK AGAIN   New Year's Day, 1928   There were 20 dead men on board

On request Robert L. Ripley will send proof and details of anything depicted by him.

Boxing with a kangaroo in Australia, and wrestling with a bear in New York

U. S. NAVAL TRAINING STATION,
GREAT LAKES, ILLINOIS
REAR ADMIRAL, JOHN DOWNES U. S. NAVY,
COMMANDING OFFICER

This anchor is made out of Blue Jackets . . . God bless them.

Good luck to you, my good friend Nat Fliescher, who has never turned an old fighter dow
He has taken care of many of them. He always gives a belt to a champion who real
deserves it because he knows his boxing.

Abe the Newsboy
Gives Blood to
Save Boy's Life

Abe the Newsboy Hollanderky of this city, famous as the navy's newsboy, yesterday gave of his blood to prolong the life of George Mosher, 14, of New York, who is critically ill from a malady known as Kala-Azar, a form of black fever. The transfusion took place at Seaside hospital, New Dorp, Staten island.

The boy has been ill with the disease for the past eight weeks. Physicians at the hospital announced that frequent transfusions were necessary to prolong life, and Abe, learning of the fact, volunteered about a week ago. He sent a telegram to the boy expressing his wish to help him.

Abe was a guest at dinner on the U S & luka yesterday.

2, 1926

Thug's Attack
Rouses Abie's
'Irish' Temper

"Abie the Newsboy" fought his 1060th battle last night, but there were no seconds, no timekeepers, no referee to the fight. For that matter, the engagement wasn't even fought in a ring and there were very few spectators. Abie's purse was the only purse at stake, for his battle was with a holdup man. Details of the fight:

Abie Hollenderskay

Abie, whose last name is Hollenderskay, and who has sold Hearst newspapers all over the world, was accosted at First and Figueroa streets and at the point of a gun ordered to put up his hands. Abie did—he put his right fist right up under the bandit's chin and knocked him cold. It was a knockout in the first 10 seconds of the first round. Abe was awarded the decision.

Never having reported any of his official ring battles to the police, Abie didn't bother reporting last night's engagement.

Abie has carried the Hearst papers to the four corners of the earth with the U. S. Battle Fleet, one of the few ordinary citizens ever permitted to ride on them.

ABE THE NEWSBOY TAKES ON FOUR
MEN ON BOARD U. S. S. DENVER

Abe the Newsboy was in his element on Sunday among his many friends on board the U.S.S. Denver.

To give the jackies a Sunday afternoon's entertainment he gave a boxing exhibition, taking on four of the crack boxers of the gunboat in one, two, three, four order. And finished fresh as a daisy after the sixteen rounds of continuous boxing.

At times during the bouts Abe offered his unprotected jaw to his opponents, and received the full force of the blows sent to him without rocking him in the least. The last bout proved to be the fastest, as he fought Jiran, the hard hitting oiler, and during that bout Abe was more careful about protecting his jaw, keeping well covered and giving him no chance to land his blows on it, although he could block as well as hit.

In the first four rounds Abe took on F. Musshel, who is known all along the Pacific coast as a clever boxer and who carries a kick in either hand. Musshel, with a little training, would be hard to stop.

In the second four rounds G. Medino gave a good account of himself, although only 115 pounds heavy. He handled himself well and Abe predicts that he will be a comer and with a little more training and ring experience will be a dangerous man at his weight to meet.

H. Koch was the third man to don the gloves with the Newsboy. He proved himself very clever and if he had been in good condition would have kept Abe busy.

Phillips and O'Toole seconded all the bouts and Kroder and Jiran, were the referees.

After the exhibition Abe was given a rousing sendoff for his endeavor to drive dull care away on a Sunday afternoon.

ABE, THE NEWSBOY, IS HEAVYWEIGHT CHAMPION

(Continued from Page 1)

up in which Abe had the best of it, Ortega rushed his man against the ropes and pushed him through them. Abe was partly in the ring and partly out of it, spectators on the ground trying to prevent his falling from the platform, and Ortega, without really realizing what he was doing, but fighting madly, swung low and landed on Abe's groin.

The crowd saw the foul instantly and said so in no unmistakable terms, but Charley Johnson saw it just as soon and promptly raised Abe's hand to indicate that he was the winner.

Ortega was ring general enough to realize what he had done and walked to his corner. Abe, who did not fall when the blow was delivered, walked to his corner, across the ring, and then laid down on the floor to recover from the effects of the punch. The injury he received was apparent to all who were close enough to see him when he was undressed by his seconds. It was some 15 minutes before he was able to leave the ring.

Crowd Orderly.

The crowd was tremendously pleased at the result and cheered until the roof was almost lifted, but there was no disorder—there never at any of the other bouts held at the National Sporting Club—and in a few minutes the arena was clear of people.

Although the ending was unfortunate, the battle was a big feather in the cap of the National Sporting Club, which ran off the affair in a clean, orderly manner, just as it does all of its bouts. The American congressmen who sat at the ringside with their wives enjoyed the sport greatly and were much pleased with the way in which the bout was conducted.

The semi-final fight of the afternoon also ended with a foul, when Young Ricardo, a lightweight from London, who had all the best of the milling up to that time struck Willie Howard of Balboa, better known as Arthur Du Free of Brooklyn, after knocking him down in the fourth round, just as Howard was rising.

There was a red hot preliminary of eight rounds between Battling Prince and Kid Carrier, which ended i. a draw.

Plans are on foot to take up a subscription for a belt emblematic of the championship, to be presented to Abe, the Newsboy, which he will defend against all comers.

ABE WILLING TO
HELP SUFFERERS

Ready to Wrestle or Box With Anyone Provided Receipts Go to the Relatives of Victims.

POKES REVOLVER IN FACE OF
NEWSBOY ABE IN BANK ST.

Unidentified Man Menaces Passing Pedestrian But Does Not Carry Out Apparent Threat.

Eddie R_ battled 20 noon at th_ for the we_ the Isthm_ which Ref_ a draw,_ with the_ fans prese_ should hav_ he did all_ times to_ other han_ livered cle_ eree Stein_ Eddie landed it counted for four of Abe's wild swings.

While coming up Bank street near Rialto theatre at a late hour last evening, Abe Hollanderky, 211 Huntington street, was held up by an unidentified man, who brandished a revolver under Mr. Hollanderky's nose. The man was standing in one of the doorways just as Mr. Hollanderky passed, the robber stepped out and moved in back and eree Stein...

Abe deserves all the credit that can be given him as he showed the fight fans that he can open up when he is defying a man near his own weight, being willing to mix it at all times throughout the bout. On the other hand Ryan proved that he is as game a boy as ever climbed through the ropes on the Isthmus, as in the second round he was injured his left hand, and practically fought the remaining eighteen rounds with one hand.

FAMOUS ABE, THE
NEWSBOY, HERE,
HAS APPEARED IN
1039 RING BOUTS

Abe the Newsboy, world famous figure who has fought 1,039 boxing bouts and grappled in 147 wrestling matches, besides gaining a big reputation by selling newspapers to famous personages the world over, is in El Paso. Abe arrived yesterday afternoon and leaves this afternoon for Los Angeles, after visiting J. Goldstein here. He is called the "world's greatest newsboy."

Abe has quit the professional ring game, with an enviable record, having met many famous boxers, but says he is ready at all times to appear on cards staged purely for charity.

He is en route to California and will soon leave with the U. S. fleet from a California port. He has sold newspapers on battleships for 22 years, he recalls.

Abe met Sam Langford when Sam was a welterweight. Joe Gans, and a legion of others, as his total of 1,039 fights shows.

The report book shows him born in Russia in 1888, a Hebrew-American, and that he started boxing in 1896. His name is Abraham Hollanderky. His home is New London, Conn.

Abe has autographed photographs and letters from famous statesman and army and navy men the world over, having been around the world twice. He says: "I've boxed under every flag there is." He is paid he is "the only fighter with three million. My first million is my health, my second million is my nerve and my third million is my friends."

be deware.

Waiting for Abe's autograph
so the boys can send his great
book home, for their folks to read
about the great Navy we have.

(Top): Captain W. F. Amsden, Abe, and Comdr. C. E. Battle. Center illustration shows U.S.S. Louisville, which figured in two rescues at sea. In one of these rescues 490 people were saved when the S.S. Harvard went on the rocks off California. In the other rescue, 9 people were saved off Honolulu. Lower photo shows U.S.S. Quincy, which carried refugees from Spain to French ports, making several trips.

Iron men of the old Navy, who have bought papers from me and did me many favors. They have over 100 years of service. Each has from 20 to 25 years of service.

"The fellow is all right.   He is a man who has been around a lot and he meets all kinds."

"Yes," I told the girlie.   "I just made that remark because I meet all kinds in my business, and I have to stand them off."

"Never mind explaining," she said.   "I am waiting on you because I'm hired to wait on all kinds."

The fleet was at San Pedro, and I went there and served the boys with newspapers and magazines.

When I got back I went in that store and apologized to her again.   But she wouldn't pay any attention to me.

I learned her name was Miss Freda Weinberg. The fleet cruised to Australia and I went with them.   That was the land where I had boxed a kangaroo some fifteen years previously and got badly beaten.

A year and a half later, the fleet got back to California, and I went into the stationery store where Freda still worked.

I again apologized to her for hurting her dignity.   She was very cool to me.   Every morning I would drop in and say:

"Good morning, everybody."

Finally she got so she would answer with the rest, "Good morning."

Then I asked her out to lunch.   She wouldn't go.   She told another girl:

"Did you see that awful homely man who asked me out to lunch?"

The other girl said:

"Why don't you go with him? Give him a chance to show his good qualities or queer himself forever."

Next she went to lunch with me. I outdid myself as host. When I was taking her back to the store, she said:

"Do you know, you're not such a bad fellow, after all."

I made it a point to get acquainted with her friends. She introduced me to her closest chums and invited me to her home for the sacred holidays.

One of her girl friends who lived on Temple Street, Los Angeles, met me one day and asked me to dinner at her home. During dinner she inquired if I was seriously impressed with Miss Weinberg.

"If you are," she concluded, "I will undertake to arrange a match."

I replied:

"I am a lone fighter. I have gone around the world several times with the Navy and arranged my own matches in every port. And I can make this match if anybody can."

And so, after a three-year's courtship, I am engaged to Freda Weinberg, and I won by square fighting. I am the homeliest man in the world and yet I won the sweetest girl in the world. And so my long career of fighting comes to an end.

Some of my married friends tell me the big fight is just commencing.

CHAPTER TWENTY-THREE

N JUNE 7, 1931, Abe the Newsboy lost a one-round technical decision to Dan Cupid. The happy wedding took place at the Hebrew Sheltering Home, in Los Angeles, California.

Many civic leaders, actors, and sporting figures honored Abe by coming to his wedding. And don't ever think that my Naval friends let me down.

Among the many high-ranking Naval officials who attended the ceremony were my good friends Admiral J. V. Chase, at that time Commander-in-Chief of the United States Fleet, the highest ranking officer afloat; Rear Admiral W. T. Cluverius, and the late Lieutenant-Commander R. H. Skelton.

Some turnout for Abe, the Newsboy!

Admiral Chase told me: "Abe, you've come a long way since you first met up with the Navy, and I hope your married life will be just as big a success."

I told him that I knew it would be, because I intended to live up to the Navy shipmate standards of honesty and fair play.

The Admiral was right about Abe going a long way with the Navy. When I first started out with the Navy, under my old friend "Teddy" Roosevelt, I was a half-starved little immigrant kid, with the responsibility of keeping a family in grub and shelter.

With the Navy, I prospered, traveled, and received what the professors call a liberal education. Of course, I never got much book learning; but I was too busy hustling papers, fighting, wrestling bears, or anything else that could walk into a squared ring prepared for a battle.

With the Navy I became the Champion of Panama. With the Navy I traveled the seven seas; with the Navy I developed my scrawny figure into a strong, healthy body. How much more fortunate was I than hundreds of others of my race who never succeeded in coming to America and getting the opportunity of making something of themselves.

All that I am I owe to my many thousand dear friends in Uncle Sam's Navy. Thank God for the Navy!

As it is not the custom to hold a celebration ball in the synagogue, I later gave a free dance for all my Navy friends, at Long Beach, California. I had nearly 7,000 guests. Some crowd for a newsboy!

My Navy pals had helped me make my wedding possible by helping me publish the first edition of this book, so I wanted to show my appreciation.

When you spend forty-one years with the Navy it becomes a part of you; and believe me, it was hard for me, at first, to break away from my usual associations with the Navy. Of course, I never entirely severed relations with the Navy; I just assigned myself to shore duty. In taking orders for my new book by contacting the personnel of the Fleet on the West Coast, I am really still with the Navy up to the present time.

When the Fleet is away I sell copies of my book, or take "bit" parts in the Hollywood studios. I have many good friends in Hollywood, and they are always glad to cast Abe, the Newsboy in a picture.

Of course, I don't give Clark Gable any competition; but when they need a character for a seaport scene, boxing, or a "tough mug" bit, I usually get a call. I can act without much making up on, which saves the studios some money.

The Navy men often ask me about the Hollywood stars. I have played with Wallace Beery, George Raft, Max Baer, Myrna Loy, Zasu Pitts, Monte Blue, Mary Astor, Fred Kohler, George O'Brien, Victor McLaglen, Douglas Fairbanks, Jack Dempsey, Mary Pickford, and a host of others. They're all real folks, and good friends of Abe, the Newsboy. The bigger they are, the more human they are.

Sometimes the directors hand me a big laugh, especially when they are shooting a scene supposed to represent some foreign port or a Navy background. Of course, I don't offer to correct them, because I learned, during my long association with the Navy, to obey orders strictly and willingly. After all, I got paid only for acting, and not directing. If they make a mistake in a movie, the public will probably not notice it anyway.

I often wonder what my dear mother would say if she could see her son act in the movies. Or if she ever dreamed, while in the old country, of such a nice home as she later owned in America. Thanks again to the opportunities I received through my associations with the Navy.

The Navy has always been ready to perform any humanitarian work that offered itself, and I was soon to be in the midst of such an activity.

I had worked with the Navy at the Santa Barbara earthquake, in 1925, when the Navy landed and took the situation well in hand. But the Santa Barbara disaster was just a lightweight champion compared with the heavyweight monster that was to strike Long Beach, in March, 1933.

Winding up a fairly good business day, and attending the Navy fights, I was leaning against the side of a brick building, waiting for a ride back to Los Angeles. Suddenly I felt something push me forward, and I quickly turned to square off with my adversary, when Wham! the whole building collapsed. If the wall had fallen outward I wouldn't be dictating this story now. I shook the dust off me. The ground seemed to roll like the deck of a destroyer in a heavy sea.

"Abe," I told myself, "it's time you started moving."

I looked about for a safe avenue of escape. The street-lamp overhead was waving wildly, and

I jumped from beneath it as it crashed to the street.

I could hear dull thuds all over the city as building after building fell to the heaving earth. Boy, this was no spot for Abe the Newsboy! The public wasn't interested in buying newspapers when the whole city was folding up—and I wasn't interested in selling them.

People began to run up and down the middle of the streets in wild disorder. Hurrying over a block I saw the side of a five-story hospital fall outward, exposing the rooms to the light of day. Many of these rooms were occupied by patients.

In all my forty-one years with the Navy, I had never witnessed a sight like this. A voice from the street shouted, "Hey, Abe!" I turned around quickly, and there was one of my pals from the Fleet, driving one of those rented autos the sailor boys hire when they want to make a big flash. "Come on, I'll take you to Los Angeles," he invited. I ran to the car, jumped in and yelled, "Let's get out of here." He slammed the car in gear, and we tore down the street full speed ahead.

Turning to take a short cut out of town, another series of tremors began, and the street in front of us split wide open. The crack crossed the street and was about four feet wide—we were blocked off. As we got out of the car to investigate, an oil-pipe, buried beneath the street, burst and drenched us with black, gummy oil. I turned to my buddy. He looked like that big black bear I wrestled with for a dollar, in a museum on

Fourteenth Street, New York.

"I think we'd better retreat, Admiral," he grinned. So we did.

It took us three hours to get to Los Angeles. We were safe, but badly shaken by the sights we witnessed along the way, particularly at Compton. This little town was really wrecked—a picture of devastation.

The next day I decided to go back and investigate. After all, the Fleet was anchored in the harbor at Long Beach and San Pedro, and the boys might need Abe.

The Navy had not only landed, but had thrown a cordon around the stricken area, to keep out looters and morbid curiosity seekers. There were sentries at every crossroad. I would never have gotten past the sentries without my Navy passes.

Finally, I got to Long Beach. Instead of needing assistance, the Navy was landing boatload after boatload of blankets, medical supplies, etc. However, I was glad to help unload the boats at the dock.

Twelve thousand Navy men had landed in the devastated area, and had taken over the district, under command of the late Captain Smythe. Temporary hospitals were set up for the injured. All electric wires were down, or out of commission, so it was necessary to set up emergency lines and supply current from the generators on board battleships in the harbor.

Martial law was established, temporary food canteens and shelter for the homeless were set up. The men worked feverishly on telephone and telegraph lines, to restore communication with the outside. The Navy was really swinging into action.

Not only did the boys in blue save hundreds of lives in this emergency, but they proved a godsend to the thousands of injured and those suffering from exposure and hunger. In one day the Navy made thousands of friends.

It is said that history repeats itself. This might be true, because I remember the Navy relieving distressed people at Martinique in 1902, San Francisco in 1906, Jamaica in 1907, Messina in 1908, Chile in 1922, Tokyo Bay in 1923, Leeward Islands in 1924, Santa Barbara in 1925, and now Long Beach in 1933.

These relief workers recall the daring rescue work performed by the U. S. S. Louisville in 1931. As the Louisville was making a speed trial run she received the Harvard's SOS call at 3:28 a. m. on the morning of May 30, 1931.

Steaming 115 miles to Point Hondo, the ill-famed "Graveyard of the Pacific," the Louisville arrived at 7:25 a. m.

Launching boats, the Navy boys took 575 men, women and children, all of them in various stages of dress, and all cold, wet, and suffering from exposure to the raging sea.

These people were all landed safely in Wilmington, California. Again the Navy boys "came through" in an emergency. And Abe was on hand with his newspapers which told of the heroic work of the boys of the U. S. S. Louisville.

When you look at a record like this, is it any wonder that Abe says "Thank God for the Navy?" That's why I am proud of my many years of association with the Navy, and of my part in helping the Navy boys.

In all the world there is no navy like ours. It has never lost a war. Its work for humanity has actually saved more lives in peace time than its guns have taken in war.

As Amos says, "Ain't that somethin'."

CHAPTER TWENTY-FOUR

OST people think of the Navy in terms of war. But I look at it in another way; maybe because I never went to war. During the World War I served my bit as a boxing instructor with the Navy, without charge; not even a dollar a year.

Of course, the Navy has always been the "first line of defense." Just like the boxer with the longest reach has an advantage over his opponent, the country with a strong navy can reach out and protect itself and all its interests. But I think the Navy is great because of other reasons.

For example, those many times the Navy has given aid to suffering people all over the world. It never asked about race, nationality, or religion; it just pitched in and performed its humanitarian mission.

Then, too, the Navy has helped to promote medical science and research, as in the case of the dreaded Chargres fever in Panama. When people were dropping like pins in a bowling alley, the Naval medical officers with the Marines in Panama went right ahead with their research; and this work helped to bottle up this killing disease.

The Navy has introduced modern medicine to

all of Uncle Sam's island possessions. And the Navy is always willing to help in national or international health problems. These errands of mercy are the best kind of diplomacy, and promote more good will than a flock of statesmen can ever do. After all, a Greek, a Japanese, or Frenchman might not understand a peace treaty; but they all understand a bowl of hot soup when they're hungry, or a fresh bandage around an injured head.

My friends on the ships have often told me how Naval engineers have helped commerce and industry by solving their problems with actual experience in the Navy. For instance, the Navy gave to the world of trade a now much-used metal—duralumin.

The Navy has also perfected communication devices under actual trial conditions. It has developed aviation by its inventions and research.

Naval engineers have developed new kinds of engines, steels, batteries, ships, paints, and hundreds of other valuable finds that we use in our everyday life. And Abe the Newsboy thinks all these things more important than war.

I picked up my education by association with the Navy. I never had the chance to attend regular schools. I even picked up my lessons in boxing a sock at a time.

While waiting on the dock at San Pedro for a launch to go out to a ship for a little bumboating, I was approached by a pleasant looking chap of about eighteen.

"Going out to the ship?" he asked.

"Yes," I replied, "Would you like to go out?"

"Would I?" he answered, "I sure would; I'd like to join the Navy."

We talked it over while waiting for a boat; and it turned out that he was driving a bakery wagon, but he wanted to join the Navy more than anything else in the world. He locked up his bakery truck, and offered me half of an apple pie. It was very good pie.

I took the young man out to the ship with me, and within a week I had helped him enlist. Then I forgot all about him.

Three years later I boarded one of the ships. A smart looking young Ensign stepped over to me and asked:

"Say, there, would you like a piece of apple pie?"

It was the same young man I had helped to enlist. We sat down and had some pie and coffee, and talked things over. It was very good pie.

I tell this incident just to show that the Navy offers a wonderful opportunity to ambitious young men. If they get in, work hard, and shoot square, they have every opportunity to advance themselves.

I have a good friend, a Captain in the Navy today, whom I knew as an enlisted man.

I have watched most of today's ranking admirals work their way up the ladder of success. I knew many of the retired commanders when they were young lieutenants.

The Navy is a great place for education and advancement. But if a man is not honest, he will never get anywhere in the Navy.

Ten thousand men are trained annually and returned to civilian life by the Navy. Most of these boys have received technical training, and make honest, hard-working citizens. Most of them get good jobs in their field, and settle down to a successful life.

I know many of my former Navy pals who have been successful when they went into civilian life. After the great World War, Uncle Sam sent many of his sailors to college, or to schools where they received technical training.

Many of these boys are leaders in their field today. One of them, Joseph Fainer, is one of the most successful attorneys in Los Angeles. Another is the Governor of Texas. Most of these ex-sailors have made good.

America's famous juvenile judge, Judge Ben B. Lindsey, once remarked that he had sent hundreds of problem boys into the Naval service.

"The Navy not only straightened them out, but gave them an opportunity in life that they would never have gained anywhere else." And the Judge is right.

In the old days they had wooden ships and iron men; now, the Navy has steel ships and super-men.

One must have a high school education to get in the Navy now.

There is no more dumping of riff-raff into the Navy. You have to be good to get in—and you have to be good to stay in.

Looking back over my forty-one years as the

Navy's newsboy, I can see how the type of sailor in our service has improved year by year. Today, I think the Navy has the finest bunch of enlisted men on earth, and the finest class of officers. They're all gentlemen.

Not only do the Navy boys have a chance to promote themselves, they are encouraged to do so. Education is made attractive for them. Willard Ridings, an educator and publicity man in Los Angeles, reminded me of this fact. The last time I saw him I had to give him all the latest news. He got a kick out of how I stopped some sailors who tried to pull a fast one on me. The boys were talking about their last intelligence test, when they thought they'd catch me on one of the questions.

"Tell us, Abe, if you found a battleship steaming toward you in Lake Merritt, and you were ordered to destroy it, what would you do?"

They thought they had me. "Why, I'd take a submarine and sink it," I told them.

"But where would you get your submarine?"

"The same place you got your battleship," I replied, and walked away.

You don't have to have an education to answer intelligence tests like that. Anyhow it must have been the right answer, because everyone kept repeating it on board ship for a whole week.

I don't know much about naval ratios, or which country has the best battleships, but I know which country has the best sailors. After all, every nation has about the same kind of guns and war tools. But take it from me, the way to measure a navy is by its manpower.

Lots of times, people have asked me: "Abe, how does our Navy stack up with this or that country?" "Aren't the boys in our Navy younger and less experienced?"

I always answered: "They are young, maybe younger boys on the average than those of other navies; but they're full of the old 'Navy Spirit,' and you don't have to worry about their taking care of us."

I remember when the World War started; in just a year our Navy grew from 85,000 to 350,000, and seven months later to 532,000. Almost as soon as these new men were mustered in, they absorbed the old "Navy Spirit."

You can't explain the real meaning of "Navy Spirit"; you have to feel it. Many times I felt it come over me when I was in a tight spot, or when some heavyweight was punching me in the belly. It helped me pull myself together and battle through to victory.

Whenever the going got tough, I'd give myself a fight-talk and say: "Abe, the Navy's looking up to you; never mind the odds; let's go out and win!"

Folks, a Navy man just can't let the Navy down. So I say to the citizens of this country, "Don't worry about the Navy—just give it a fighting chance."

I began my life with the Navy under my good friend, President Theodore Roosevelt, and I watched the Navy grow and improve until today the Commander-in-Chief is another great Roose-

THE MIGHTY MISSOURI, FLAGSHIP OF THE UNITED STATES FLEET, AT THE HEIGHT OF
HER CAREER AS SHE HURLED SHELLS (UPPER RIGHT) AT JAPANESE MAINLAND
In every port city in the nation fleet units from huge battleships to tiny patrol craft
will be on display today to the American public which made the fleet possible.

—Navy photo

Colorful parade to open Navy day, Victory Loan fete in Los Angeles

★   ★   ★   ★   ★

'Abe, the navy's newsboy,' is legend with U. S. fleet

By GAYLE GIBBS

There's just one thing that "Abe, the navy's newsboy," likes to talk about, and that's the navy—from brass to bell bottoms, from a captain's gig to a battleship

—Navy photo.
ABE, NAVY'S NEWSBOY
Roosevelt I said, "Bully"

And Navy day is the biggest day of the year for the 57-year-old battle-scarred boxer who's a legend in the fleet.

Abe has been all over the world and around it more times than he can remember, but always with "my navy." He couldn't join up because of defective eyesight so for nearly 50 years he's stayed with the navy as newsboy for thousands of blue jackets.

When he was 7 years old, Abe, whose real name is Abraham Hollandersky, started selling newspapers to officers and men from the ships that came in for fueling at the New London, Conn., coal base. A few years later he took up boxing.

During the last war he taught the boys at the New London submarine base how to "use their dukes." During this war he was too old to box so he recruited 1700 men for the navy.

The small stocky guy with the knuckle nose and cauliflower ears claims he's been knocked down plenty, "but never knocked out." That's quite a record for a fighter whom Believe-It-Or-Not Ripley once featured as "The Newsboy Who Fought 1043 Battles."

One day way back in 1906 Abe went aboard the yacht Mayflower to sell his newspapers. On the starboard side of the Mayflower's quarterdeck a visiting gentleman stood talking with some of the officers. He noticed Abe distributing papers and magazines among the men. The same visiting gentleman asked Abe for a paper and said to him.

"Where did you get that cauliflower?"

Abe answered him by squaring off with a swift right hook to the gentleman's jaw.

"I got it this way," was all the brawny little newshawk said. Immediately several secret service men rushed the pugnacious news vender, because the target at the other end of Abe's fist was Theodore Roosevelt.

"The kid's all right," President Roosevelt said, and waved the guards back.

The incident occurred while the president was reviewing the fleet under "Fighting" Bob Evans at Oyster Bay. When Roosevelt returned to the White House, he gave permission to the admiral to create the post of newsboy of the navy for Abe.

It gave Abe the right to go anywhere in the world on U. S. naval vessels and sell papers.

Later Abe decided to become an author so he wrote a book about the places and the people he'd known. He gave it the title, "The Life Story of Abe the Newsboy," and filled it with autographed pictures and stories about every salt water fan from Franklin Roosevelt to "Bull" Halsey.

In 1931 Abe married Freda Hollandersky and since then he's become something of a land lubber, selling his book aboard ships that come into the harbor at San Pedro and San Diego. Occasionally he goes up to San Francisco, when part of the fleet is anchored there.

But Abe is getting a hankering to see the world through portholes again and he'd kind of like to ship out for awhile.

"There's something about the navy that you can't forget," Abe told the Daily News reporter yesterday. "I haven't got any kids, but there are thousands of kids who've been fighting who are my boys," the navy's newsboy added.

——Give to Victory Chest——

A little story of Abe and Navy Day

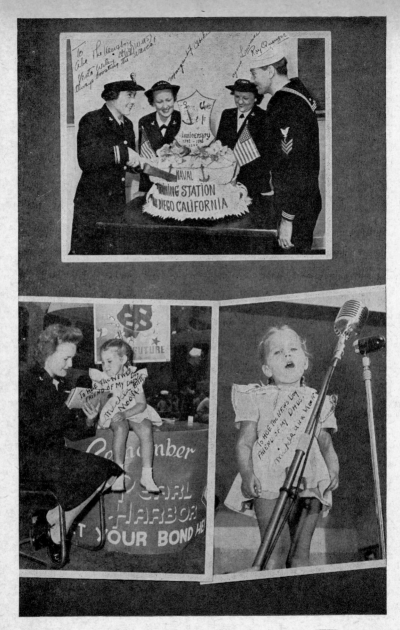

Lt. Vesta Wiley cutting the cake for the Waves' anniversary. The Waves have done a good job. (Bottom): Miss Mickle Ann Moon, daughter of Lt. (j.g.) M. B. Moon, entertaining patients at a bond rally, U. S. Naval hospital, San Diego; she purchased two $1000 bonds to start the show. Picture yourself at 4 years old helping Uncle Sam to win the war. My dad saw service and helped to do a good job. I have known Moon for 20 years in the Navy. No wonder his little daughter is all for Uncle Sam—God bless her for doing such a swell job.

Abe showing his Award of Merit for recruiting many Waves and men for the Navy.

S. D. Sports Figure Saw World As Navy Newsboy

San Diego Journal March 28-44

Selling President Theodore Roosevelt a newspaper while the Commander-in-Chief was aboard his yacht, Mayflower, reviewing the fleet in 1906, started a tough newsboy on the road to fame.

The well known San Diego sports figure, Abraham Hollandersky, became Abe the Newsboy after President "Teddy" Roosevelt created the post Navy Newsboy for him. This permitted him to travel all over the world with the U. S. fleet as newsboy and boxer.

Once mentioned in Ripley's "Believe It or Not" cartoon as the man "who fought a thousand fights," this 145-pounder started selling papers and fighting in New London, Conn., in order to help support his mother and a blind father. As a pork-and-beaner he picked up from $1 to $15 for preliminary bouts.

Between selling papers and fighting he kept busy boosting the Navy and planning an autobiography. Abe may be seen any day in San Diego with his book under his arm, his ambition to write his life story fulfilled. His latest collection to

ABRAHAM HOLLANDERSKY

his scrapbook of pictures of Presidents and Navy notables is an Award of Merit given him by the Navy department for recruiting more than 1,700 enlisted men and Waves.

Abe is proud of the fact that the Navy keeps his life story among the books in the shipboard libraries.

The newsboy reached his peak as a fighter in Central and South America. In Cuba, a Catholic chaplain took the Jewish boxer under his wing and steered him to a fight with the welterweight champion of the West Indies. Abe beat the champ and netted 30 cents on this fight.

At the suggestion of a Naval friend he went to the Canal Zone where, he immediately beat the Isthmus heavyweight champion, even though he had to give the local fighter a 40-pound advantage.

He fought in the larger cities of South America and took on all comers regardless of size or weight He once wrestled a bear and knocked the animal out. He also tangled with a kangaroo.

During the first World War he served as a boxing instructor for the Navy. Now he is an unofficial Navy booster. He credits his success to the Navy and says that any boy who wants to learn a trade and see the world should join this branch of the service.

Abe says that he follows this simple philosophy: Everything material and physical wears out in time, but honesty lasts forever

THE HOIST

San Diego Naval Training Station
January 14, 1944.

He's Mighty Proud of This Citation

Abe the Newsboy, for 37 years unofficial newsboy of the U. S. fleet, visited NTS last week to say "hello" to his bluejacket friends and to proudly display an Award of Merit presented him for recruiting more than 1700 enlisted men and Waves.

NAVY CITES ABE THE NEWSBOY
★ ★ ★ ★ ★ ★ ★
Booster for Fleet Gets Recruiting Award

You new recruits may never have heard of Abe the Newsboy, but stand by, mates—you're bound to meet him sooner or later.

Veteran shellbacks need no introduction to Abe, for he's been around Navy ships and Navy men ever since President "Teddy" Roosevelt sustained a poke in the ribs from the pugnacious youngster 37 years ago and, as a result, created the post of Navy Newsboy for Abe.

Since then Abe has become a familiar figure to men of the Navy, following the fleet as a newsboy and boxer throughout the world.

Last week he visited NTS, one of his favorite shore bases, and proudly displayed an Award of Merit, recently bestowed upon him by Lieut. Comdr. L. D. Blanchard, officer in charge of naval recruiting for Southern California for Abe's part in recruiting more than 1700 enlisted men and Waves.

He is on friendly terms with Admirals and Captains and considers himself every enlisted man's best shipmate.

But now that the war has temporarily denied him his right to travel with his beloved ships of the fleet, Abe is doing his bit as a one-man recruiting blitz. His scrapbook, pictures and stories of the Navy have influenced hundreds of young men and young ladies to don Navy blue since Pearl Harbor.

"It's the least I can do," says Abe. "Once I wrestled a bear and once I boxed a kangaroo. Those fights are nothing compared to the one our boys are fighting these right now."

Some of Abe's latest clippings

Happy victory with my friends. I am happy too.

The late President Theodore Roosevelt congratulating the men on the
U. S. S. Missouri. Bottom U. S. S. Dolphin, the President's Yacht.

Entering the U.S.S. Connecticut in 1908. Pres. 'Teddy' Roosevelt was aboard to see Bob Evans. Sold them both papers.

Looking at 'Teddy's' picture on Navy Day —October 27th. I can never forget him.

New York Journal-American
Thurs., Sept. 11, 1947-BROOKLYN

'JOIN THE NAVY, SON! . . . Abe Hollandersky, center, official "Newsboy of the Navy," brings some good news to the Navy recruiting program. At Borough Hall, he's signing up Stanley Siegel, right, of 1717 54th st., as Chief Recruiter De Angelo, left, looks on. During the war, Abe obtained the enlistments of more than 1,700 Navy men.

Famed Newsie Signs 'Em Up for the Navy

A new touch was added to Navy recruiting today, when Abe the Newsboy (Abe Hollandersky) arrived at the Navy Recruiting Station, Post Office Building, Brooklyn, and announced he was ready to help.

Chief De Angelo took Abe up on the offer and they set out to sign up enlistees.

They were quite successful, too.

Abe showed his mettle as a salesman to prospective Brooklyn recruits.

The U. S. Navy was the making of Abe the Newsboy. He was a good sailor, too.

Abe recently received an award from Secretary of the Navy Forrestal, for his "patriotic contribution to the war effort in obtaining the enlistments of more than 1700 recruits."

He says:

"My advice to the poor or rich boy who wants to rise in the world, is to join the Navy, where he will learn a trade, see the world, gain a wide education and have the opportunity for a career that will gain him glory in time of peace as well as war."

Abe is now proprietor of a gift shop at Long Beach, Calif. He's also written an autobiography, "The Life Story of Abe, Hero of a Thousand Fights."

It's about his 1,068 boxing fights and how he became the best known newsboy in the country.

Our beloved late Presidnt, making his last speech.

Iron Master and Philanthropist — Andrew Carnegie, whose donations to our Public Libraries the American People will never forget. He even bought a paper from me and gave me a five-dollar gold piece for it. He died at the age of 83.

To "Abe" newsboy of
The Old Navy
Ray Tarbuck
U.S.S. IOWA '46

(Top): Capt. Ray Tarbuck, U.S.S. Iowa, one of my many friends. (Bottom): Vice-Adm. (then Captain) Gifford, inspecting his ship. He is a great sport.

433

(Top): Comdr. Lawrence F. Reifsnider, Abe, and the late Capt. David A. Weaver.
(Bottom): Floyd Gibbons, the great hero and war correspondent,
and Capt. William J. Giles.

Two of my Navy friends at the Naval Training Center, whom I have known since midshipman days. Commodore R. Haggart, who saw me box in 1908 on the Olympia, and Capt. J. J. Curley, who saw me box at the Training Center.

Commodore O. M. Forster, who is looking at my Award of Merit, and said,
I did a good job.

(Top): Capt. W. R. Smedberg, aide to Secretary of the Navy, and (Bottom) Capt. John Ross, whom I have known for many years. Great Navy men, and good fellows.

THE
NAVY GREETS
PRESIDENT
HOOVER
ON
NEW YEAR'S
DAY

◆

Photo shows
Naval Officers in
line preparing to
meet President
Hoover at
White House
Reception
Admiral
Charles E.
Hughes and
Rear Admiral
J. C. Cowie,
(SC)
L. to R. front
row

velt. No wonder Franklin D. Roosevelt is a great President; he has the Roosevelt blood in his veins, and he's a true Navy man.

All of the Presidents for a period of several years back have been friends of Abe the Newsboy. I sold papers to all of them. They have all sent me their finest autographed pictures. And all of them were good friends of the Navy.

President Franklin D. Roosevelt has shown that he is a real Navy booster. He has worked with the Navy Department, and knows the value of our Fleet. And he has shown that he intends to keep Uncle Sam's Navy up to par and in good fighting trim.

Believe me, with a lot of dictators trying to run the world, it is imperative to have our Navy in top shape. A champion never loses when he's in condition.

CHAPTER TWENTY-FIVE

LOOKING back over my life I recall hundreds of happy occasions. I remember many thousands of great men who have been good friends of Abe the Newsboy. The unpleasant experiences I ignore. After all, there's no use worrying about smoke that has gone out of the funnel.

Every day some friend asks me about some famous person I have known, some statesman, some fighter, some fine Navy man, or the like. And I naturally remember some of them because of some little incident.

I remember Andrew Carnegie, the capitalist, when I sold papers to him on his yacht at New London, Conn. One day he gave me a five-dollar gold piece for a paper and said:

"Here's a pound for your paper, lad."

Believe me, it did look like a pound of gold to me. We had steak for supper that night. After that, I never accused the Scotch of being tight. You will notice his picture in my book.

Mr. Carnegie has made thousands of people happy by his generous gifts for libraries, thus providing books for people who could not afford to buy them.

I remember selling papers to Herbert Hoover

who never talked to me as much as did Calvin
Coolidge; and Mr. Coolidge had a reputation of
being a person who talked little. Every time I
sold him a paper he would always "kid" me about
being the "world's best looking newsboy." The
really big people in life are always the most
democratic.

I have many fine friends in the newspaper
world, and have sold papers to good friends such
as Damon Runyon and Robert Ripley. Mr. Runyon has helped me so many times I can't find
words to express my feelings of gratitude to him.
He is as good a fellow as he is a writer. Mr. Ripley illustrated me in one of his famous "Believe It
or Not" cartoons, which you see in this book.

I remember selling papers to Irving Berlin,
another poor boy who made good in this wonderful country of ours. Mr. Berlin is a very friendly
man when you know him. He also autographed
one of his pictures for me. Once he told me, "Abe,
you have the most musical voice of any newsboy
I ever heard"; but I think he was "kidding" me.

Floyd Gibbons, the famous war correspondent, was another of my good customers. He is
a real Navy booster.

William Fox, Arthur Brisbane, Claude Swanson, Rube Goldberg, Mrs. Theodore Roosevelt,
the late Sir Thomas Lipton, and James Rolph,
Jr., of California, were all customers of mine. I
made friends with all of them.

I have standing invitations to call upon most
of the outstanding personages of today at any
time. I have had written invitations to visit the

White House many times in my career. Imagine, Abe the Newsboy being invited to the White House!

This is a real land of opporrtunity, and I do not agree with anyone who says otherwise.

When you figure that I have sold papers to every great person in America during my past forty-one years with the Navy, and have conducted an honest business, on top of my world's record activities in boxing and wrestling, you can see why I am called "The World's Greatest Newsboy."

I don't like to brag, but I think I have earned that title, for I have sold newspapers to great people all over the world.

A chief petty officer from the Fleet took me to see a wrestling match in Los Angeles. I watched a bearded hill-billy tug and jump around with another two-hundred-pound coal heaver for half an hour. The winner got three thousand dollars.

I wrestled at Miner's Bowery Theatre in New York, in 1907, for five hours and eighteen minutes. My purse was seven dollars.

"How did you like it, Abe?" asked my Naval friend.

"Well," I replied, "once I wrestled a bear for a dollar; but then I didn't have to make so many faces as those guys."

In the preliminary, two wrestlers spent most of the time fighting in the front-row seats. Another preliminary bout ended when both wrestlers started slugging the referee.

Modern wrestling is mostly show.

Of course, everyone knows how the wage scale for boxers has advanced. Just compare the cut modern fighters get with the wages I received. I boxed Kid Norfolk, who weighed 170 pounds, for twenty-five rounds; and my purse was $250. (ten dollars a round.) Of course, the Navy boys took up a purse for me after the fight, as they cleaned up by betting that I could stay for the full twenty-five rounds. Their purse amounted to $1,680. The Navy boys are always good sports.

Today, the Navy offers the best opportunities in the world for the young man who is interested in good, clean sports. Every ship has its athletic teams, and these are coached by men who know their business. Annapolis graduates, some of them All-Americans, coach the Fleet football teams.

They can even play baseball on the airplane carriers.

Each ship has its rowing crew, a ball team, a boxing team, a basketball team, etc., all aiding in the Navy's aim of skilled hands, a trained mind, and a strong body.

I have lived an adventurous life and had many close calls. If I had my life to live over again, I don't believe I would change it, save that I might have married earlier.

Before marriage, twenty dollars seem like a dollar; but after marriage, a dollar seems like twenty.

I believe that if I had married ten years ago I would have been wealthy today. But that's life.

Outside of that I have no regrets. The Navy

gave me a chance in life, and I took advantage of it.

To any poor boy who feels that he lacks the opportunity to advance himself, I say, "Join the Navy."

For what the Navy has done for Abe the Newsboy, it has done for thousands of others. For this fine work I shall be always grateful. I offer my services to the Navy at any time I can be of help.

What more can a man say?

"Thank God for Our Navy!"

THE END

My dear Mr. Hollaniersky:-

     Thank you very much for your letter and good wishes. Come in and call when you are going through Washington. I would like to see you.

     Yours very truly,

     Theodore Roosevelt

WESTERN UNION
TELEGRAM

RECEIVED AT

65 N N 9

    FY Newport R I Dec. 28 1923 1110A

Champion Abe The newsboy

      N ew London Conn

Best wishes for a sucessful amd a happy new year

        Admiral William Sims

             1122A

Greeting cards received from the President and Admiral Sims.

THE SAILOR'S PRAYER

Now I lay me down to sleep,
I pray the Lord my soul to keep,
Grant no other sailor take
My shoes and socks before I wake.
Lord guard me in my slumber
And keep my hammock on its number,
May no clews nor lashings break
And let me down before I wake.
Keep me safely in thy sight
And grant no fire drill tonight,
And in the morning let me wake,
Breathing scents of sirloin steak.
God protect me in my dreams
And make this better than it seems.
Grant the time may swiftly fly
When myself shall rest on high.
In a snowy feather bed,
Where I long to rest my head.
Far away from all these scenes
From the smell of half done beans.
Take me back into the land
Where they don't scrub down with sand
Where no Demon Typhoon blows,
Where the women wash the clothes.
God thou knowest all my woes
Feed me in my dying throes.
Take me back, I'll promise then
Never to leave home again.

FOUR YEARS LATER

Our Father who art in Washington
                    (Heaven)
Please dear Father let me stay
Do not drive me now away.
Wipe away my scalding tears
And let me stay my thirty years.
Please forgive me all my past
And things that happened at the mast
Do not my request refuse,
Let me stay another cruise.   AMEN.

ABE, THE NEWSBOY
(Abraham Hollandersky)

Welterweight Champion of Panama and South America

Home Address, New London, Conn.

Born 1888.

Abe, the Newsboy, is Fistiana's most unique son. During his picturesque career, begun in 1905 and yet unfinished, and which is really a collection of records, he has had 387 wrestling matches and has fought 1039 bouts under every flag of the world. Abe won the world's welterweight wrestling title in 1907 after 4 hours and 18 minutes; and at one time, in Panama, wrestled for five hours and twenty-two minutes. He fought five champions, among them Jack Ortega, who weighed 220 pounds and from whom he won the heavyweight title of Panama and South America in the 19th round of a scheduled 45-round bout. Today Abe offers his services, gratis, to any boxing show held for charity. Below is a list of his opponents that Abe could recall. Abe started his boxing career in 1905, boxed 27 years and retired in 1932.

Some of my toughest fights: Kid Norfolk, Negro light heavyweight champion, 25 rounds, Colon, Panama; Panama Joe Gans, middleweight champion, 25 rounds, Panama City; Joe Dailey, middleweight champion of Chile, 25 rounds, Valparaiso, Chile; Eddie Ryan, welterweight, 20 rounds, Panama, Columbia; K. O. Pollits, 20 rounds, New London, Conn.; Jack West, exhibition, 4 rounds, father of the famous Mae West; Jack Ortega, heavyweight champion, I won on the 18th round of a 45 round fight on a foul.

WON FROM

Young Matthews, 12.

Young Sullivan, 10; Young Sharkey, 6; Young Jeffers, 10; Batt Conley, 10; Young Samson, 6; Patsy Oregon, 6; Eddie Chambers, 10; Young Conners, 6; Young Robeder, 10; Young Miller, 6; Young Sharkey, 4; K. O. Pollits, 10; K. O. Pollits, 20; Austin Rice, 10; Austin Rice, 4; Austin Rice, 6; Young Harris, 10; Young Terry, 10. Joe Gardner, 4; Charley Baker, 4; Young Miller, 6; Jack Larsen, 4; Young Stores, 5; Soldier Lewis, 1; Frank O'Brien, 1; Jack Jencey, 7; Charley Murphy, 3; Jack Smith, 2; Sailor Lucas, 2; Young Speedy, 5; Kid Cumberledge, 20; Young Jackson, 10; Young Joe Jeanette, 10; Young Jack Johnson, 10; Eddie Ryan, 20. Johnny Hines, 14; Mickey McDonald, 8; Johnny Hines, 4; Jack McLean, 1; Jack Dobbs, 4; Kid Green, 1; Fighting Dick Miller, 7; Steve Jackson, 21; Charley Lawrence, 6; Sam Keller, 6; Jack Ortega, 18 (foul); Charlie Johnson, 6; Shaun Sullivan, 1; Kid Carter, 9; Jimmy Kelly, 5; Jack Burgess, 4; Batt Marshall, 6; Batt Marshall, 5.

Patty Green, 10; Young Dillon, 10; Andy Thomas, 12; Young Sam Langford, 6; Young Kid Thomas, 12; Young Gunboat Smith, 8; Kid Lewis, 12; Young Sailor, 10; Young Gans, 12; Young Gallagher, 7; Mike Mooney, 12; Willia Hearn, 10; Young Jones, 12; Young Martin, 12; Kid Sauers, 12; Jim Kennedy, 12; Kid Nelson, 12; Kid Williams, 10; Young Ketchell, 6; Young Larry, 10; Jack Perry, 10; Frankie Louis, 10; Young Mullin, 10; Young Statton, 10; Kid Burns, 10; Kid Burrows, 10; Jackie Wallace, 10; Young Lolly, 10; Young Ketchell, 10; Young Britt, 10; Young Fitzsimmons, 10; Young

Fitzsimmons, 10; Young Murray, 6; Batt Jones, 15; Young Chester, 15; Eddie Callan, 15.

Young Peck, 15; Kid Thomas, 12; Young Solomna, 8; Sidney White, 4; Young Fitjimits, 12; Jack Dukoe, 10; Frank Sutzor, 10; Abe Kostelo, 8; Young McCoy, 10; El Thomas, 15; Young Manfact, 10; Young McDonald, 10; Young Conway, 12; Kid Jones, 4; Young Johnson, 10; Thomas Sullivani, 10; Frank Fay, 6; Young McCoy, 10; Young Mar, 10; Young Wollis, 10; Young Phillips, 12; Pete Millone, 10; Phil Harrison, 10; Kid Lambert, 4; Young Conner, 4; Eddie Rullen, 4; Joe Dailey, 6; Young White, 6; Kid Black, 8; Young O'Brien, 6; Kid Wagner, 6; Patty Sullivan, 8; Eddie Conners, 6; Young Wolfe, 8; Young Terris, 10; Eddie O'Conner, 6; Kid Jones, 8; Young Mills, 6; Young McCoy, 6; Young Mackintosh, 1; Young Galagar, 1; Terry Edwards, 10; Young Langford, 10; Young Burke, 10; Young Papke, 10; Mike Flynn, 10; Young Bawell, 10; Young Jones, 10; Billy Jones, 10; Kid Flyn, 12; Kid Jones, 12; Billy Heavens, 10; Young Smith, 10; Young Egan, 10; Tom Ogen, 10; Tom Ogen, 10; Mosy King, 6; Young Thomas, 9; Young Moran, 10; Young Sommers, 8; Young Wolgast, 10; Young Kelhan, 10; Young Klein, 10; Patsy Brenen, 10; Young Jones, 10; Frankie Jones, 10; Young O'Brien, 10; Eddie Martin, 6.

NO DECISIONS

Eddie Conway, 15; Jack Walker, 12; Kid Murray, 12; Young White, 12; Young O'Neill, 15; Bernie Yanger, 6; Joe Tippins, 4.

Young Monday, 6; Young Monday, 6; Young Joe Gans, 6; Austin Rice, 6; Jack McLean, 8; Joe Pickett, 6; Jimmy Allen, 6; Mosey King, 6; Zamonski, 6; Buck Falvey, 8; Tommy Teague, 10; Jack Batterick, 8; Young O'Neill, 4; Jimmy Ross, 6; Willie Moody, 6; Kid Cunningham, 10.

Young Galor, 8; K. O. Pollits, 4; Austin Rice, 8; Austin Rice, 10; Austin Rice, 10; Harry Greenhouse, 4; Sam Delmont, 6; Sam Delmont, 10; Pat Conners, 3; Jack Doorman, 4; Jack Denning, 6; Tode Moran, 3; Jack Cohen, 3; Jack Smith, 8; Lew Turner, 4; Mike Ninan, 6; Jimmy Gardner, 6; Dick Grand, 8; Austin Rice, 6; Kid Norfolk, 25; Buck Falvey, Young Sherman, 8; Kid Carter, 6; Young Langford, 9; Frank McLean, 8; Black Harris, 8; Joe Gans, 6; Terry Mitchell, 6; Paley Haley, 6; Young Blackburn, 15; Dick Miller, 6; Jack Farrell, 6; Jack Harrison, 6; Young Ross, 4; Willie Lucas, 6; Young Shea, 8; Young West, 8; Young Jackson, 10; Young Thompson, 4; Tommy White, 4.

Buck Thomas, 10; Joelivar, 10; Jackie Norman, 6; Seder White, 15; Hugo Polits, 8; Kayo Polits, 10; Kid Black, 4; Harry Brooks, 10; Willie Jennings, 10; Young Canole, 10.

Teddy Ritchie, 10; Young Gorman, 15; Kid Green, 12; Buck Harris, 12; Harry Turner, 12; Kid Schay, 10; Billy Smith, 12; Billy Jones, 12; Jimmy Harris, 15; Grover Aze, 6; Grover Aze, 10; Young Johnson, 10; Panama Joe Gans, 25; Kid Baspie, 15; Young Langrod, 10; Italian Joe Gans, 4; Italian Joe Gans, 4; Mickey Kenin, 6; Young Terry, 10; Kid Williams, 4; Young Sharkey, 4; Young Smith, 10; Young Evan, 10; Young Sheppard, 10.

DRAW

Tom Law, 6; Tom Law, 6; Tom Law, 6; Young Thompson, 12; Harry Thompson, 8; Buck Miller, 6; Young McCoy, 10; Young McGovern, 6; Young Burke, 6; Young Sheffield, 8; Kid Chambers, 10. Tom Stewart, 10; Grover Hayes, 12; Young Sommers, 12; Jeff Dorothy, 12; Jim Island, 12; Young Edwards, 12; Charles Strong, 8; Kid Larkey, 12; Young Terry, 12; Kid Saunders, 12; Frankie Faye, 4; Lew Shepperd, 6; Kid Thomas, 5; Jerry Ryan, 12; Sailor Thomas, 12, Kid Young, 15.

Joe Walkit, 4; Young Sevenee, 10; Young Burke, 10; Young Phillips, 6; Kid Burke, 10; Kid Fox, 10; Mike Jones, 10; Jimmy Kelly, 6; Young Kelly, 6; Dick Miller, 6; Jimmy Murphy, 10; Jack Denning, 6; Young Harris, 10; Young Johnson, 6; Young Edwards, 10; Kid Cambie, 10; Young Thomas, 10; Kid Newman, 10; Young Dorothy, 10.

Kid Sullivan, 15; Young Leonard, 6; Batt Jones, 6; Tommy Disent, 6; Young O'Neill, 10; Young Briggs, 10; Young Thomas, 10; Thomas McFallin, 10; Young Cox, 12; Peter Donovers, 12.

Pete Dunn, 6; Young Montana, 6; Jimmy Winters, 10; Sailor Donovan, 6; Young Sharkey, 6; Maurice LaMonyne, 6; Jack Goodney, 4; Ed Chambers, 6; Jack Austin, 6; Jimmy Russell, 10; Sailor Rappo, 6; Joe Bernstein, 6; Billy Costelly, 12; Billy Collins, 8; Willie Riley, 6; Jerry Cole, 20.

Kid Schay, 10; Young Rullen, 4; Steve Dorlton, 4; Sailor O'Roake, 4; Young Ketchell, 8; Kid Sullivan, 4; Joe Island, 6; Lou Shepard, 4; Harry Stone, 4; Dick Miller, 5; Billy Kepelle, 4; Tiger Flowers, 4; Kid Wilson, 4; Kid Wilson, 4; Young Donald, 4; Eddie Kelly, 10; Frank West, 4; K. O. Pollits, 10; K. O. Pollits, 10; Austin Rice, 6; Austin Ric, 6; Lew Turner, 4; Zalmonski, 6; Young Monty, 8; Mickey McDonald, 8; Jack Gardner, 6; Frank Walton, 4; Terry Young, 10; Jack Smith, 6; Jack Lowery, 6; Tommy Moran, 6; Dick Miller, 6; Phil Harrison, 10; Young Jones, 10; Young Ketchell, 10; Kid Miller, 10; Young Fisher, 15; Young Jeffers, 10; Young Johnson, 20; Young Sam Langford, 15; Young Sharkey, 10; Young Johnson, 10; Young Danlhall, 12; Harry Myers, 12; Young Jones, 15; Red Daniels, 15; Young Kirk, 12; Young Shocky, 12; Bill Harris, 15; Young Jackson, 12; Billy Smith, 15; Young Henry, 15; Young Salvin, 6; Young Rulen, 8; Young Terry, 10; Young Harrison, 11; Young Nolan, 12; Young Jack Johnson, 15; Young Nelson, 15; Billy Jones, 15; Kid Palmer, 5; Billy Walker, 4; Tommy Ferguson, 4; John Wilson, 2; Young Marins, 5; Joe Marino, 4; Tommy Perry, 4; Young Connoly, 3; Harry Kremme, 4; Young Gasey, 4; Young Marinan, 4; Young Ritchie, 4; Jack Smith, 4; Aron Clark, 3; Kid Williams, 5; Kid Black, 4; Kid Brown, 4; Kid Davis, 4; Sailor Gordon, 4; Young Jackson, 10; Young Tomson, 4; Tommy White, 4; Harry Wing, 2; Kid Black, 10.

Red Sullivan, 12; Tommy Ketchel, 15; Eddie Chelmars, 12; Young Donohue, 4; Eddie Ryan, 10; Austin Rice, 10; Young Langford, 15; Billy Jones, 12; Harry Harris, 15; Harry Curly, 4; Young Chong, 10; Billy Kantan, 10; Kong Lee, 6; Young Harrison, 6; Mike Donohue, 6.

Young Sullivan, 6; K. O. Moran, 10; Billy Walsh, 6; Batt Jones, 10; Austin Rice, 10; K. O. Pollits, 10; K. O. Pollits, 6; K. O. Pollits, 5; K. O. Pollits, 12; Kid Carter, 12; Jack Gerry, 4; Young Bryan, 10; Kid Ferguson, 10; Eddie Kelly, 4; Billy Keppele, 4; Sailor Jones, 6; Steve Dalton, 4.

LOST

Young Morris, 10; Young Deaffy, 10; Fred Bone, 10; Jack Smith, 10; Sailor Jones, 10; Soldier Camby, 10; Harry Jones, 10; Young Phillips, 10; Young Jeffers, 10; Tommy O'Conners, 15; Jack Robinson, 9.

Al Rogers, 15.

Young Bakers, 10; Young Perrelly, 6; Young Jones, 10; Billy Jones, 10.

KNOCKOUTS

Harry West, 4; Sailor Brown, 4.

Kid Roberts, 10; Kid Jackson, 4; Young O'Brien, 4; Kid Brown, 4; Young Miller, 4; Joe Clark, 7; Young Buck, 5; Kid Black, 10; Young Levins, 6; Kid Goodman, 4; Young Powers, 10; Harry Brooks, 5; Kid Williams, 4; Eddie Wallace, 10; Young Regan, 4; Eddie Kelly, 10; Soldier Rich, 10; Johnny Matthews, 10; Kid Sailor, 10; Young Robson, 4; Red Morris, 4; Tommy Jones, 7; Young Candiate, 1, Young Sullivan, 6.

THE WHITE HOUSE
WASHINGTON

June 3, 1926

Dear Abe:

I have your letter of May 25th, with en-
closed clippings which I have noted with interest.
I shall, of course, be very glad to see you any
time you come to Washington.

Sincerely yours,

Ernest Lender
Secretary to the President.

"Abe", The Newsboy,
120 S. Grand Ave.,
Los Angeles, Calif.

THE WHITE HOUSE
WASHINGTON

March 17, 1925.

My dear Sir:

As requested in your letter of March
15th I am sending herewith a copy of the
letter to which you refer.

Sincerely yours,

E. H. Sanders
Secretary to the President.

Mr. Abe Hollandersky,
120 S. Grand Avenue,
Los Angeles, California.

Enclosure.

THE WHITE HOUSE
WASHINGTON

November 7, 1924.

My dear Abe:

The President has been greatly
pleased to receive your message of congratulations. He asks me to communicate
to you the assurance of his deep appreciation.

Sincerely yours,

C. B. Slemp
Secretary to the President.

Abe, The World's Greatest Newsboy,
96 Canal Street,
New York City, N. Y.

U. S. S. DOBBIN

Guantanamo Bay, Cuba.
11 February 1925.

TO WHOM IT MAY CONCERN:

The bearer, Abe Hollandersky (known throughout the Naval Service as Abe the Newsboy), is known to me personally. For nearly thirty years he has been selling newspapers and bumboating to the Naval vessels.

During the war he was a boxing instructor at Naval Station, New London, Conn. Prior to the war and after he took part in numerous boxing and wrestling matches at numerous Army camps and Naval vessels. He has always shown his willingness to entertain the service men and has always given his best.

This vessel leaves Guantanamo Friday for California. Abe is making the trip overland and will rejoin us there. Anything that can be done for him to speed him along will be appreciated by the Naval service in general. I have known him for a period of ~~seventeen~~ years and can vouch for his character.

H. C. Gearing Jr.

H. C. GEARING, Jr.
Commander, U. S. Navy.

I am grateful to the Captain for this letter.

NEW LONDON CHAMBER OF COMMERCE

NEW LONDON, CONNECTICUT

Walter S. Garde, President   Prentice M. Hatch, Vice-President   C. C. Costello, Vice-President
Bank of Commerce, Treasurer   Wm. L. Apley, Secretary   James G. Hammond, Manager

OFFICE OF THE MANAGER   ✒   ✒   ✒   MERCER BUILDING

PHONE 1642

New London, Conn.
Jan. 20th., -1927.

'Abe' The Newsboy,
120 S. Grand Ave.,
Los Angeles,
Calif.

Our Dear Abe-

Municipalities and 'home folks' are not without the very splendid spirit of appreciation and sentiment, evidenced by the high esteem in which you are held by the thousands that know you. This is especially so in your instance, Abe., when we stop to measure up your valued services to us.

There are thousands of us who have followed your career with interest. We have many times observed you in action. We have seen you under 'fire' in the white heat of action in the 'squared circle' pitted against a worthy opponent. Yours is a reputation to be proud of. Your name has never been touched with the slimy breath of scandal which has seared and ruined so many professional athletes. You have lived a clean life. No one can say that Abe the Newsboy has been crooked and 'fixed' a fight. Clean living, clean thinking, clean acting can and does pay in professional sports.

You are a seasoned veteran of more than 1000 battles, Abe, and you have come through clean and four square. Your long period of service in professional sports exemplifies the fact one can play the game and still be a gentleman. You have reflected credit alike on your profession, on your legion followers, your Home City and State.

Your former friends and business associates in the City of New London, Conn., join with the writer in extending to you their compliments and good wishes, and are proud to subscribe themselves as champions of a Champion, of Abe Hollendersky, the World's Greatest Newsboy.

In renewed assurance of the warm esteem of the writer, I am, my dear Abe,

Most Cordially and Courteously,

James G. Hammond   Sec'y.,

New London Chamber of Commerce.

This letter was given to me from the Great Little Town, New London, Conn.

Admiral S. S. Robinson, (Ret.), U. S. Navy, President Admiral Farragut Academy,
Toms River, N. J.

Rear Admiral C. W. Cross, USN ret. A good friend of mine since midshipman days.

My good friends, Rear Adm. Frederick I.
Entristle, and Comdr. L. C. Quigge, who
is now Captain. Taken on board the
U.S.S. Iowa.

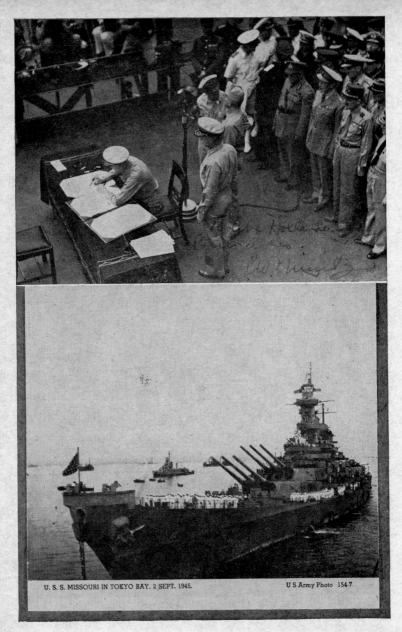

U. S. S. MISSOURI IN TOKYO BAY. 2 SEPT. 1945.   U S Army Photo 154·7

Admiral Chester W. Nimitz signing peace on U.S.S. Missouri in Tokyo Bay.

Japs arrive aboard the U.S.S. Missouri to sign the peace in Tokyo.

U.S.S. ENTERPRISE

Six times "SUNK" by Japs

Admiral Halseys flagship from early days of Pearl Harbor till end of bloody invasion of Okinawa.

Claimed sunk six times she has the envaible record of 911 Jap aircraft shot down and 71 enemy Ships sunk by her pilots

Pas por the President ial Unit Citation.

Official U.S NAVY PHOTO

Admiral W. F. Halsey, on his flagship U.S.S. Enterprise who did a marvelous job in the war.

USS ROOSEVELT

USS PHILIPINE

U.S.S. Roosevelt—the ship named for our beloved President Roosevelt. Our Navy Day is for our beloved Theodore Roosevelt. These two great men will never be forgotten. They were both good friends of mine—may they rest in peace.

USS PRINCETON

USS VALLEY FORGE

USS·LEYTE

USS·MIDWAY

Aircraft Carrier Franklin D. Roosevelt. Top: model cake of ship.

U.S.S. Bennington, which did a great job in the war.

USS ANTIETAM

USS RANDOLPH

USS WASP

USS BUNKER HILL

Aircraft carriers who did a great job.

U.S.S. MIDWAY. 45,000 ton Aircraft Carrier. Length 986'0" 200,000 h.p. speed 30 knots.   Main Battery 18-5"/54.   Aircraft 100.   Crew 3000.

U.S.S. SHANGRI LA, 27,100 ton Aircraft Carrier, length 855'10" speed 30 knots. Main Battery 12-5"/38. Aircraft 80. Crew 2500.

U.S.S. BUNKER HILL, 27,100 ton Aircraft Carrier, length 855'10" 150,000 h.p. speed 30 knots,   Main Battery 12-5"/38.   Aircraft 80.   Crew 2500.

OFFICIAL U.S. NAVY PHOTO

U.S.S. ESSEX

Aircraft carriers, who did a marvelous job, and the planes made it tough on the Japs.

U.S.S. WASP, 27,100 ton Aircraft Carrier, length 855'10" sp.30 knots. Main Battery 12-5"/38.Aircraft 80.Crew 2500.

U.S.S. BOXER, 27,100 ton Aircraft Carrier, length 855'10" 150,000 h.p. speed 30 knots. Main Battery 12-5"/38. Aircraft 80. Crew 2500.

U.S.S. INTREPID, 27,100 ton Aircraft Carrier. Length 855'10" 150,000 h.p. speed 30 knots. Main Battery 12-5"/38. aircraft 80, crew 2500.
"Official U.S.Navy Photograph"

U.S.S. BENNINGTON, 27,100 ton Aircraft Carrier. length 855'10" 150,000 h.p. speed 30 knots. Main Battery 12-5"/38. aircraft 80, crew 2500.
"Official U.S.Navy Photograph"

Aircraft carriers, who did a marvelous job. Their planes made it tough on the Japs.

One of the Aircraft Carriers who did a big job knocking out so many Jap airplanes as you can count on the turret.

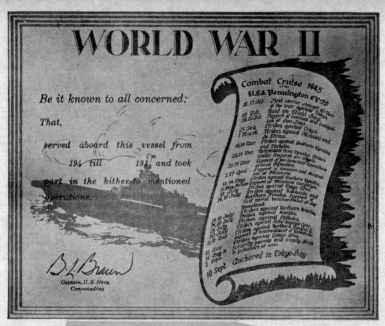

WORLD WAR II

Be it known to all concerned:

That,

served aboard this vessel from 194_ till 194_ and took part in the hither-to mentioned operations.

B. L. Braun
Captain, U. S. Navy,
Commanding

Combat Cruise 1945
of the
U.S.S. Bennington CV-20

16, 17 Feb. First carrier aircraft strikes of the war against Tokyo
18 Feb. Raid on Chichi Jima
20, 23 Feb. Support of America and scraped.
25 Feb. Iwo or Iwo Jima and scraped.
1 March Strikes against Tokyo. Je Shima.
14, 19 Mar. Strikes against Southern Kyushu and Shikoku.
20, 21 Mar. Retirement from Kyushu Strikes under frequent air attack.
23, 31 Mar. Support of Pre-invasion operations ground Okinawa.
1, 27 April Support of invasion and capture of Okinawa.
13, 14 May Strikes against Southern Kyushu.
12, 13 to 14 June Support of Okinawa campaign.
10 July Strikes against Tokyo charge.
14, 15 July Strikes against Hokkaido and Northern Honshu. Support of first naval bombardment of Jap homeland.
18 July Strikes against Northern Honshu.
24, 28 July Strikes against Honshu.
28 July Strike against Kobe supply area.
30 July Strikes against Northern Honshu.
9, 10 Aug. Strike and Bombardment of Kamaish support against Tokyo drive.
13 Aug. Strike against Tokyo drive.
16 Aug. Security patrols and supply drops to prisoners of war.
8 Sept.
10 Sept. Anchored in Tokyo Bay

The U.S.S. Bennington, who did
a marvelous job in the war.

470

USS DULUTH

U S NAVY PHOTO 118-4

USS CLEVELAND

U S NAVY PHOTO 118-17

USS OAKLAND

U S NAVY PHOTO 117-10

USS SAN JUAN

U S NAVY PHOTO 116-6

Some Cruisers who helped knock the hell out of the Japs

471

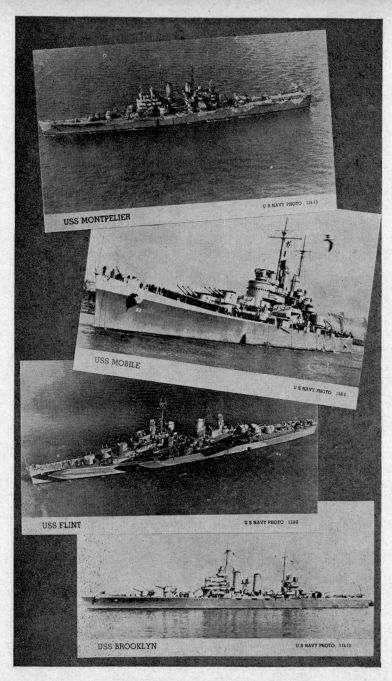

USS MONTPELIER

U S NAVY PHOTO 118-13

USS MOBILE

U S NAVY PHOTO 118-3

USS FLINT

U S NAVY PHOTO 118-2

USS BROOKLYN

U S NAVY PHOTO 118-10

Some Cruisers who made it tough on the Japs

U.S.S. SPRINGFIELD

U.S.S. WILKES BARRE

OFFICIAL U.S. NAVY PHOTO

U.S.S. ATLANTA

U.S.S. FALL RIVER

Cruisers who made it tough for the Japs.

U.S.S. Phoenix, U.S.S. Los Angeles, U.S.S. Tucson. Cruisers who made it tough for
for the Japs.

U.S.S. FREDERICK FUNSTON

U.S.S. PASADENA

U.S.S. ASTORIA

U.S.S. NASHVILLE #589

OFFICIAL U.S. NAVY PHOTO

New Cruisers who made it tough for the Japs.

U.S.S. TUSCALOOSA 25-A

U.S.S. VICKSBURG

U.S.S. CANBERRA — — 13,600 ton Heavy Cruiser. Length 673'0" 120,000 h.p. speed 30 knots. Main battery 9-8"/55. Anti aircraft 12-5"/38. Crew 1,200.

U.S.S. COLUMBUS

Some Cruisers who made it tough on the Japs

USS SPRINGFIELD

USS ST PAUL

USS MANCHESTER

U.S.S. HELENA

USS TOLEDO

New Cruisers who made it tough for the Japs.

477

(Top) Comdr. Simon L. Shade, training officer during war time at the Naval Training Center, San Diego. He had charge of hundreds of thousands of Navy men—and sent them out to war. The job was well done. (Bottom) Lt. Comdr. Harold J. Richardson, who helped Comdr. Shade at the Station. They are both swell people—and their job was well done. Wherever they are—I wish them both good luck.

Co. COMD'R.   11 APRIL, 1949
T.M. PFIFER B.M.C.
U.S. NAV. TRA. CEN.   SAN DIEGO, CALIFORNIA

Company 081, Top Fighters on the center. Record time of 16½ seconds to extinguish tank fire. Again proving teamwork and cooperation the prime essential. Congratulations from your old shipmate, Abe the Newsboy. Everyone can make good if the effort is there.

3 April, 1949

Co. Comd'r.   N.E. Timm G.M.C.
Asst. Co. Comd'r.   A. L. Lester A.O.C.
U.S. Nav. Tra. Cen.   San Diego, California

Company 49 - 080 won 13 pennants, 8 of them major pennants. Graduated as one of highest companies of the year in over-all average.

480

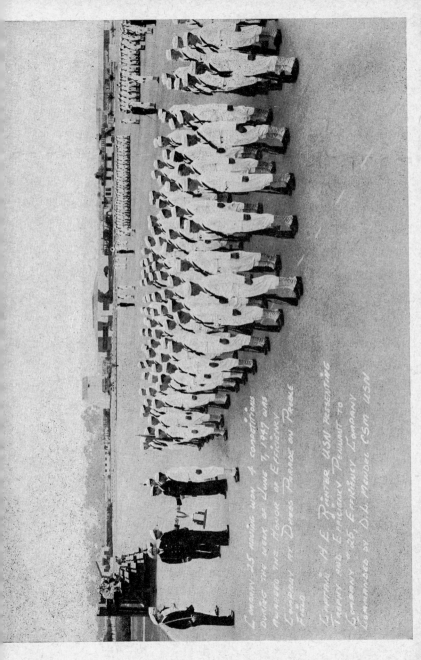

CO. 25—Receiving the Trophy for the good work they did. Now the men are ready to go out to sea on the ships and do their job. The Training Officers in the Training Center, believe me, are working hard—always on the job.

THE SECRETARY OF THE NAVY

WASHINGTON

15 November 1946

Abe, The Newsboy
715 West Seaside Boulevard
Long Beach, California

Dear Abe:

I understand that you are about to publish a Victory
Edition of your Autobiography, and I want to send you
my best wishes and appreciation of your forty-seven
years' service to the officers and men of the Navy.

I was glad of the opportunity to meet you on Navy Day
at the Biltmore Hotel.

Sincerely yours,

James Forrestal

Thomas Kelliher jr
       Commodore U.S.N.

[signature]
Vice Admiral US Navy

W. S. Parsons
Rear Admiral, U.S.N.

[signature]
Vice Admiral U.S.N.

W.B. [signature]
Vice Adm. US Navy.

[signature] Oldendorf

E M Pace Jr

R W Bimey Captain,

C. S. Thomas

[signature] Captain USN

Rear Admiral I. C. Johnson

Captain [illegible] Potter U S

Captain Richard D. [illegible] USN.

Maj. Gen William D Old U.S.A.

L. L. Bennett Comdr US CG

L. S. Hermle, Brig Gen. U.S.M.C.

H B Roberts Comdr U.S.C.G.

Jack Bolton, V. Gen.

James Forrestal

Harry R. Sheppard M.C.

W. A. Sundberg III, Captain U.S.N.

[illegible] Capt. USN

[illegible] Col. USMC

A. G. H[illegible] Capt USN

Wm Fox Radm (SC) USN

W. H. Perry Capt. (MC) U.S.N.

W. W. Bird Captain U.S.N.

J. A. Ahman Comdr. U.S.N.

W. J. Smith, Captain, U.S.N.

A. R. Inslow Jr. Captain, U.S.N.

Oscar Hagberg, COR. U.S.N.

Ray Miller Lcdr. U.S.N.

S. M. Archer, Comdr USN

W. R. Phieeips R. Adm. USN

L. B. Farrell Captain USN

F. W. Bruning Comdr. USN.

W. T. Thomas Jr. Comdr. USN.

Ga Pierce, Cmdr. USN

W. R. Ogan Capt U.S.N.

J. W. Adams Captain U.S.N.

J. H. Carson Rear Adm. USN.

W. B. Moore, Captain, USN '30

S. F. Rifsnider, Rear Adm., U.S.N.

T. W. Rimer, Captain U.S.N

G. F. Boone, Lieut USN

S. Johnson Lt. Comdr. USN

J.V. Neff Capt USN

J.G. Benjamin, Capt U.S.

J. E. Lee Capt USN

Ward Captain USN

J.W. Havland Capt USN

M.M. Leonard Capt (dc) USN

H.J. Nelson Capt USN

W.W. Rockey Capt. U.S.N.

W.P. Buford Capt. U.S.N.

E.C. Ewen Capt USN

W.C. Farr, Capt. U.S.N.

J.S. Downs Cmdr, USNR

John T. D. Lewis Capt

A.M. Gugen Capt USN

Phelps Hickerman, Capt. US Navy

J. J. Ferguson   Comdr. US Navy

Ray Vanhuck   Captain USN
                     U.S.S. Iowa.

W. Hogue   captain, USN
                  U.S.S. Hector

B. B. Biggs Capt USN

                  USS St. Paul

J. W. Sears   Capt. USN

Jack Kennedy. Capt. U.S.N. (Ret)
                         again.

L. M. ieue — Rear Admiral U. S. Navy

C. T. Hunt. Capt. U.S.N.

Halvain   Comdr USN.

R. C. Libby, Captain, USN.

Paul B. Colony Captain USN. —

R. E. MacFarlan, Lt Col. USMC

F. S. Steinwachs, Capt. U.S.N.

O. O. Kessing Capt. U.S.N.

E. R. "Andy" Anderson Capt., USNR

N. H. Sanders, Jr.   Capt. U.S.N.

J. D. Murphy   Capt. USNavy

J. Fisk   Commodore U.S. Navy

A. H. Gray   Capt. U.S.N.

B. B. Adell   Capt USNavy

F. S. Lee   Rear Admiral USN.

L. R. McDowell   Captain US Navy

Walter Hart   Captain U.S. Army Retd.

Peter R. Lackner   Captain USN

A. Moore   Captain USN.

Bruce McCandless   Comdr, USN.

J. Alex Kinney, Capt. USN

John Ross   Capt. U.S.N.

George T. Simms   Commodore U.S.N.

E. Carmick, Capt, USN.

L. M. Glasser, Cys, USN.

C. H. Stallings   Capt USN

C. COFFORD
U.S. NAV TRA CEN.
SAN DIEGO, CALIFOR.

E.E. PATTERSON
SAN DIEGO, CALIFOR.

The pennant, with five interlocking gold circles on a gold field, is awarded the company accumulating the greatest number of points in intramural competition.

ADDRESS REPLY TO
BUREAU OF NAVAL PERSONNEL
AND REFER TO

Pers-620-RS

20 November 1943

Mr. Abe Hollandersky
"Abe", The Newsboy
715 West Seaside Boulevard
Long Beach, California

Dear Abe The Newsboy:

Before making a trip out of town Admiral Jacobs instructed me
to write you in his behalf. He remembers you and so do I.

It is gratifying to know that you have helped the Navy secure
so many good men and arrangements are being made whereby you
will receive appropriate acknowledgment of this service from
the Officer-in-Charge, Los Angeles Recruiting Station.

With best wishes,

Sincerely,

Webb C. Hayes
Captain, USNR
Director of Recruiting & Induction

**Thanks to Uncle Sam and to my good friend, Vice Admiral Jacobs for presenting
to me my Award of Merit for recruiting seventeen hundred men for the Navy.**

U. S. NAVAL TRAINING STATION
SAN DIEGO, CALIFORNIA

17 July, 1940.

TO WHOM IT MAY CONCERN

I have known Abe Hollandersky, better known as "Abe the Newsboy", since 1907. He has delivered newspapers, periodicals and "bum-boated" on various ships and stations to which I have been attached over a period of twenty-seven (27) years. He is honest, industrious, dependable and has never to my knowledge abused any privelege or courtesy which has been extended to him. Furthermore, he has assisted and cooperated with all of the officers and men of the Navy. He is exceptionally industrious and has always supported and discharged his obligations to his own family and I feel sure that he will always provide adequately for his immediate relatives and those living in his own household.

Abe is also well known over a period of forty (40) years by my brother, Rear Admiral Randolph Ridgely Jr., U.S. Coast Guard.

Lieutenant Commander, USN Ret.
Provost Marshal.

22 July 1935

TO WHOM IT MAY CONCERN:

My friend "Abe the News Boy" has spent almos
his entire life in serving the Fleet in one capacity or
another, but principally as News Boy.

I have known "Abe" personally for a period o:
some thirty odd years and this experience confirms the
reputation he has throughout the Service for honesty and
straightforwardness, and a cheerful readiness to give
service to the Fleet in whatever capacity it might be
needed.

Any one considering the employment of "Abe"
can be assured of honest and faithful service.

W.H.Standley,
Admiral, U.S.Navy,
Chief of Naval Operations.

U. S. NAVAL TRAINING CENTER
SAN DIEGO 33, CALIFORNIA

March 3rd 1947.

Mr. Abe Hollandersky:
715 West Seaside Blvd.
Logg Beach 2.Calif

Dear Abe-;

From the "Last of the Apprentice Boys in active duty
to the "Last of the Famous Navy News Boys" Greetings. Hows the
byy? It seems as yesterday although it is many years since the
good old days in Panama when you had them rolling on the mat
and crying help. Do you remmember the days on the old USS May
flower when "Good old TEDDY" was our Commander in Chief. I will
never forget the day you squared off at him and you nearly landed
in Atlanta. But he being the fine fellow that hewas said " let
him alone "Ill take him on" He then made you Newsboy to the USN
I remmember one day in Guahtanamo when you came down in a small
boat all the way from New York how you ever made the trip I will
never know but the Sunday Papers were always delivered on time.

I have read your book with great interest and can
say from personal knowledge it is accurate How many of those
grand old fellows have I met and known and arenow passed ond.
I hope you have great success with your new book and every on
in our Navy will ready it. You and your book have done a great
job for the USN and you have been a great part of the Navy for
over 40 years that I know of, and I trust that you will live to
be so for many more years to come.

Best wishes and good luck.

Sincearly your Pal and Shipmate

Harry S. Morris CTM USN
Provost Matshal's Office
U S Naval Training Center
San Diego Cal.

This 100,000 men—I am proud of them for doing a great job—they helped to win the war. This is Uncle Sam—always ready!

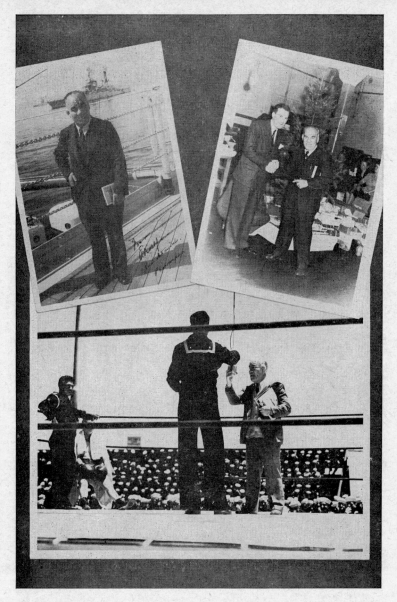

Top—Abe aboard the U.S.S. Virginia. My good friend, Adm. Edward C. Kalbfus, took this picture—a great hobby with him, and a good fellow. Two above—Eddie Peck, the son of my great friend, Mr. Peck, who is printing my book. He may not be a good fighter—but a hulluva good fellow. Bottom—Abe making a speech, helping to sell millions of dollars worth of bonds at the training station during the war. God bless the Navy—they bought plenty of bonds.

Abe, the Newsboy, who gave over a gallon of blood in his life, to save a life.
Champion, Hero of a 1,000 fights.

Top: Abe and Jimmy Hackley giving exhibition at North Island, San Diego.
Bottom: Harry Brabang and Abe, giving exhibition at Training
Center, San Diego.

Abe in his early days of boxing.

Top. Abe when he was champion.
Bottom: Abe boxing on the Mayflower for a Congressional party.

Top: Jimmy Durante and Abe entertaining the boys to help sell bonds.
Bottom: Comdr. Gene Tunney, undefeated heavyweight champion of the world, looking at Abe's book.

Top—We are all paying tribute to our great riend, Capt. Jack Kennedy, one of the grandest sportsmen in America—the most honest referee in the boxing game—it is just too bad we do not have many more like him. I have known the Captain 41 years. I saw him go into the Navy and saw him retire twice. Joe Fisher, Mike Ekter, Georgie Hetzel, Mushy Callahan, Billy Vincent, Lt. Joe Shugrue and Jimmy Looks.

Bottom—James J. Jeffries autographing a boxing glove for the highest bidder for a bond— Six or seven of our fighters and myself put our names on the glove—sold for many thousands of dollars worth of bonds.

Some of the great fighters of all times: 1.John L. Sullivan. 2. Jake Kilrain. 3. 'Yank' Sullivan. 4. A. J. Lennon. 5. J. D. Loughlin. 6. John H. Rice. 7. Abe the Newsboy, Champion of Panama. 8. Tommy Ryan, undefeated middleweight champion of the world. 9. James J. Jeffries, ex-heavyweight champion of the world.

My old friend, Bob Ripley, a good friend and a good sport. A man who proves everything he says.

BEST O' LUCK TO YOU ABE

Ripley

"BELIEVE IT — or NOT."

Comdr. Gene Tunney, once heavyweight champion of the world. He is well liked in the Navy for his sportsmanship.

THE SWEET SCIENCE

by Trevor C. Wignall
p.33

Even here, as will be seen, the Jew does not shine
very brightly. But there is one Jewish boxer-- I
admit I never heard of him until I read of his achieve-
ments in the "Everlast" record book--who deserves to
have monuments built in his honour. He is known as
Abe, the Newsboy, but his real name is Abe,
Hollandersky. Born in 1888, he is justly spoken of
as fistiania's most unique son. During his career, which
was begun in 1905, he has had 387 wrestling matches,
and 1,039 boxing bouts under every flag in the world.
He is credited with having won the world's welterweight wrestling title in 1907, and with having fought
five boxing champions. To borrow from the phraseology
that would probably be used by his biographer, Abe,
the Newsboy, is some baby!

published by Duffield and Co.   New York
MCMXXVI

MONDAY, MARCH 24, 1930

Between You and Me!

Abe, the Newsboy, Author Wants to Get Married Book Needs Profits His Fiancee Is Waiting

By Damon Runyon

FEW authors possess the rare good judgment of Mr. Abraham Hollandersky, whose latest book is to hand. I find toward the end of this enthralling tome a page given over to two illustrations, one of the author, Mr. Hollandersky, himself, posed with his arms folded across his manly chest, in true authoresque style, and the other of a pleasant looking young lady.

DAMON RUNYON

This, as I gather from the cut-lines, is Freda Weinberg, fiancee of Mr. Hollandersky, "who is patiently waiting for Abe's book to be published and supply them with the means to begin their married lives together."

How many of our authors marry first, and write their books afterwards, not waiting to see if their royalties will supply them with the means to begin their married lives? How many, I repeat? Well, too many, according to my operatives who have been around interviewing the wives of authors.

So I contend Mr. Hollandersky is an author of rare sagacity. I bow, too, to Freda Weinberg, the lady who is patiently waiting. I hope and trust that Mr. Hollandersky's book, "The Life Story of Abe the Newsboy," meets with immediate, and great success. I haven't got far into it as yet, but you can see it is a deserving tome.

No Shrinking Violet

MR. HOLLANDERSKY, by the by, is none other than Abe the Newsboy, himself. I was greatly surprised to learn this. I have known Abe the Newsboy for many years, and I always thought his name was Abe the Newsboy. But here it is Hollandersky. It shows you how little we know of our fellow citizens, after all. I think I prefer Abe the Newsboy.

He bounced in on me the other day to favor me with a copy of his book. Abe the Newsboy is a short, chunky built little man, of swarthy complexion, with two mangled ears, and a slight mumble to his speech, the aftermath, no doubt, of 1,039 ring battles, of which, according to the book, Abe was the hero.

"I had to get my book printed at my own expense," Abe explained to me, as he handed me my presentation copy. "It cost me $12,000, but what's the difference—it gives me a life job selling it."

It is a solid looking, well-bound volume, this "Life Story of Abe the Newsboy," and from a casual perusal of the text, I am inclined to think Abe had some expert assistance on it. But he supplied all the illustrations, beginning with a full length photo of himself carrying a traveling bag covered with labels from all over the world.

The book contains photos of both the Theodore Roosevelts, of Calvin Coolidge, and Herbert Hoover, all autographed to Abe. There are photos of distinguished officers of the Navy, and of scores of celebrities in other fields, also autographed to Abe. These pictures bespeak for my friend both a wide acquaintance and considerable crust. A shrinking violet wouldn't tackle Al Smith, for example, for an autographed photo, would it? but here's Al beaming right at you from a page of Abe's book.

He's a Champion!

NOW don't think Abe's 1039 battles the bunk. He had 'em. In all parts of the world. He also had 387 wrestling matches, once wrestling a bloke in Panama 5 hours 22 minutes, which is really longer than I would care to sit through a wrestling bout. The 22 minutes would suffice.

He once licked Jack Ortega, who weighed 220 pounds, for the heavyweight championship of Panama and South America, although Abe the Newsboy never hefted much above the welterweight mark. The bout was scheduled for 45 pounds, and Abe won in the nineteenth. Along came Willie Ward, of Baltimo', otherwise Kid Norfolk, otherwise "The Little Black Thunderbolt," to relieve Abe of the title in 25 tough heats.

So you see my friend Abe was no geezer in the manly art, Kid Norfolk was afterwards quite a distinguished fistic figure. In 1907 in Panama, Abe grappled with a guy for 4 hours, 18 minutes to win the welterweight wrestling championship of the world. Anyway, Abe claims it was of the world. If it was only of the nearest cantina, it was good enough.

For a man who has held the world's welterweight wrestling championship, the heavyweight boxing championship of Panama and South America, Abe the Newsboy is somewhat reduced in titles as he moves into the forty second year of his life. In fact, the only title he now claims is "World Champion Newsboy." He probably is all of that.

He sells his papers up around New London, Conn., where the war cano above in and out. Abe has always followed the Navy. In fact, his book is dedicated "To my dearest friends, the officers and men of the U. S. Navy." They have always been kind to Abe the Newsboy. His pages are filled with letters from officers of the Navy vouching for his character.

In fact, the contents of the volume generally—the photos and the letters—are to me striking testimony that there is a lot of kindness in this world, after all. Some very distinguished citizens have gone out of their way to extend courtesy to this battered up little gladiator with the thickened speech. I find in Abe's tome evidence that great movie stars, noted journalists, famous cartoonists, renowned pugilists and prominent politicians have paused to be nice to him.

He presents photographic reproductions of newspaper clippings which depict incidents in his life that prove he is no mug. He has given his blood for transfusion to weaker veins time and again. He has heroed in rescues of human life. He has boxed for charity. He has had his love affairs, too. There was a gal named Carlotta—but let's not go into that.

1039 Ring Battles

I BELIEVE Abe's record of 1,039 ring battles to be authentic. Also I believe it to be a world's record. True, a lot of his opponents were just fellows around, but he fought many tough 'uns. I note that most of his opponents were "Young" So-and-so, if they weren't "Kid." He records his first fight in 1905, and his last about 1918, but he makes no pretense that his printed record is complete. Abe the Newsboy couldn't recall more than half his battles to save his neck.

I never saw Abe the Newsboy when he wasn't hustling, and I never knew him to ask anyone for anything except perhaps an autographed photo, and now that I am apprised of the waiting Freda Weinberg, I hope and trust that Publisher Abraham Hollandersky will commence paying liberal royalties to Author Abe the Newsboy forthwith, if not sooner.

Copyright, 1930, by N. Y. American, Inc.

My great friend, the late Damon Runyon, who always helped me with my book, and gave me advice. I never will forget him. He was one of the finest sport writers in the world. He never turned an old-timer down. He was something like my good friend, Walter Winchell, who does the same.

Abe, the Newsboy, Who Once Struck Teddy Roosevelt, Helps Recruit WAVES

One way to get ahead in the world is to sock the President of the United States. Anyway, that is what Abe the Newsboy did, and he seemed to get places!

It was in 1906 and a tough little kid by the name of Abe Hollandersky somehow got aboard the presidential yatch Mayflower, and the first thing he did was to sell President Teddy Roosevelt a newspaper.

The famous Teddy, amused, started kidding the newsboy. He pulled the newsy's right ear and asked, "Where did you get that cauliflower?"

"I got it this way," Abe said, immediately squaring off, ducking under the President's arm, and administering a good stiff poke in the ribs.

President Roosevelt grunted and a group of secret servicemen jumped in and grabbed the boy.

"The kid's all right," the President said, waving the secret servicemen away. The two talked for a while and Roosevelt took a liking to the boy. Upon returning to the White House he had the post of navy newsboy created for Abe. It carried no pay, but gave Abe the right to go aboard or travel on United States naval vessels.

Since that time Abe Hollandersky, the tough kid who socked the President of the United States, has been around a lot with the fleet and can number among his close friends almost every famous admiral, skipper, or common gob in the United States navy.

Abe the Newsboy is well known in Long Beach, and now has his own little business down on Seaside avenue, where the men of the navy come in to buy newspapers or curios.

To Abe, the sun rises and sets in his beloved navy. All his life he has steered boys toward the sea, but now, in wartime, he is working hard to get new recruits, especially for the WAVES, who release men held on shore posts for sea duty.

"We all of us got to work hard at this," Abe said. "My friends in the navy, the oldtimers who have been in the service for 30 years, are proud of our girls."

Oftentimes Abe the Newsboy will meet a girl he considers a likely recruit for the WAVES, then will drag out his scrapbook of pictures and stories of the navy, tell her of the vital work she will be doing and, in many cases, will persuade the girl to enlist.

"Our navy is the best in the world," Abe says proudly, usually adding wistfully, "wish I was young enough to get in."

Abe delivering papers to the USS
Connecticutt.

My good friend, Chief Morris. I
knew him when he enlisted in the
Navy 44 years ago.

The First Meatball Company of 1950 at USNTC, San Diego, California.
These men worked hard and did a good job. Company Commander T. M. Pfifer, B.M.C., U.S.N.

U.S.S. Missouri in action.

MEATBALL COMPANY HONORED—Company 320 stands at attention as a third gold star is affixed to their company flag at brigade parade on Preble Field last Saturday. The group, under the guidance of Company Commander J. R. Trammel, CSC, garnered the personnel, bag, barracks, and infantry pennants to win the coveted "meatball" award.

Another Meat Ball well done by Company Commander D. L. Carr, G.M.I.

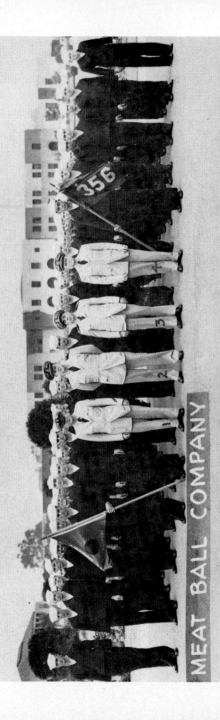

MEAT BALL COMPANY

To: ABE With Best Regards.

1. *[signature]*
2. *[signature]*
3. Lieut. C. A. Duffy U.S.N.
4. B. A. Maxwell

28 May 1951

RECORD FALLS AS CO. 356 COPS FLAG AGAIN, 16 PENNANTS TO STELLAR COMPANY—Few recruit companies have achieved such heights of efficiency or claimed such outstanding goals as has Co. 356, to whose record is 16 pennants topped by their winning the efficiency pennant two consecutive weeks. A company of Regiment Three, Co. 356, graduated last Tuesday with the long line of pennants trailing only as prelude to their unusual record of accomplishments. Of the many records broken or set by this company, the most outstanding was winning the efficiency trophy for two consecutive weeks—a Training Center record. The saga of the "Meatball" began two weeks ago when 356 won their first efficiency pennant. Prior to the formal presentation of the efficiency trophy, made in conjunction with the Meatball Pennant, Co. 356 marched front and center last Saturday to receive a gold star for being honor company of the week. "Congratulations, Chief Boatswain Mate Blaylock," Captain Copeman said to the chief standing by his company of well-trained recruits "for untiring efforts and devotion to duty, you are presented the highest award of Recruit Training . . . the efficiency trophy."

The above are Chief Petty officers, who are known as Company Commanders. They teach new recruits for the Navy. A good job well done.

Top row—Duncan Wells, V. M. Doescher, G. A. Faurot, J. F. Griffin.
2nd row—H. D. Clark, W. G. Sperling, M. O. Perkins, C. W. Wilhelm.
3rd row—W. E. Waldren, O. T. Bozeman, R. E. Cleek, F. V. Schmittou.
4th row—E. Robertson, C. F. Jones, J. A. Schisler, J. Q. Homan.

The above are Chief Petty officers, who are known as Company Commanders. They teach new recruits for the Navy. A good job well done.

Top row—M. R. Ellison, R. T. Logan, D. J. Schultz, W. T. McCann.
2nd row—A. Singer, A. D. Kisson, C. R. Lacour, S. F. Steele.
3rd row—H. J. Yeager, J. L. Pea, K. W. Draper, L. C. Poole.
4th row—J. D. Steger, D. L. Williams, G. F. Thomas, D. D. Campbell.

The above are Chief Petty officers, who are known as Company Commanders. They teach new recruits for the Navy. A good job well done.

Top row—F. I. Jones, R. E. Bryant, C. W. Swanson, J. T. Tribble.

2nd row—J. D. Harris, A. L. Lester, E. P. Kirchgessner, C. L. Mallard.

3rd row—R. C. Altwein, V. E. Monaghan, E. J. Andrews, B. B. Akridge.

4th row—J. O. Hill, W. J. Moore, A. B. Longtin, P. B. Mason.

The above are Chief Petty officers, who are known as Company Commanders. They teach new recruits for the Navy. A good job well done.

Top row—W. W. Nance, F. B. Dodge, D. D. Dungan, J. C. Henderson.
2nd row—D. C. Park, M. L. Coon, Q. O. Fagans, E. D. Mulvihill.
3rd row—R. F. Charlebois, A. W. Johnson, H. E. Hunt, H. M. Kirkland.
4th row—M. O. Redding, G. A. Pyle, M. A. Aves, R. A. Lewis.

The above are Chief Petty officers, who are known as Company Commanders. They teach new recruits for the Navy. A good job well done.

Top row—A. L. Seymour, J. W. Drake, A. D. Stone, C. A. Uri.
2nd row—T. N. Pitts, E. H. Lennington, J. W. Overton, A. W. Bullard.
3rd row—R. R. Bunz, C. L. Morrow, R. L. Vandagriff, G. C. Armstrong.
4th row—C. F. Graham, J. H. Evans, E. F. Ehringer, R. L. Donnett.

The above are Chief Petty officers, who are known as Company Commanders. They teach new recruits for the Navy. A good job well done.

Top row—J. B. Pitts, R. J. Breen, E. Bonds, L. G. Vann.
2nd row—M. D. Hoeft, G. Wilson, W. R. MacLain, I. Silversmith.
3rd row—J. R. Burns, W. P. Bradley, E. E. Patterson, M. O. Perkins.
4th row—J. W. Leslie, T. R. Young, V. A. Wilson, J. R. Hutchins.

The above are Chief Petty officers, who are known as Company Commanders. They teach new recruits for the Navy. A good job well done.

Top row—A. Kozak, H. C. Thompson, P. D. Crutchfield, J. M. Mackey.
2nd row—E. N. Holder, H. A. Stevenson, A. J. Sherwood, J. E. Ellis.
3rd row—T. R. Moodie, J. R. Coyne, D. L. Renedbaugh, R. D. Hawkins.
4th row—M. Yurosko, W. O. Ederveen, H. L. Brown, Q.M.C.; Miles R. Matthews, Q.M.C.

The above are First Class Petty Officers, they teach new recruits for the U. S. Navy.
I hope they will make Chief Petty Officers soon.

Top row—A. G. Erber, G. F. Woodward, L. W. Woodall, J. W. Reese.
2nd row—B. G. Ladd, J. M. Dahlquist, G. S. Ebbs, J. T. Mitchell.
3rd row—R. A. Brett, R. E. Engledow, R. D. Lee, N. W. Hacker.
4th row—William C. Toney, R. W. Alston, Q.M.Co.449; C. E. Saunders, Q.M.1;
F. H. Evans, Q.M.1

Impressive ceremony at commissioning of U.S.S. Recruit. Rear Admiral Wilder D. Baker, Commandant 11th N.D., and Captain Connolly, U.S.N., Center Commandant; Captain Malone in command of training recruits.

ADMIRALS AND EVEN PRESIDENTS 'ABE'S' CUSTOMERS FOR 50 YEARS

By J. VICTOR FONTAINE,
Telegram Staff Reporter

Meet "Abe The Newsboy."

He is Abraham Hollandersky, 59, of Long Beach, Calif., who has woven his life around the Navy by selling newspapers to its personnel for more than 50 years.

Born in Russia, he came to this country at the age of seven. Two years later, he began selling papers in his home town of New London, Conn. He's been selling them since and has made a very profitable living.

Met Seven Presidents

His more than half a century of business has brought him a wealth of friendships with the top men and thousands of 'gobs' in the Navy. He also has met seven presidents of the United States.

Although he never joined the Navy, he has made three trips around the world on battleships.

And "Abe's" pride has been collecting autographed pictures of the prominent men he has met.

He called on Adm. Wat Tyler Cluverius, U. S. N. (ret.), president of Worcester Polytechnic Institute.

It was in 1931 at Los Angeles, Calif., that "Abe" got acquainted with Adm. Cluverius. At that time Adm. Cluverius was chief of staff to Adm. V. T. Chase, then commander in chief of the Pacific Fleet.

Adm. Cluverius was a paper customer of "Abe's." And says "Abe," Adm. Cluverius attended my wedding that year in Long Beach. "Abe" brought along some photographs of his wedding in which Adm. Cluverius appears.

Abraham Hollandersky — "Abe the Newsboy"—of Long Beach, Calif., who has spent his life selling newspapers to "gobs" and admirals.

As a boy of nine he was "adopted" by the Navy gobs near the New London base. Before long he got "inside the yard" selling papers. The Navy boys, said "Abe," soon taught him to box and during the prime of his life he was in 1068 bouts.

But it was in 1906 that "Abe" really got to know the Navy—which today is part of him.

On a Summer day that year, President Theodore Roosevelt appeared at the base to review the fleet, "Abe" somehow got on

Turn to "ABE," Page Eighteen

Abe

Continued from Page One

board the ship where he met the President.

"Abe" told "Teddy" about his admiration for the Navy, how he would like to sell papers, etc. "Abe" said that "Teddy" grabbed him by his ear and said he would see what he could do about it.

Several days later, "Abe" says he got "permission granted" by the Navy.

In his newspaper selling "Abe" has met Presidents Taft, Wilson, Harding, Coolidge, Hoover and Franklin D. Roosevelt on inspections of Navy yards at New London or Long Beach.

War Activities

"Abe," whose father operated a tailor shop in New London and became permanently blind when "Abe" was 10 years old, taught boxing at the New London Navy base during the first World War.

In World War II, he helped recruiting for the Navy and sold War Bonds. He received an Award of Merit from Secretary of the Navy James Forrestall for his bond-selling efforts.

"Abe" knows many of the top men and he has not only their autographed picture but his picture shaking hands with them. Fleet Admirals Chester W. Nimitz, William F. Halsey, Jr., Ernest J. King and William D. Leahy are but a few.

"It's a wonderful democratic country," says "Abe." "I've had a wonderful experience in my life, something I know could never happen where I was born."

Writes Book

Abraham Hollandersky's newspaperboy career has been so full of incidents that he has written a book about himself. It's entitled "Abe the Newsboy." He had it published himself and he says since 1931 he has reprinted 12 editions. Another edition is ready to run off the press. But the book hasn't made any money for him yet, "Abe" admits.

"Abe" plans to return early next month to Long Beach where he has his newstand and gift shop. His wife has been operating the business since he left on his trip.